CALIFORNIA STUDIES IN FOOD AND CULTURE

Darra Goldstein, Editor

The publisher gratefully acknowledges the generous support of the Ahmanson Foundation Humanities Endowment Fund of the University of California Press Foundation.

The publisher also gratefully acknowledges the generous support of the Humanities Endowment Fund of the University of California Press Foundation.

Popes, Peasants,
and Shepherds

Popes, Peasants, and Shepherds

RECIPES AND LORE
FROM ROME AND LAZIO

Oretta Zanini De Vita

Translated by Maureen B. Fant

With a foreword by Ernesto Di Renzo

UNIVERSITY OF CALIFORNIA PRESS

BERKELEY LOS ANGELES LONDON

Series page: Cauliflower grower selling his harvest in the streets of Rome (Biblioteca Clementina, Anzio)

Frontispiece: Bartolomeo Pinelli, Temple of the Sibyl at Tivoli (Biblioteca Clementina, Anzio)

University of California Press, one of the most distinguished university presses in the United States, enriches lives around the world by advancing scholarship in the humanities, social sciences, and natural sciences. Its activities are supported by the UC Press Foundation and by philanthropic contributions from individuals and institutions. For more information, visit www.ucpress.edu.

University of California Press
Berkeley and Los Angeles, California

University of California Press, Ltd.
London, England

A revised and expanded edition of *Il Lazio a tavola: Guida gastronomica tra storia e tradizioni,* originally published in Italian and simultaneously in English as *The Food of Rome and Lazio: History, Folklore, and Recipes.*

Library of Congress Cataloging-in-Publication Data

Zanini De Vita, Oretta, 1936–
  [Lazio a tavola. English]
  Popes, peasants, and shepherds : recipes and lore from Rome and Lazio / Oretta Zanini De Vita ; Translated by Maureen B. Fant.
      pages   cm.—(California studies in food and culture ; 42)
  A revised and expanded edition of Il Lazio a tavola : Guida gastronomica tra storia e tradizioni, originally published in Italian.
  Includes bibliographical references and index.
  ISBN 978-0-520-27154-8 (cloth : alk. paper)
  1. Food habits—Italy—Rome.   2. Food habits—Italy—Lazio.
3. Cooking—Italy—Rome.   4. Cooking—Italy—Lazio.   5. Italians—
Food.   I. Title.
  TX723.2.R65Z3613   2013
  394.1'20945632—dc23

                                                    2012038610

Manufactured in the United States of America

22 21 20 19 18 17 16 15 14 13
10 9 8 7 6 5 4 3 2 1

The paper used in this publication meets the minimum requirements of ANSI/NISO Z39.48–1992 (R 2002) (*Permanence of Paper*).

For my daughter, Chiara De Vita

The Lazio region of Italy

CONTENTS

FOREWORD: LAZIO'S GASTRONOMIC ROOTS

ERNESTO DI RENZO

The region of Lazio is a mosaic invented on paper between 1860 and the 1930s. The morphology, climate, and landscape of its territory are heterogeneous. Mountains alternate with plains, hills with coastal areas, valleys with lakes. Calcareous soils alternate with volcanic, woods with marshes, and maritime climates with continental.

The interaction of these varied features, together with demographic dynamics that have more than once remade the ethnic composition of the population, has been felt in the economic-productive sphere as well as the gastronomic, predisposing the guiding principles of development in a fragmentary and heterogeneous sense. With the exception of the Rome metropolitan area, Lazio has always had a markedly rural identity, one in which the authentic "genetic" matrices of its territory can be seen in its agriculture and stock raising.

Up to the end of World War II, agriculture, the true backbone of the regional economy, was practiced in a regime of substantial autarky, especially in the mountainous interior. The local communities grew grains, fruits and vegetables, vines, and olives, followed, under Arab influence and the discovery of the New World, by corn (maize), legumes, and tomatoes. The local biodiversity subsequently expanded to include a number of autochthonous foods that can be considered typical of certain localities. The list includes the green beans of Arsoli, the chickling vetch of Campodimele, the chestnuts of Vallerano, the *pizzutello* (pointed) grapes of Tivoli, the broccoli rabe of Anguillara, the wild strawberries of Nemi, and the artichokes and romaine lettuce of Rome.

Ever since antiquity, stock raising has symbolized Lazio, and it remains an important source of income for the region, though it employs many fewer people than in the past. Animal-related activities provide the inhabitants of Lazio with essential sources of nourishment, which the local cuisines have turned into a multiplicity of dishes, such as the *abbuoti* of the Ciociaria, flavorful rolls made from the intestines of Roman milk-fed lamb and filled with lamb innards, onion, parsley, and pecorino.

In the region today, such so-called typical products are at the center of a renewed collective interest following a lengthy cultural renewal that began with the post–World War II boom years. It was a period that saw the depopulation of the rural world, the growth of urban sprawl, the introduction of food-preservation methods that ensured supply far from the time and place of production, and the acceptance of women in the workplace. Naturally, there were consequences for food preparation.

The combination of these factors sparked the irreversible decline of peasant-pastoral culture, with its precarious existence and limited resources, and transformed traditional gastronomy, bringing an abrupt halt to the transmission of culinary know-how. A corollary has been the disappearance of centuries-old foodways and the establishment of new ones. The gradual acceptance of the new ways has increasingly restricted the space afforded to local flavors, considered synonymous with an archaic world from which it was felt necessary to take as great a distance as possible. It evoked poverty and could not guarantee modernity.

In the last two decades, as often happens when deculturation is excessive, the need not to lose oneself, or to return to being oneself, has activated a growing movement of identity revival. A similar operation has brought about the rediscovery of foods, recipes, and eating habits "of the old days," as evidenced in the widespread phenomenon of gourmet shops, *agriturismi,* farmers' markets, and peasant lunches. Thus in Lazio, as in the rest of the Western world, genuine, authentic, typical, and home style have gradually become the features of a manner of eating that is healthful and consistent with traditional values, as well as with the found-again balance between man and the environment.

This pastoral and agricultural heritage is an inextricable part of Rome itself, as well. Albeit residence of kings, emperors, and popes, seat of government and its bureaucracy, the capital's genetic imprinting has ensured that the peasant soul of Rome coexists with its urban dimension. Rome has always contained gardens, meadows, and places for food storage. Even the place names from the historic center to the periphery echo the themes of rural life. Such street names as Via dei Fienaroli (hay sellers), Via dei Caprettari (goat sellers), Via dei Fienili (haylofts), Via degli Orti (vegetable gardens) di Trastevere, Via del Frantoio (oil press), or Via dell'Aratro (plow) are not chosen arbitrarily by the ruling class, but capture true aspects of the agropastoral sphere existing within the city.

However, the reason why Rome can still be considered the most "peasant" of European capitals is something else. There are agrarian estates even inside the roads that ring the city. Sheep still graze along the urban stretch of the Aniene River and the Via Appia Antica. Green spaces have everywhere insinuated themselves into the city fabric, even right up to the arches of the Colosseum. Numerous small neighborhood markets still survive, their vegetable stalls often managed by farm women from the *agro romano*. Thanks to their presence, such dishes as *carciofi alla giudia, cacio e pepe, aliciotti all'indivia, coda alla vaccinara,* and *pajata* still constitute the "markers" of a kitchen that, although simple, expresses intense and original tastes.

Traditional Roman gastronomy (*cucina romanesca*) in fact represents a puzzle characterized by its creativity and its heterogeneity, in which the products of the countryside coexist with the specialties of the forests, the fish caught in the rivers with the cheeses of the pastures, the typical products of the coastal Maremma with the dishes of the urban Jewish tradition. The latter custom contains that arithmetical paradox known as the *quinto quarto,* the "fifth quarter," which comprises everything edible that remains after the animal has been quartered and the more prized cuts removed. From this offal (tripe, heart, liver, spleen, thymus gland, brains, tongue, tail), *cucina romanesca* has managed to derive flavorful dishes to offer to gourmet palates from the world over in the trattorias of Testaccio, Trastevere, and San Lorenzo.

But studying *cucina romanesca* does not mean only taking into account its innumerable horizontal layers that are the result of contributions from its surrounding area. We must also consider its age-old history, during which many food products and recipes were handed down both through oral tradition and in writing. The latter, an extensive literature, includes the names of Horace, Cicero, Columella, Apicius, Juvenal, Martial, and Petronius. They speak of an extraordinarily imaginative gastronomic culture that distinguished everyday meals from festive banquets, the tables of the rich from those of the poor, the emperors' menus from the *parvae cenulae* of the citizens. It is also possible to outline a picture of a diet in which the range of the courses alternated from antipasti to soups and from roasts to vegetables—without disdaining snails, cabbages, fava beans, chicory, and borage. Some combinations of ingredients survive to our own day, such as olives spiced with chile or fennel or aniseeds; the custom in the *fiaschetterie* (wineshops) of eating hard-boiled eggs with Frascati wine; the persistence with which the *padellotto* (mixed offal), *arzilla* (skate), *animelle* (sweetbreads), or *trippa* (tripe) are cooked along the lines of dishes described in the pages of *De re coquinaria,* the *Satyricon, De re rustica,* or the nineteenth-century *sonetti* of Gioacchino Belli. Think, finally, of all the cheeses, such as *caciofiore, marzolino, caciotta,* or pecorino, that grace the tables of the capital every day.

Of this gastronomic universe that embraces in a single, organic reconstruction of Rome and its region, past and present, the tables of popes and common people, the work of Oretta Zanini De Vita constitutes an important and complete account.

TRANSLATOR'S PREFACE

MAUREEN B. FANT

It was only when the supply and prices of farmhouse fixer-uppers in Tuscany and Umbria reached a critical point, twenty or so years ago, that English-speaking visitors to Italy began to notice the large region to their south. In addition to affordable real estate, it offered rugged natural beauty and inhabitants who couldn't have cared less about attracting tourism, a refreshing alternative to the manicured, Anglophone Chiantishire model. Those of us who hiked the region's hills and mountains, explored its wilder Etruscan rock-cut tombs, admired its medieval towns, and kayaked in its volcanic lakes felt adventurous even just knowing this wonderful land existed. The food was good too and in many ways indistinguishable from that over the border. The region's olive oil was often better than that of its more famous neighbors, as were the many local beans, greens, and mushrooms. Meanwhile, in the southern part of the region, adjacent to Campania, water buffalo gave excellent mozzarella. The political and geophysical-gastronomic distinctions were similarly blurred on the mountainous east, where there is a long border with Abruzzo and short ones with Molise and the Marche. But since the region's restaurants and trattorias until recently largely ignored its rich gastronomic heritage, food tourism continued to go elsewhere.

As a result, when, in the early 1990s, I would tell friends that I was translating a gastronomic history of the Lazio region, the usual response was, "Huh?" I've been explaining the Lazio region to English-speaking visitors ever since. Allow me to summarize. The regional borders of Italy can, with a moderate stretch, be compared to the national borders of Africa: just substitute "foods" for "tribes." They often represent political boundaries that may work on paper but do not necessarily reflect the divisions practiced by the actual people who live there or cut much ice with the sheep in the Apennines and the water buffalo in the former Pontine marshes. Like all Italian regions, Lazio is divided into provinces: Rome, extending in all directions from the national capital; Viterbo and Rieti to the north; Frosinone and Latina to the south. Unlike, say, Tuscany and

Emilia-Romagna, which contain numerous cities with strong identities of their own (think Pisa and Arezzo, Parma and Modena, in addition to Florence and Bologna), the small provincial capitals of Lazio have always been overshadowed by the Eternal City. How could they not be? Thus we have a region—one of tremendous natural variety dominated by agriculture and pastoralism—at the service of a capital city ruled for much of its history by emperors and popes. In this book (a greatly revised and expanded edition of that earlier translation), Oretta tells the captivating story, through its people and their food, of the continuity and coexistence of this unique capital and its surrounding countryside with its multifaceted hinterland—not just popes, peasants, and shepherds, but Jews, poets, politicians, paupers, priests, nuns, brides, grooms, innkeepers, fishermen, and movie stars.

The revisions to and expansion of the original Italian book have been made for this edition and have not been published in Italian. Oretta writes for educated Italians in a spirited and lighthearted way. We have tried to gloss or annotate allusions that educated English speakers would find mysterious. Such notes are necessarily laconic, but—I would suggest—could be jumping off points for explorations in Latin and Italian literature, history, political theory, geography, sociology, urban planning, and agronomy. Oretta touches all these subjects, and more.

I've preferred to use the Italian Lazio to the Latin Latium, though that archaism still turns up in English. Modern Lazio only partly coincides with ancient Latium and so should have a different name. The Italian adjective form of Lazio, *laziale,* offers no solution in English, so for this I have kept with the Latin and use Latian.

Since Rome and its river, the Tiber, are household words in English, Roma and Tevere are translated. Otherwise, the region's toponyms have no equivalents and are necessarily given in Italian. Ancient names are left in Latin. For example, aqueducts that existed in antiquity are spelled *aqua* (Latin), while papal constructions are called *acqua* (Italian), which is how both sets are known in English.

The recipes may be historic, but they are meant to be cooked—not that we are expecting frog frittata (recipe on page 194) to become all the rage—and have accordingly been recast to bring them closer to the format Anglo-American cooks have every right to expect. The Italian future and future perfect tenses have been eliminated so that most actions are now in chronological order. Ingredients are presented in order of appearance instead of importance, the Italian way. Nevertheless, we've tried to keep a lid on the Anglicization so that the recipes would still convey something of the traditions they represent. For this reason, most prepping is in the body of the recipe, as Oretta wrote it, not the ingredients list, as is current in modern English-language cookbooks. I have more to say on the specifics of the recipes, such as measurements and substitutions, at the beginning of that section. We are less accommodating about substitutions than modern cookbooks like to be, but if you make some allowances for eels, frogs, some of the offal, and some of the game, the recipes are really quite accessible (and delicious).

Translating Oretta is a privilege, a pleasure, and a challenge. You don't even want to know what translating Italian recipes is like (add enough salt and cook it till it's done?). The recipes would not be so easy to follow without the careful ministrations of our copy editor, Sharon Silva, nor, for that matter, would the text. For her skill, knowledge, and patience she has our profound thanks. Oretta joins me in thanking too our agent, Jennifer Griffin. And finally, our most affectionate thanks to Darra Goldstein, Sheila Levine, Kate Marshall, and Dore Brown at the University of California Press, who have given this book, long after its initial low-profile publication in Italy, the home I have always felt it deserved.

ACKNOWLEDGMENTS

Many people have accompanied me in this long and exciting journey through the *cucina* of Rome and Lazio, and all have my heartfelt thanks. First among them must be mentioned Ernesto Di Renzo, who introduced me to the world of food anthropology and who has kindly written a foreword to this book. Maureen Fant has translated me admirably, putting heart and soul into the work as only she is able. Mariano Malavolta led me by the hand through the intricate maze of ancient Roman politics, and Marcella Pisani made me see the beauties and remains of Rome with fresh eyes. Finally, I thank the staff of the library of the Fondazione Marco Besso, Rome, for the kind and professional help they have always given me in my research.

(previous page) Arthur J. Strutt, wagon for carrying wine into the city
(Biblioteca Clementina, Anzio)

Introduction

The food of Rome and its region, Lazio, is redolent of herbs, olive oil, ricotta, lamb, and pork. It gives pride of place to the genuine flavors of foods, making it a very "modern" cuisine. It is the food of ordinary, frugal people and had no role in the development of the kind of cooking that over time became elaborated and codified in the palaces of the nobility and later in the temples of haute cuisine. The introduction of products from the New World, such as the tomato, the potato, and corn (maize), did not transform the hearty popular cuisine; they merely enriched it.

From earliest antiquity, Roman and Latian cooks were thrifty[1] and remained so even in the period of the famous Lucullan banquets—rare privilege of the wealthy few. The most important meal for the ancients consisted of *puls* (plural *pultes*), a porridge based on a grain, notably *far,* or emmer, to which fava beans, chickpeas, or lentils were added. With it, they ate mostly vegetables and to a lesser extent milk and cheese. Meat was extremely rare, and what little was used was from chickens, rabbits, or game.

In the last centuries B.C. and the first centuries of our era, the typical daily menu consisted of bread, oil, milk, olives, honey, and eggs. On those few occasions when meat was served, it was almost exclusively in soups seasoned with garlic and onion. Meat did not include beef or veal, since oxen were too valuable as work animals to slaughter them for the table. Protein content was provided mostly by eggs, which the Romans loved.

A primitive unleavened bread was made by mixing water and flour and then shaping the dough into a flat focaccia. The same dough could be used to make what was probably a sort of tagliatelle or *maltagliati,* called *laganum* in Latin. A simple recipe using *lagana* has come down to us (recipe on page 134).

Meals always included vegetables, most commonly turnips and cabbage. Every family, even the poor, had a little garden sufficient for the daily requirement of greens. Salt for food preservation came from immense deposits under the southernmost of Rome's canonical seven hills, the Aventine,[2] which were in turn restocked from the salt marshes at the mouth of the Tiber.

Even the common people's kitchen enjoyed the effects of contact with Greek civilization and trade with the East. The Sabine hills, northeast of Rome (bordering present-day Abruzzo), came to be covered with olive trees, and the use of olives and olive oil was introduced. To this day, the oil produced there is one of Italy's best.

By the height of the empire, the middle and upper classes were consuming more meat. But in the countryside, people went on as before and continued to eat simply, relying above all on homegrown fruits, legumes, and vegetables.

In the Middle Ages, the struggles among baronies caused hard times, including famine, in Rome and Lazio, both city and country.[3] The splendid gardens that had adorned houses within the city walls under the empire were converted to the growing of vegetables. These kitchen gardens contributed to feeding the people of Rome until the mid-nineteenth century, when they were swallowed up in the building frenzy that accompanied the arrival of the Kingdom of Italy.

With the Crusades, contact with the East was reopened. The tables of the rich became laden with such exotic products as sugar, spices, and oranges, all of them imported by the maritime republics (Genoa, Venice, Pisa, and Amalfi), which dominated trade in their day, and not just in the Mediterranean. But unlike them, Rome remained highly conservative in its cuisine and anchored in tradition. Romans continued to make their sweets with honey and ricotta, to make their wine with the grapes grown in their own vineyards, and to cook their vegetables, fish, and meat in lard, *guanciale,* or olive oil.

For centuries to come, the population of Rome was only a few tens of thousands. Cut off from the political scene and its troubles, the people continued to live and cook simply, bringing in most of their food needs from the various surrounding zones that today form the region of Lazio—Tuscia and Sabina[4] to the north, Campagna to the south, and Marittima,[5] or coastal area. The rural population and the people in the small surrounding towns had thus maintained and cultivated a cuisine that remained very close to that of the city: a roast kid cooked near Sora, in southern Lazio, or one in Amatrice, at the region's northern tip (and formerly in Abruzzo), differed little from what was eaten in Roman homes. For this reason, many of the recipes in this book can be considered as belonging to the region as a whole.

The same holds for pasta: poverty and imagination lay behind the proliferation of all the many types that changed name from town to town: the *stracci* of one become the *fregnacce* of another, and the Sabine *frascarelli* differ little from the *strozzapreti* of the Ciociaria, the region's southern hinterland. The popular imagination gave whimsical names to the simple paste of water and flour, and only rarely eggs, worked with the hands or with small tools. Thus we have *cecamariti* (husband blinders) and *cordelle* (ropes), *curuli, fusilli* (also called *ciufulitti*), *frigulozzi, pencarelli, manfricoli,* and *sfusellati,* as well as *strozzapreti* (priest stranglers), the *lacchene* of the town of Norma and the *pizzicotti* (pinches) of Bolsena, while the *fieno* (hay) of Canepina has, accompanied by *paglia* (straw), been absorbed into the repertory of the pan-Italian *grande cucina.* All these pastas were served with much the same sauce, plain tomato and basil, though on feast days, pork, lamb, or beef would be added. It is impossible, as well as historically incorrect, to make hard-and-fast distinctions among the dishes of the region's separate geographical areas—whether Tuscia, Sabina, or the Ciociaria— since by this time the Roman popular cuisine had adopted and absorbed almost all these dishes and made them its own.

At the beginning of the twentieth century, residents of Rome's Prati quarter—in the shadow of Castel Sant'Angelo—could still see the Tiber flow and hear the crickets and cicadas inside the fortress. Public transport from there to Viale Manzoni was a horse-drawn trolley that started at Piazza Navona. The best salamis came from Ignazio in Via della Scrofa and the finest fresh cheese from Bernardini, the milkman in Via della Stelletta. The best *panpepato* was from the baker Gioggi at the Circo Agonale (Piazza Navona), and lamb and sweetbreads were booked ahead with Giorgi, the butcher.

In the evening, people dined at home by gaslight, and after dinner they went out to the *caffè* to chat with friends till late. In summer, there were concerts in Piazza Colonna or at the Caffè Guardabossi in Piazza Montecitorio. But those with a sweet tooth left the music to others and concentrated on the famous *cassata siciliana* or sorbets at Aragno.[6]

And that was decades, not centuries, ago.

The Agrarian Landscape of the Campagna Romana

In his *Grand Tour in Italy,* Goethe, who saw the Roman countryside, the *agro romano,* at the beginning of the nineteenth century, recounts how he found it as it must have been when, in the fifth century B.C., Cincinnatus[7] was persuaded to leave his plow and return to public life. We have no way of knowing where

Cincinnatus's farm at Prata Quinctia was actually located, but it was probably along the Via Salaria, near the present-day Borgo Quinzio, and there he was, bent over his hoe, when the senators arrived from Rome to beg him to return. Nor do we know what he was growing, but surely there were onions, cabbages, and beans and perhaps a few olive trees from which to press oil for soups and to light his lamps. Goethe's point, and he was right, was that no advances had been made in the intervening millennia. Unless impeded, the waters of the marshes would take it over. During the Roman Republic, the wise administration promoted drainage projects and channeling of the waters. The Etruscans, the best farmers of antiquity, had tackled the same problem by harnessing the waters for irrigation. And in the countryside, the people lived by farming also in nonoptimal environmental situations.[8] This was still, in Cicero's day, the agrarian situation in the *agro romano,* which he mentions in his orations on agrarian law.[9]

The villas and large farms of the Roman patricians were placed on salubrious hillsides, while slaves tended the extensive holdings on the plains. With the fall of the empire, conventionally dated to A.D. 476, the countryside became an *ager desertus.* No one took care of the drainage, and the road system was abandoned to the brush; the ruined aqueducts were not repaired, and malaria took more and more victims. This is partly why, at the turn of the sixth century, most of the immense territory passed into the hands of the Church, mainly through donations of lands by this time unfarmed and unprofitable, or even through donations of barbarian kings, not always and not all marauders, as tradition would have it. For example, it is known that, during the third siege of Rome,[10] the Goth king Totila invited the peasants to work in peace and bring him the tribute they would otherwise have delivered to their legitimate masters.

After the invasions by the Visigoths and Vandals in the fifth century, agriculture in the countryside briefly resumed. The Church, led by Pope Gregory the Great (590–604), the careful organizer of the ecclesiastical holdings, had three large *patrimoni* (assets) at the time, each of which was composed of many estates, or *massae.* These were in turn made up of numerous *fundus* (farms) that included *casali,* or "farmhouses," that were so important that their names have survived to this day where the buildings stood.

It was during the pontificate of Gregory that the Lombard hordes fell on Lazio and put the countryside to fire and sword. But as soon as peace was made with Agilulf,[11] work in the fields gradually resumed. The donations registered by Anastasio Bibliotecario,[12] following the invasions of the Goths and Lombards, describe the *campagna romana* as sown with farms and covered with crops and orchards.

The eighth century was the century of the foundation of the *domuscultae* by Popes Zachary (741–52) and Hadrian I (772–95), with the intent of giving a new breath to agriculture. *Domuscultae* were small clusters of houses near a main road, served by a modest church, hospice, warehouses, taverns, fountains, and barns. These villages initially appeared in the lower Tiber valley north of Rome; later they multiplied over the whole *agro romano*. The first *domusculta* was Sulpiciana (ancient Bovillae); a second was on the Via Tiburtina, five Roman miles from Rome; Pratolungo rose on the Via Nomentana; Laurento and Massa Fonteiana were on the Via Laurentina; Campomorto was established on the Via Nettunense; Antius was on the Via Severiana; and Casale di Galeria was on the Via Claudia.

The economy of the *domuscultae* must have been truly flourishing: the revenues from their products could finance part of the works for the construction of the Leonine wall.[13] *Triticum* (wheat), barley, wine, oil, and legumes were produced, and pigs were raised in the surrounding forests. Some of the *domuscultae* were huge. Sacrofanum covered an area of some thirty-nine square miles (one hundred square kilometers) and fed five fortified citadels: Formello, Campagnano, Mazzano, Calcata, and Faleria.[14] The *liber pontificalis* documents how every year the *domusculta* of Capracorum supplied the Lateran stores with wheat, barley, wine, vegetables, and some one hundred hogs, which the Church kept in warehouses adjacent to the Basilica of St. John Lateran. Each day, under the loggia of the basilica, it was the custom to distribute to the poor fifty loaves of bread, two amphorae of wine, some bowls of soup, and some rations of pork.

The *domuscultae* survived between 750 and 850; most of them were destroyed by the raids of the Saracens,[15] by internal struggles, and by the spreading malaria that made the lands unlivable for much of the year. Some of them survived beyond the ninth century, perhaps because they were built on the more salubrious and defendable hilly areas.

With the disappearance of the *domuscultae* begins the metamorphosis of the *campagna romana:* the people who took refuge in more defendable positions built fortified villages, as at Mazzano and Calcata, both also true *castra,* as at Castelgandolfo, Castel Malnome, Castel Romano, and Castel Fusano, which preserve their history in their name.[16]

At the dawn of the second millennium, the *campagna romana* was fairly well populated. There were castles, but there were also churches with farmhouses next door, with both placed near the castles in more easily defended positions. These arrangements allowed significant improvement of the vineyards, olive orchards, and especially the vegetable gardens, which were usually located next to the walls of the built-up areas, giving the peasants greater security.[17] The foundation of the Confraternity[18] of the Vegetable Men and that of the Oil Men, which, in addition to helping the working members of the organizations, also provided assistance for the sick and for burial of the dead, date to those years.

Meanwhile, the numerous Roman monasteries, which had extended their holdings outside the walls with the intent of boosting their production of grapes and vegetables, proceeded to cut down large expanses of forest, replacing them with canes useful for supporting the vines. They abandoned the ancient drainages to create wells of irrigation water, thus inevitably encouraging the recrudescence of malaria. The numerous watercourses that ran down the hills were often deviated to carry water to the gardens within the city's walls, with the old aqueducts demolished in the process. Such was the case when Pope Callixtus II (1119–24) redirected water to the Porta Lateranense (Lateran Gate), where a watering trough was to be built. Altering the routes of the watercourses also allowed for more work at the numerous mills that operated in the city and the hinterland.

It was at this point that the lands used for pasture began to predominate over the ever-less-profitable agriculture fields. And thus the animal rearers, the *boattari*, began to pull ahead of the farmers. The *Ars bobacteriorum urbis*[19] was already active in 1088.

The numerous towers that still punctuate the *campagna romana* were built during the sixteenth century, together with *casali*, or large farmhouses, almost all fortified, of which every trace has generally been lost. They include the *casali* of Olgiata on the Via Cassia, of Lunghezza on the Via Tiburtina, of Crescenza on the Via Flaminia, and, south of Rome, of Torre Astura and the fort of Nettuno. Michelangelo designed Tor San Michele at the mouth of the Tiber. The list continues with the towers of Olevola and Vittoria, the Torre Flavia, Tor Vaianica, and the tower of Maccarese.[20] Little by little, something in the *agro* was moving, slowed by the marshification of the lands, in turn aggravated by the neglect of the owners and the floods of the Tiber, which left stagnant water everywhere.

The roads, almost nonexistent and especially unsafe, did not permit the regular supply of food to the city. For this reason, over the centuries, the popes tried to help agriculture any way they could. For example, Julius II (1503–13) prohibited both the passage of armies over cultivated or sown fields and the buying up of foodstuffs by farm owners, and imposed severe penalties on anyone who impeded the passage of goods across their property.[21] Between the end of the sixteenth century and the beginning of the seventeenth, the situation was grave. To make it even worse, the plague arrived, accompanied in the summer of 1581 by a heavy new outbreak of malaria. It sent almost one-third of the farm population to the cemetery, leaving the countryside without manpower. The situation, which worsened further over the next two years, convinced the few survivors to leave the fields and withdraw into the less pestilential high hilly areas. At the end of the 1600s, these debilitating circumstances, along with the slow but unstoppable spread of the *latifundium* (large farming estate), meant that only one-tenth of the lands would be cultivated. Pasturage gave good revenue and few worries to the land owners, and therefore the trading of farmland for pastureland continued until the end of the 1800s. The situation began to improve only after World War II.

Alarmed by the situation, many newly elected popes enacted provisions, but their solutions soon fell into the void. Their measures were tediously replicated and the content of the dispositions monotonously repeated, which shows how widely they were ignored. Much of this failure was due to the excessive power of the barons, who could do much as they liked, with well-armed militias in their employ. Deaf to any imposition of law and impervious to any change that might improve the situation of the countryside, the large landowners were, in the centuries to follow, those truly responsible for the crisis of the *agro*. A land register from the end of the seventeenth century records that the more than 500,000 acres (205,000 hectares) of the *campagna romana* were divided among 362 estates, 234 of which, for a total of nearly 311,000 acres (126,000 hectares), were owned by 113 nobles. The remaining 195 acres (79 hectares), more or less, were in the hands of religious institutes, monasteries, churches, and the like. Small farmers owned practically nothing. Of all of these farmlands, fewer than 60,000 acres (24,000 hectares) were in agriculture at the end of the eighteenth century.

Meanwhile, corn arrived. From the middle of the eighteenth century, its market prices were competitive, and as a result it was also used to make bread: a *gabella* (tax) on flour meant wheat cost eight giuli[22] per *rubbio*,[23] while a *rubbio* of corn cost only two giuli. In this situation, it is obvious that the gardens and the vineyards just outside the city were intensely cultivated to satisfy the demand, as were the lands on the banks of the Tiber. Curiously, to stress the fertility of the unexploited lands, the quality of what was actually produced was celebrated in Europe: from the famous romaine lettuce, celery, artichokes, and cabbages to the excellent fava beans grown on the lands of the Caffarella estate[24] and that already were eaten with pecorino (recipe on page 220). There were also the fruits, of course: peaches, cherries, apples, pears, almost all from cultivars that today have disappeared and that amazed travelers and painters almost up to the dawn of the twentieth century.

The produce that arrives daily at Roman markets today is of exceptional quality, thanks especially to the variety and fertility of the terrain, much of it of volcanic origin. That soil makes possible the particular biodiversity that ensures that the products of the *campagna romana* are truly unique.

The Tiber and Fish in Popular Cooking

Of all of Rome's honorary citizens, Father Tiber merits a particularly special place. For centuries the river took an active part in city life, for good and ill, often destroying lives and homes with the devastating floods that periodically invaded the low-lying neighborhoods.[25] That is why, when Rome became the capital of Italy and the whole city underwent a major makeover to make it look like a great European capital, the Tiber was enclosed in heavy embankments.[26]

The river now lives, alone and imprisoned, between the stout walls that isolate it from the city's life, and the time when it was home to boats, mills, and fishermen is long gone.

In earliest antiquity, the catch was plentiful and constituted an important element of the popular diet, though fish, freshwater and saltwater alike, was considered unworthy to serve to company. Gentlemen who liked to go fishing were regarded with suspicion. Later, however, Antony and Cleopatra, as well as the emperors Augustus and, later still, Marcus Aurelius and Commodus, were passionate anglers.

Contact with the refined civilization of Greece taught the Romans to appreciate the delicate flesh of fish and the masterly preparations cooks could make from it. Demand for fresh fish, especially rare varieties, reached the point that aquaculture was introduced. Some installations were veritable masterpieces of hydraulic engineering, accommodating both fresh water fish and those requiring seawater. The fourth and fifth levels of the Markets of Trajan, in the center of Rome, contained aquariums filled with freshwater and with seawater brought from Ostia, the port of Rome. The demanding gourmet could order salmon trout from the Moselle or Danube, or fish from the Black Sea, or sturgeon imported from Greece[27] to be caught live by specialized slaves. The markets of Ancona and Ravenna supplied large quantities of *pesce azzurro* (see page 274), while from Sicily arrived the greatest delicacy of all: the moray eel, *muraena* in Latin, *murena* in Italian.

The fashion for private fish farms exploded, and the nouveaux riches outdid themselves to see who could stock the rarest fish. The largest fish farms were built in Campania, where Licinius Murena launched the fashion in about 90 B.C., to be followed by the consul Sergius Orata, the first to raise oysters (at Baiae).[28] He was followed in turn by such famous jet-setters as L. Licinius Lucullus, who had a hole cut through a mountain near Baiae to bring the water from the sea to his fish farm. Against these characters stood the moralists—notably Cicero—who called them disparagingly "an aristocracy of fishermen" who cared more about their fish farms than about affairs of state.[29]

In addition to the moray eel, the Romans' favorite fish included tuna (especially the belly), red mullet, gray mullet, eel, sole, and mackerel. No pike could equal those pulled from the Tiber where the sewers emptied. Large fish were much sought after and were often given as gifts to the emperor. A satire by the poet Juvenal tells of an enormous turbot given to the emperor Domitian, who supposedly consulted the Senate as to the best way to cook it.[30] A true gourmet treat were the mollusks: oysters, date shells, mussels, clams, warty Venus, scallops, and razor clams. Particularly prized were the oysters of Lake Lucrinus, in Campania, and, later, those imported from northern Gaul.

The invasions of the migrating tribes, who swarmed down from the east onto the fertile Italian plains, wiped away all memory of the gourmet life. Wars, famines, and plagues left the lands abandoned for centuries, and so they ceased to produce. The road back to civilization was long and hard.

In successive waves, the so-called barbarians canceled entire inhabited and cultivated regions from the map of Italy, erasing more than merely eating habits. Medieval man had to begin again from scratch, living in houses no longer worthy of the name, nourishing himself when he could with game, wild grains, and roots. The people forgot the great Roman cuisine almost entirely.

With the economic upturn of the year 1000, the waters of the Tiber once again became a major channel for the movement of people and goods, including foodstuffs. Business was conducted in the crowded ports of Ripetta and Ripa Grande,[31] where the traffic of large and small craft grew steadily until boats and ships created frequent bottlenecks, comparable to those on today's roads and streets.

While it was still active, the port of Ostia fed the major part of commercial traffic directed toward Rome, since the Tiber was navigable as far as its tributary the Nera, in Umbria. For centuries, small and large craft[32] were pulled upriver by water buffalo treading a sheep track along the left bank. This service, called *alaggio*, or "haulage," was in use as early as the Roman Empire. In the Middle Ages, the monopoly was given to the bishop of Ostia, who engaged a subcontractor to supply the animals for traction.

The flow of shipping in the ports and the activity of the boatmen and stevedores who loaded and unloaded all sorts of freight, including food, were regulated by papal proclamations and *motu proprio,* or decree.

The Tiber also participated in city life by making its rich, unpolluted waters available to fishermen. The humanist Paolo Giovio (1483–1552) maintained that ninety-six varieties[33] of fish could be caught in the Tiber, and fishing on the river was always one of the marvels of travelers. There were trout, pike, barbel, carp, eel, salmon, and sturgeon. As late as the mid-nineteenth century, sturgeon, salmon, and their caviar were sold in shops in the city and in the outlying areas. Sturgeon had given rise to a curious and ancient tradition. In the Middle Ages, the heads of the largest specimens—those longer than 47 inches (1.2 meters)—were brought as gifts to the Conservatori del Campidoglio (the political hierarchy that governed the city), for whose tables they were transformed into delicious soups. Most of the brutes were caught in the short space between the Tiber Island and the Ponte Sublicio. A marble plaque spelling out the rules for sale was supposed to be displayed wherever fish were sold. An amusing example can still be seen on the Portico d'Ottavia, next to Via di Sant'Angelo in Pescheria.

Capita piscium
hoc marmoreo schemate longitudine
majorum usque ad primas pinnas
inclusive Conservatoribus
danto

The text says that the head, up to the first fins, of any fish longer than the diagram had to be given to the *conservatori*. The diagram in question is a picture of a sturgeon incised on another marble plaque, now in the Palazzo dei Conservatori, one of the buildings of the Capitoline Museums, on the Piazza del Campidoglio.

Of the many species that the then-clean waters of the Tiber used to offer, the most famous were perhaps *ciriole*, small, strong-tasting eels, different in both size and flavor from those fished (then and now) in the lakes of Lazio. They were cooked *in guazzetto*, or else fried, according to an ancient and unvarying recipe.

The University of the Fishermen, as the guild to which all those who worked with fish was called, was one of the oldest and most important in the city's guild hierarchy. It included the fishermen of the upper Tiber, as well as those who fished the river's middle course and mouth. The guild was regulated by a charter: one that has come down to us dates to 1665. It is more or less from this moment that fishing, formerly a laissez-faire activity, was regulated.

The fishmongers belonged to their own guild, whose charters are documented from 1536. The guild established rules and regulations for both hygiene and retail sale of fish. They could now only be sold in specific markets or in the city streets by special license from the consuls. Fishmongers also had to use a particular kind of basket, called a *celigna*, both to transport the fish and to measure it: according

Fish was sold in the Portico d'Ottavia, and nearby shops,
such as the one shown here, sold cured meat, cheeses, and spices
(Fondazione Primola, Rome)

to law, the tail had to remain outside the container and could not be considered
in the price (which was based on length, not weight). For reasons of hygiene, the
sale of fish, in the street or in the market, was prohibited during the hottest part
of the year, from July 8 through September.

The main fish market, from antiquity down to the beginning of the twentieth century, was in the Portico d'Ottavia, in the Ghetto. There was a second

market at the Pantheon, and another in the quarter, or *rione,* called Ponte. A large exhibition market of fish, the *cottio,* took place two days before Christmas, after midnight. The opening was marked with a solemn ceremony attended by city authorities, prelates, patricians, and members of the press, even at the beginning of the twentieth century. Three piazzas were rented by the University of Fishmongers and the proceeds were handed over to the Camera Apostolica (in other words, the Vatican), which also collected rent on the stone used as a sales counter. The fish market did not move until 1922, when it was transferred to the General Markets—the main wholesale food market—on Via Ostiense.[34]

The 1536 charter even dictated rules for correct behavior on the job: "It is prohibited to play with dice on the stones of the fish market.... It is prohibited to throw down money for the *riffa* [raffles] on top of the fish ..." and so forth. Curiously, the charters authorized fishmongers to sell "wild animals," defined as "pigs, stags, goats, hares, pheasants, partridges, pigeons, doves, thrushes, starlings, and other tiny birds." The University of Fishmongers, like all the other guilds of the city, ran a home and a hospital that assisted its own members. Aid was extended not only to the sick and to pilgrims of the trade who were passing through Rome but also included dowries for poor or orphaned girls, support for spinsters, help with burial, and other forms of assistance. The home and hospital were located next to the church of Sant'Angelo in Pescheria, in the Ghetto, where the fishmongers had a chapel dedicated to their patron saint, Saint Andrew.[35]

Fish flowed to the markets in abundance and at a good price, even if the largest specimens invariably ended up on the tables of the rich clergy and the nobility. Freshwater fish were the most common and the most prized, both because they were less complicated to catch and because they traveled a much shorter distance to market. Marine fish were carried along the Tiber from Ostia to the ports of Ripetta and Ripa Grande and were distributed to the city's markets from there.

Fish were never as important in the regional cuisine of Lazio, nor indeed of any Italian region, as other foods. This is quite odd when one considers that Italy is almost completely surrounded by a sea full of fish, and that for centuries the Lenten fast, by forbidding consumption of meat, in effect imposed a fish diet. The problem lay in the internal transportation, where roads were almost nonexistent and travel times made it impossible to deliver fresh fish to the towns of the interior.

Preserved fish had already appeared in popular cooking in antiquity. During the famous Roman Carnival, the people loved to stop at the wineshops (osterias) to eat *tarantello*—belly (*ventresca*) of tuna preserved in salt—and wash it down with a nice glass of wine. *Alici,* fat, tasty anchovies caught along the shore, were also preserved in salt, in large wooden barrels. Salted anchovies are used in many traditional Roman dishes.

Salt cod and stockfish are found in almost all the cuisines of the Mediterranean area. The very ancient practice[36] of preserving cod by drying or salting occurs in Roman cooking in numerous specialties.

Many of the Roman meatless dishes are associated with Lent, Fridays, or any of the other 130 days of the year when, until recently, meat and its derivatives were prohibited for practicing Catholics. On Good Friday, a day of particularly strict fasting, it was usual to visit the thousand tombs of the beautiful Roman basilicas. At twilight, there wasn't a housewife whose table did not have the famous Good Friday soup, the sumptuous *luccio brodettato* (recipe on page 195), or the delicate pasta and *broccolo romanesco* in ray (skate) broth (recipe on page 143).

In Rome, the feast of Saint John, on June 24, means snails (*lumache*), also permitted on meatless days. It falls in the season when the tasty gastropods are fat and full of flavor. After the plentiful rains of early summer, they were collected in abundance in the vineyards and gardens that, until the early 1900s, covered much of the area of today's city. The best snails are those with striped white shells, called *vignarole* (of the vineyards). Even today, on the night of San Giovanni, the "true" Romans gather in one of the many osterias in the neighborhood of the Basilica of Saint John Lateran to eat *lumache alla romana,* cooked with tomatoes and plenty of chile. As late as the 1800s, men arrived at the feast with sorghum in their buttonholes or a few cloves of garlic in their pockets and rang a cowbell, all to keep away the witches. It was also the night when the witches came to Rome on broomsticks to honor their patron, Saint John. With the first light of dawn, they went back south to Benevento and the walnut tree that, according to legend, is national headquarters for all the witches of Italy.[37]

Only the well-off could afford the luxury of sitting at a table in an osteria to eat snails; the poor, the so-called *fagottari* (brown baggers),[38] took them home in big earthenware pots, covered with a cloth, and sat and ate them on the meadows around the basilica.

Today snails can be found, both fresh and frozen, in supermarkets. They are sold ready to cook, but true aficionados see personally to the process of purging them, which differs slightly from region to region. In Rome, the snails were traditionally put in a wicker basket along with plenty of bran perfumed with Roman mint, and the operation took several days.

On the other hand, the boom in saltwater fish in *cucina romana* did not begin until the 1980s: today on the tables of Roman homes and restaurants absolutely everything can be found. But the most traditional preparations are those in which the fish is combined with vegetables, such as artichokes and peas, or is used in sauce for pasta. This is the most typical Roman seafood cooking.

Water and Aqueducts

The decision of Romulus and Remus, the mythical founders of Rome, to build their city in this place must have had something to do with the fact that its hydrogeological situation gave solid guarantees of fertile agriculture. This wealth was subsequently ably studied by the Roman engineers, not only by the farmers. From the republic through the empire, fountains and *jeux d'eau* beautified the city and its gardens. And plenty of water must have reached Rome, if we are to believe Frontinus, who, early in the second century, wrote an important work on Roman aqueducts in which he informs readers that the city was supplied with a million cubic meters of water per day.[39]

An increase in the population, due also to migration and to the great influx of slaves, is probably why the Aqua Appia was built, around 312 B.C. The first of a series of eleven aqueducts, it started from the eighth mile of the Via Praenestina and, running almost entirely in underground conduits, emerged on the arches at the Forum Boarium.[40]

The Anio Vetus, the next of the great aqueducts, came in 272–69 B.C., paid for with the booty of the war against Pyrrhus, king of Epirus (280–75 B.C.). It took water from the Aniene River, north of Tivoli, and followed the river in underground channels until it reached the city.

The water traveled ever longer distances: in 144–140 B.C., the Aqua Marcia arrived directly on the Capitoline Hill after a trip of sixty miles (one hundred kilometers) from the upper valley of the Aniene, bringing its excellent, cold water to Rome. Much later, in A.D. 212, the emperor Caracalla added a branch, the Aqua Antoniniana.

The need for water became ever more compelling, and so, in 126 B.C., the Aqua Tepula was built, which, as its name suggests, reached the city warm from a group of springs on the Via Latina. Because the water was not the best quality, it was used for fountains and baths. In 33 B.C., Agrippa, at his own expense, built the Aqua Julia, also from the Via Latina on the Alban Hills, to supply his private baths in the Campus Martius. Not satisfied, in 19 B.C., he built the Aqua

John Zahnd, view of the ruins of a Roman aqueduct in the *campagna*
(Biblioteca Clementina, Anzio)

Virgo, which still serves Rome and which, also from the Alban Hills, had the formidable flow of thirteen cubic meters per second. In 2 B.C., Augustus brought the Aqua Alsietina to Rome from its source of Lake Martignano (Alsietina in antiquity) on the Via Cassia, which must have been used for the Naumachia (where mock naval battles were held) in Transtiberim (today's Trastevere). The Acqua Vergine terminates in the Trevi Fountain and has often been cited as the secret ingredient of the excellent tea and coffee found in the center of Rome.

The most important of the aqueducts, begun by Caligula and completed by Claudius in A.D. 54, was the Aqua Claudia, whose water came from springs on the Via Sublacensis near the sources of the Aqua Marcia, with an excellent flow. It was followed a few years later by the Anio Novus, which, again near Sublacum, present-day Subiaco, caught the waters of the Aniene.

The greater need for potable water in Transtiberim was what convinced the emperor Trajan of the need to intervene anew, and so it was that around 109, the Aqua Traiana flowed into Rome, terminating on the Janiculum Hill.[41] Finally, between 220 and 235, Alexander Severus brought to Rome the last of the ancient aqueducts, the Aqua Alexandrina, taking its water from the marshy Pantano Borghese, east of Rome. It ran for 13.7 miles (22 kilometers) on the Via Praenestina.[42]

With the fall of the Roman Empire, these giants, no longer monitored and kept in repair, stood for centuries only to bear witness to the ancient splendor. They were blocked during the Gothic War (535–553), in the siege of Rome (537–38), but Justinian, emperor of Byzantium, provided for their partial repair.

Throughout the High Middle Ages, partial restorations and recoveries made it possible for Rome to receive at least some water. In the seventh century, Pope Honorius I (625–638) restored a stretch of the Aqua Traiana. Trajan's aqueduct must in some way have functioned during the next century as well, if it was able to operate the mills set up on the Janiculum.

Pope Hadrian I (772–95) provided for the partial restoration of Trajan's aqueduct and of the Claudia. His engineers also worked on the Aqua Virgo (Acqua Vergine), but since this aqueduct ran in large part through underground conduits, it had been less damaged by neglect and time. The three aqueducts had to supply the city's hospitals.

It was almost a thousand years before someone else took a look at the situation of the city's water supply. That was Pope Sixtus V, Felice Peretti (1585–90), who had a hand in the construction of the Acqua Felice, named for him. The aqueduct took its waters from the sources of the Appia and the Marcia (Marzia) in the Castelli Romani, in Colonna territory. The new aqueduct ran underground for thirteen miles (twenty-nine kilometers) and for another fifteen miles (twenty-four kilometers) in aboveground constructions and then emerged on the plain for seven miles (eleven kilometers), reaching Rome at Porta Furba. From there, bending toward San Lorenzo, it reached the Quirinal Hill, where the pontiff built the magnificent fountain that still stands in the middle of the piazza. The flow of water of this immense work was calculated at 3.7 million gallons (14 million liters) per day. A part of all that water must have supplied the beautiful pontifical Villa Montaldo, no longer standing, in the area of the present-day Stazione Termini.

Hydraulic works continued for another century with the construction of the Acqua Paola, which took its supply from Lakes Bracciano and Martignano. Finally, at the end of the pontificate of Pius IX (1846–76), the ancient Aqua Marcia was restored and, in honor of the pontiff, renamed Acqua Pia. It is one of the aqueducts that still today quenches the thirst of Romans and tourists.

Mills on the Tiber: Bread and Pasta in Rome

Bread has been baked in Rome since antiquity, but it has not always been made with wheat. The first stalwart warriors of the republican period nourished themselves for more than three centuries on an unleavened focaccia, cooked on the hearth and certainly not made with the precious wheat we know today. It was made from various grains, such as barley and spelt, but also millet and others. Although at various dark periods of Italian history people resorted to making flour from acorns, the ancient Romans appear not to have. The most common bread was unleavened: once a year, dough was made from millet flour and formed into biscuits.[43]

It appears that it was through contact with Egypt that the ancient Romans learned to make a soft and very white bread. Soon the *pistores* (bakers) began to bake a marvelous variety of breads, later procuring the tender grains grown in Sicily and in North Africa, which displaced the old spelt cultivated by this time only in the most isolated or mountainous regions and used by the country folk.[44] Wheat was ground by mills operated first by elbow grease, then by draft animals.

At some point, bread making left the home and became public, and consumers became increasingly exigent. In the first century B.C., Roman bakers produced breads made of wheat, rye, and barley, and very white bread for the wealthy patrician tables; Egyptian bakers created the fashion of fine, white Alexandrian bread. Many different kinds of bread were produced: *panis cibarius, secundarius,* and *plebeius,* in increasing order of bran content, *panis furfureus* was for animals, while special bakeries produced *panis militaris* and *panis nauticus* for soldiers and sailors. There were breads flavored with milk, honey, wine, oil, cheeses, candied fruits, spices, and fragrant herbs. There was even a *panis ostrearius* made expressly for serving with oysters. Often bread was molded into the most imaginative shapes: the satirist Martial reports an obscene loaf, created to serve to the mistress of the wealthy host of a banquet.

It follows that the Roman *pistor* (baker) was a personage of rank, aware of his own importance. Evidence of this is the monumental tomb, worthy of a consul, of the baker Eurysaces, which can still be admired today outside the Porta Maggiore in Rome.

Then the barbarians arrived, but in Rome, as elsewhere, people continued to grind wheat and make bread. A myriad of mills ground wheat for the city. Those built on dry land, called *mole terragne* (land mills),[45] were powered by the numerous watercourses that ran through the city; others were built on the banks of the Tiber.

The historian Procopius of Caesarea, in his *Gothic War,* provides the first mentions of the Roman phenomenon of the floating mill. The Goths besieged Rome in A.D. 537, but that was not enough, and they took the drastic step of cutting off the flow of water through the aqueducts. In addition to depriving the people of water, that action brought to a halt all the city's mills. But General Belisarius,[46] in charge of defending the city, had the brilliant idea of mounting mills between pairs of boats anchored to the banks of the Tiber, alongside the

Tiber Island, where the current was fastest. For many centuries to come, mills on the Tiber were to be an integral part of the Roman landscape. They proliferated until, by the eighteenth century, they posed real impediments to river traffic, but they remained in use until the end of the nineteenth century, when people were still having their grain ground for home use.

The mills were anchored to a masonry pylon attached to the riverbank. The pylon also served as a sort of escalator by which to reach the mill, and its resilience helped absorb the movements of the mill when the river was high. The mill proper was contained in a wooden house atop a large boat anchored with ropes and chains. Between the large boat and a smaller one next to it were the wheels that propelled the mills by their movement in the water. The small boat, the *barchetto,* was also anchored with ropes and chains. It was not rare, however, for the fury of the floodwaters to rip the fragile boats from their moorings and smash them against the bridges or the riverbanks. Sometimes the owners were lucky and managed to drag their boats back to their moorings without too much damage.

Mill operations were strictly regulated. The cost, in 1597, to mill a sack weighing 450 to 500 *libbre*[47] was ten bolognini.[48] A great deal of flour must have been used if Pope Sixtus V (1585–90) forbade milling to all but the bakers in order to keep track of the city's monthly consumption of wheat.

The millers had a guild whose charter dates to 1496. They were bound by strict laws, and the wheat collected by their delivery boys had to travel with proper documents. The guild also dictated rules on the use of the *marrane,* the streams that ran through the city. The owners of the mills mounted over the waterways were not allowed to damage the surrounding gardens during loading and unloading, and once a year, they were obliged to clean the riverbed. Numerous laws and regulations administered by the state reflect the importance of the mills to feed the whole city. For example, among them was one that prohibited the requisitioning of horses in service to and from the mills.[49]

The bakers, or *fornai,* belonged to another guild. The weight of the bread was set by law, and the charter of 1481, still preserved at the headquarters of the Confraternity of Bakers in Rome, imposed a boycott on mills that "replace or ruin the flour" by adding nonwheat flour. The bakers were not allowed to sell bread to osteria operators or to *caporali* ("corporals," who were obliged to buy from special military bakers), and bread could not be baked on Sunday.

Bread was always one of the principal components of the common people's meals, and some simple bread-based recipes still exist in the cooking of Rome and Lazio. "Interpreted," as modern cooks say, and embellished, their popularity as the opener of a typical Roman meal, and sometimes much more, is growing steadily. We speak of course of the celebrated *panzanella,* humble *pancotto* (recipe page 246), and the now ubiquitous *bruschetta.*

The humble slice of chewy Roman bread, toasted, rubbed vigorously with a clove of garlic, drizzled with extra-virgin olive oil right from the press (*frantoio*), and sprinkled with salt lay long forgotten. On the rare occasions that anyone made it, it was as a snack, or for children, and in any case was more suited to country houses, where it could be easily made by toasting the bread in the fireplace. *Bruscare* means simply "to toast."

Today it is back in fashion. There is not a trattoria or restaurant, however smart, that does not serve some type of *bruschetta* as an antipasto. In other words, *bruschetta* has become the acid test of the gourmand's boundless imagination—though sometimes perhaps excessive or misguided. That humble slice of bread laden with such varied toppings and sauces has lost all sense of its poor origins, but in compensation it has risen to the honors of the most tasty and recherché recipes.

Pasta, however, at least ready-made dry pasta in the imaginative shapes we know today, has been around for centuries, but its broad diffusion dates only to the late eighteenth and early nineteenth century, when machines and industrialization, and the lower prices that followed, aided its spread all over the country. There is no doubt that, quite early and not only in Rome, every housewife every day kneaded water and flour to make the dough that, cooked in a vegetable soup, would be the main dish of the daily menu.

Homemade pasta[50] has been handed down with the generic name of *maccheroni,* but the infinite variety of shapes ranges from *gnocchetti* and small fusilli to thin fettuccine and spaghetti. Already in the sixteenth century, Rome had its University of the Spaghetti Makers (guild of *vermicellari*), which means that the production and sale of pasta was already widespread there among the middle classes. Pasta sellers opened their shops in the area around the Pantheon, where their memory endures in such street names as Via dei Pastini and Via delle Paste.

Before the tomato was widely consumed, even by the poorest residents—a phenomenon that dates from the end of the 1700s—pasta was dressed almost exclusively with grated pecorino cheese or fried pork fat, with perhaps the help of garlic or onion or herbs. The survivor of that type of seasoning in Roman tradition is the famous *battuto,* a base for sauces made of pork fat, onion, and herbs (recipe on page 251), which is used to add flavor to nearly all the ancient soups of Lazio.

Rarely could the poor afford the luxury of egg pasta, though it was quite common among the leisured classes. Beginning in the seventeenth century, culinary texts speak of angel hair, *capelli d'angelo,* a type of egg pasta cut too thin for human hands ever to have made it. These were, in fact, the specialty of certain nuns, whose convents often sent them as gifts to new mothers or to sick members of important families with a rather curious ceremony. An important scholar of things Roman, Gaetano Moroni,[51] gives an amusing description. The bearers of the precious gift, preceded by the families of the nobles, ramrod straight in their elaborate uniforms, marched ahead of the gift: "And immediately afterward, brought in by numerous bearers, one saw towering the 'pavilion of the new mothers,' that is, a grandiose machine with bizarre designs, entirely covered with long threads of *tagliolini* or other egg pasta, the whole surrounded by a swarm of capons and hens for the use of the illustrious patient."

Also well established at the time was the custom of offering a plate of pasta to the masons who had reached the roof of a house under construction. This curious practice is still alive and well in the towns of the Roman hinterland: when the last tile is placed on the roof, the Italian flag is raised and the owner makes a hearty lunch for the workers.

We must stop to talk about one of the most famous pasta dishes in all Italy, the celebrated *pasta all'amatriciana* (recipe on page 111). The dish takes its name from the town of Amatrice, where all the inhabitants are aficionados of their gastronomic monument. Today it has become a mainstay of the popular Roman kitchen, but to make it exactly right, never use pancetta in place of *guanciale,* which has a much more delicate flavor. The quantity of tomato, which was added later, as its use became more common, is just as important, since the pasta should be colored only light red. The types of pasta to use are *bucatini* or spaghetti, period.

Polenta is another important dish in the region's kitchen. Cornmeal was a late arrival on the Roman gastronomic scene. Shepherds brought it from Abruzzo, as food for the transhumance, and even today it is still less common in the capital than in the towns of the hinterland, toward Rieti to the northeast and Latina to the southwest, where it was introduced by the peoples of the Veneto who came to populate the Pontine area after the marshes were drained.[52]

The Romans make polenta with finely ground yellow cornmeal, and they give it an almost creamy consistency. They serve it with various sauces—such as *sugo d'umido* (recipe on page 253), *sugo finto* (recipe on page 254), and others—but their favorite is with sausages and pork rinds (recipe on page 126), which today can be tasted in numerous towns of the Roman countryside.

Rome and Its Gardens

Green spaces were an important feature of the Roman cityscape until the founding of the Kingdom of Italy in 1861 (Rome became its capital only in 1870). Most such spaces were parks, but some were kitchen gardens and vineyards. There was plenty of water: in addition to the Tiber, Rome was traversed by numerous *marrane,* or streams, which were canalized and used for irrigation. The largest *marrana,* known as *the* Marrana, began in the Castelli (the hill towns south of Rome), ran outside the city walls at the Via Appia, and emptied into the Tiber, after passing under the Via Ostiense at the Basilica of Saint Paul's Outside the Walls. Another one, the Aqua Crabra, ran along the walls outside the Porta San Giovanni, entered the city under the Caelian Hill, ran along the Circus Maximus, and emptied into the Tiber at the Temple of Hercules Olivarius (formerly believed to be of Vesta), where it fed a spring.

Water deviated for irrigation often wound up invading the streets, which thus became bogs. But by the end of the sixteenth century, a law attempted to impose order on the deviation of water by prohibiting drawing water without the authorization of the consuls, on penalty of a fine of fifty gold scudi and three lashes. Drinking water was sold in the street and was delivered to homes by water carriers. To quench their thirst during the summer, in addition to the *fontanelle,* or small street fountains, still a feature of the city today, passersby could, for a few coins, buy a glass of water flavored with a couple of drops of lemon juice from the *acquafrescaio* (the cold-water man), who kept it cool in special ice-filled containers.

During the Renaissance, "gardens" also came to mean green spaces owned by literary figures or artists, which became the headquarters for learned gatherings. Far from the pomp of the courts, humanists met in a serene green setting to dine and discuss arts and letters. Among the most celebrated gardens was that of Messer Coricio, near the Piazza della Cancelleria, frequented by the most illustrious humanists and men of letters of the sixteenth century, such as Cardinal Bembo, Paolo Giovio, and Pomponio Leto. The famous garden of Jacopo Sadoleto, cardinal and man of letters, was on the Quirinal Hill near the Church of Santa Susanna. In the Renaissance, Rome began to build palazzi with large internal courtyards, in the Florentine style, with the idea of having open spaces for parties and banquets, and also for growing vegetables.

The secret of the Roman gardens' luxuriance was abundant water and a particular microclimate. For centuries the gardens supplied the city. The sector was regulated by the powerful and wealthy University of the Vegetable Gardeners, one of the most important in the city's hierarchy of guilds. The members of the university and the confraternity met at the Church of Santa Maria dell'Orto (of the Vegetable Garden) in Trastevere (to this day headquarters of their spiritual descendants). By the end of the nineteenth century, this guild possessed one of the largest real-estate holdings in the city.

The produce of the gardens constituted a basic part of the people's diet. On the Colle degli Orti (Hill of the Gardens), the present-day Pincio, the best artichokes and celery in town, as well as famous cabbages, were grown. Famous too were the artichokes and celery picked in the gardens around the Trevi Fountain. Celery, rare on the table until the sixteenth century, was brought to Rome by Cardinal Cornaro, who grew it in his gardens at the Trevi Fountain and was so proud of his crop that, says one historian, as soon as the plants ripened, he would send "a pair as a gift for the pope, one to the cardinals, and one to the princes." These ingredients are still basic in Roman cooking, along with tender sweet peas and green lettuces, chards, and many different kinds of cabbage.

A feature of Latian popular cooking is the combination of vegetables with other ingredients. They can be added to fish (cuttlefish with peas or artichokes, recipe on page 200) or meat (oxtail with lots of celery, recipe on page 156), or served in tasty combinations with other vegetables and flavored with one of the many wild herbs that grow in abundance in the Roman countryside. The masterpiece of expertly mixed flavors is the sublime salad known as *misticanza,* which consists of greens collected on the banks of streams or, better yet, in the middle of vineyards, and then dressed with olive oil, vinegar, salt, and pepper. Today it is difficult to put together all the traditional greens, but some can occasionally be found in the city's markets. Among the most common were arugula (rocket), wild chicory, rampions, salad burnet, wood sorrel, *cariota,* monk's beard, borage, *bucalossi, caccialepre, crespigno,* wild endive, lamb's lettuce, *oiosa,* poppy greens, *piè di gallo,* and purslane (many with no equivalent term in other languages). To make the *misticanza* sweeter, large peeled grapes could be added.

Vegetables and legumes were widely used in the ancient Roman diet, their preparation becoming more elaborate as the citizenry developed more luxurious tastes. Practically every poet and writer has left a record in his writings of fresh salads or flavorful purées of vegetables or legumes. In antiquity, the most common vegetables seem to have been the squashes, the chards, peas, mushrooms (porcini were already greatly appreciated in ancient Rome, along with chanterelle and fly agaric mushrooms), wild asparagus, turnips, and rampions. Turnips and onions were an essential part of the diet, since they were considered therapeutic as well as nutritious. If we believe the satirist Martial, the legendary Romulus himself ate turnips, even in the afterlife. Turnips embodied republican probity when the consul Curius Dentatus, in the early third century B.C., was eating roasted turnips as he received a delegation of Samnites expecting to bribe him with expensive gifts. The humble turnips told them their man was incorruptible. The best turnips came from the Sabine country.

The ancient Romans did not have artichokes, but did eat cardoons, their relative, and their flowers. The earliest mention of artichokes is not until the Renaissance, in a fifteenth-century document on agriculture.

In antiquity, fava beans and wheat appeared on the everyday tables of the poor. Fava beans, usually boiled or grilled, were valued for their high caloric content. They were especially enjoyed by farmers, gladiators, and blacksmiths—in other words, by anybody who did heavy physical labor. Everyone loved them, except the Pythagoreans, for whom the beans were taboo: they were believed to house reincarnated souls.

Conservation of fresh vegetables was a problem then just as it is now. Apicius advised cutting off the tops and covering the stems with wormwood. To keep the brilliant green of vegetables, he suggested adding a pinch of soda to the cooking water. He has a famous recipe for leeks cooked in embers, well washed, salted, and wrapped in cabbage leaves. Pepper and a little olive oil were the only condiments needed.

Many kinds of vegetables were found on the wealthy tables of the empire. The emperor Tiberius had greenhouses that could be moved to follow the sun and produce zucchini year-round. Cooked greens were generally served at the beginning of the meal; for the poor, however, there was often nothing else.

Throughout the Middle Ages, greens were widely used, not just in the kitchen but also as medication.[53] And in this double role they remained on the tables of the poorest until after World War II.

Beginning in the Renaissance, to read the classic texts, vegetables were served mostly in the form of a sort of *torta rustica,* and not, as in modern times, as a side dish. They were mixed with cheese, especially parmigiano and ricotta, and with eggs and honey. Soups—always purées—were made in practically the same way and served between courses.

In Rome, vegetable sellers were divided into *fogliari,* or "leaf men," and *ortolani,* or "vegetable gardeners." The former dealt only with leafy vegetables, which were also used for wrapping fresh cheeses and took the place of paper for wrapping small items. The *fogliari* were allowed to sell their products only in their own gardens, while the *insalatari,* or "salad men," a subgroup of the *ortolani,* with permission of the consuls, could sell their salad greens throughout the streets. Legal holidays had to be respected. It was prohibited to pick vegetables on holidays with six exceptions: "fava beans, peas, fennel, melon, pumpkin, and cucumbers."[54] Eggplants were not common. They were believed to be slightly toxic and even Artusi himself thought so.[55] In Rome, they went by the curious name *marignani,* which was still in use in the 1800s. The same term was used (especially in the nineteenth century) to describe the prelates *extra urbem* (that is, those sent on missions outside the city), who could be seen walking through the city wrapped in flowing eggplant-colored cloaks.

Mushrooms that are highly prized today—such as porcini and *ovoli*—often appear in popular Roman recipes. The woods all over Lazio were full of mushrooms, and as early as the sixteenth century, wild mushrooms, both dried and fresh, were sold in the streets.

It is difficult to date the arrival of permanent markets, but they may go back to the eighteenth century. The city's oldest market, the picturesque Campo de' Fiori, was still being used as the site of executions as late as the 1600s. The statue of Giordano Bruno that dominates the piazza memorializes his death at the stake there on February 2, 1600. The piazza's name—"field of flowers"—scarcely befits the use made of it.

Much has been written on the agriculture of Lazio's rivers, and the sources have not always been objective and in agreement: the absolute desolation described by the travelers on the Grand Tour has been counterbalanced by more in-depth and serious studies. It is not that the situation was not grave, but the absolute absence of cultivation on the plain and the Castelli Romani has been contradicted by many scholars and writers, including ancient ones. Something must have survived in the *ager desertus* if Procopius of Caesarea in his *Gothic War*[56] tells how, when the Ostrogoths arrived in 537, the fields of wheat almost reached beneath the walls of Rome.

As late as the nineteenth century, in the agricultural lands of the *campagna romana,* the question of the *latifundium* remains absolutely open. Agricultural work was done by hired hands, who did different jobs depending on the season. In the late spring, for example, in the area of the Castelli Romani, there was the strawberry harvest, done mainly by women; then, in October, after the first autumn rains, it was time to gather mushrooms, which were copious in the woods. Large baskets were filled with *ovoli,* porcini, chanterelles, *famigliole,* and morels, loaded onto mules, and sent along the tracks of beaten earth to the Roman market. In June, the workers left the woods, dropping everything to go cut the hay in the fields. The hay stayed dry on the ground for some days, and everyone kept an eye on the sky and prayed it would not rain. Then the women, equipped with the characteristic wooden hairpin-shaped pitchforks, tossed and piled the hay up in stacks. Finally, they used a curious hand press to form it into bales that were collected and stored for the winter.

In summer, the horse owners, who transported the wood from the forests, met in the fields to gather the sacks of wheat and deliver them to the Annona

Garlic vendor in the Campo de' Fiori market, Rome (Fondazione Primoli, Rome)

Romana.[57] This office governed the grain sector according to an extremely complicated system, made more so by a slow and unsafe transport network.[58]

When in 1801 the Vatican liberalized the food market, and thus the wheat trade, the price of both wheat and, especially, bread began slowly but inexorably to rise, and peasant families were hard-pressed. The situation resulted in protests that today would make us smile. The women would go as a group, singing as though it were a happy jaunt in the country, often accompanied by the parish priest and some carabinieri, with no instances of violence or disorderly conduct.

Agronomists and travelers from around the world have dedicated pages and pages to what was grown in the region, some in very fertile volcanic soil. But the transition from an agrarian society to an industrial one, the effects of which were felt in Italy from the end of the nineteenth century, in Lazio occurred within a short period of time and therefore was a dramatic and intense process. As late as the years between the two world wars, the agriculture of Lazio was stagnant: official statistics of the period indicate a grain production per hectare unchanged for centuries. At the same time, the amount of land under cultivation increased enormously, from some 180,000 hectares (444,790 acres) in the biennium 1910–11 to 300,000 hectares (741, 316 acres) and more on the eve of World War II. In the same period, the whole region registered a drop in productivity of olive trees and vines, despite the substantial increase in cultivated land. This is the explanation for the drop in gross domestic product (GDP) between 1929 and 1937. Stagnation in stock raising and the decrease in the profitability of fruit and vegetable growing also contributed to the weakened GDP, even though significant transformations had taken place in these sectors, too.

Starting between 1920 and 1940, the Italian state launched a central agricultural policy, echoing what was already occurring in other advanced-economy countries. These were the epic years of the "battle of the wheat,"[59] of the constitution of the agrarian consortia, and of the big drainage projects. In the *agro romano,* peasant demands and the distribution of the lands by the Opera Nazionale Combattenti[60] began to exploit many small parcels of farmland, which developed especially along the so-called consular roads:[61] on the Via Nomentana, toward Tivoli, on the Via Appia in the direction of the Castelli Romani, and then along the Flaminia, Trionfale, and Aurelia.

In September 1944, with the Gullo decree (named for the agriculture minister in the second Badoglio government[62]) enacted, the assignment of un- or undercultivated lands to the peasants on the condition that they form cooperatives finally began. Owing to the usual bureaucratic hang-ups, however, the measure did not produce great results, which prompted fresh exasperation among those who worked the land. In September 1947, a large group of peasants, but also of veterans, artisans, and the unemployed, occupied the uncultivated property (2,965 acres/1,200 hectares) of the National Institute of Insurance in Genzano and Lanuvio. It was only the beginning: the number of occupations continued to grow into the 1950s, and began to die out only after the equalization of agricultural wages and the general economic conditions of the country began to improve.

The 1960s were the years of the Italian "economic miracle," when agriculture made a fundamental contribution to development that took concrete form in the modernization of the whole country in the following decade. Thus, the growth of Latian agriculture should be seen within the framework of the improvement of Italian agriculture as a whole, which today is regulated by the agricultural policy of the European Union.

Sheep, Shepherds, and the Pastoral Kitchen

The rich grazing lands and woods that once covered all of Lazio favored the inclusion of the meats of sheep, cattle, and game in the diet. In antiquity, game was prized more highly and considered tastier than the equally common meat of domestic animals.

Wealthy Romans squandered fortunes to equip their estates for the large-scale raising of fish and wild animals—in total disregard of the sumptuary laws that every so often attempted to put limits on excessive spending for edible delicacies and other luxuries. For example, a law enacted in 161 B.C. specified that no more than one chicken per day could be served, and it could not be artificially fattened.[63]

Bovine meat was still uncommon, and that of the cow was considered more tender than that of the bull. Game was by far the favorite source of meat, however. The Romans built *leporaria,* sophisticated enclosures for raising hares. By 37 B.C., when M. Terentius Varro wrote his treatise on agriculture, these had become capacious enough to hold deer, wild boar, and other large animals.

The *leporarium* of the great first century B.C. orator Q. Hortensius Hortalus, on the Via Laurentina just outside Rome, occupied thirty acres (twelve hectares) and was surrounded by a high wall. That of Q. Fulvius Lippinius, built in Tarquinia around 50 B.C., extended over twenty-five acres (ten hectares) and was also used to raise wild sheep captured on the islands of Corsica and Sardinia.

The less wealthy made do by raising dormice (*glires*) in *gliraria,* feeding them acorns and chestnuts. Or they raised snails (*cocleae*) in *coclearia* set up near ponds, and fed them on grasses and leaves: the most sought-after specimens came from Sabina, as well as from Africa and Illyria (an area on the Adriatic coast of the Balkan Peninsula extending from Slovenia down to northern Greece).

Anyone who had even a small farm could easily raise geese, ducks, and peacocks, as well as chickens, whose tender and flavorful meat (obtained by feeding the animals food soaked in milk) the Romans liked.

Large and small aviaries housed pigeons, doves, beccaficos (fig peckers), thrushes, francolins, peacocks, gray partridges from the Alps, guinea fowl from Numidia (roughly today's Tunisia), pheasants imported from Colchis (a part of today's western Caucasus), and the prized alpine wood grouse.

Pork was widely used, as much for its ease of preservation as for its tasty meats. The documents available to us acknowledge the great skill of Roman cooks in transforming pork into salamis, sausages, and pâtés and in salting and drying. Even during the so-called barbarian invasions of the Middle Ages, when consumption of meat was necessarily limited, swine and sheep were still seen on the Latian landscape.

By the Middle Ages, the meat trade was regulated by strict contracts directly between the Camera Apostolica and the *boattari* (small-scale raisers), whose guild was one of the most powerful in the city. Heavy taxes were levied on the animals, which had to enter town on the hoof with proper documents; these were verified at the entrance by the "custodians of the city gates."

From the beginning, taxes on food products, which were especially important because they provided the most reliable revenues, were allocated by law to fund public works, health facilities, works of beneficence, and other critical needs.

A 1566 *motu proprio* of Pope Pius V set a tax on meat (one quattrino[64] per *libbra*) and on table wine[65] (five giuli per barrel), provided that the revenues were used for the repair of two bridges, the Ponte dei Quattro Capi (Fabricio), leading to the Tiber Island, and the Ponte Sisto.

Meat was butchered in the Forum Boarium and sold in the markets. The actual butchering was done by *vaccinari* (literally, "cow men") and as compensation they received the hide, with the tail and cheeks. Here undoubtedly lies the origin of the famous dish *coda alla vaccinara* (page 156), one of the most typical dishes of popular Roman cooking.

A document from the end of the sixteenth century describes how the *vaccinari* had their own quarter, near the city's main slaughterhouse in Testaccio. The neighborhood, called *scortichiaria* (skinnery), was centered around a street that connected the Ponte dei Quattro Capi with the "site, popularly called 'of the cow tanners.'" They tanned the hides in the quarter itself and hung them to dry in the sun from the walls of the houses.

But people ate less beef than lamb, poultry, and pork, which most people raised in the city. Both sheep and pigs were driven through the city streets to graze on the banks of the Tiber or on undeveloped urban land, thus making the city's already precarious sanitary conditions even worse. Toward the end of the sixteenth century, Enrico Caetani, the *camerlengo* (the cardinal in charge of the city administration), issued a widely disregarded edict prohibiting sheep grazing within the city walls.

Of all meats, lamb (*abbacchio*) occupied the place of honor. The name probably derives from the *bacchio*, or "stick," with which the animals were struck on the head and killed. Dictionaries of Roman dialect define *abbacchio* as a baby lamb just weaned whose season lasts all spring, roughly from Easter to the feast of Saint John (June 24). For the next three centuries, consumption was so high that the papal government halted slaughtering between October and the end of April each year.

Every part of the lamb was eaten: head, innards, and flavorful flesh. All are still represented in the rich heritage of classic recipes of genuine Roman and Latian cooking, often in conjunction with the wonderful vegetables of the Roman gardens.

The considerable diffusion of lamb consumption was due to the enormous expansion of the pastures on which sheep raising was concentrated. Sheep husbandry was already widespread in the pre-Roman and Roman periods and continued uninterruptedly during the subsequent centuries, making it the most important food-related activity in the *agro romano*. The pastoral life of tenth-century Farfa is found in registers[66] that document the norms regulating the sheepfolds and shelters and the working of the milk. The first town statues of Rieti, Guarcino, and Aspra[67] established rigid norms for pastoral activities, with precise times set for pasturage. The statutes of Tivoli, which had always been on one of the routes the flocks traveled from and to Abruzzo, dictated precise rules on when the flocks could stop, on the obligation to pay taxes, on the use of the pens, and so forth.

Starting in the twelfth century, improved security in the countryside heightened the rivalry between the farmer and the shepherd, and from exactly then dates the Roman Dogana dei pascoli, or "customs office for pasture," whose duty was to check the number of head in transit at the Mammolo, Nomentano, and Salario bridges.[68] The livestock must then have set off on the Via Tiburtina, toward Sant'Antimo and thence toward the mountain pastures. From there the supervisors of Tivoli and Carsoli had charge of the passage of the sheep and the organization of the pens. From all this complicated legislation, we infer that the flocks must have been numerous. One of the first documents written about pasturage, dated 1402, during the pontificate of Boniface IX (1389–1404), describes the comings and goings of the livestock in the *agro* and refers to the transit permit for the flocks and the grant of a safe conduct to the shepherds. The tax on sheep and the working of the milk were a precious contribution of money to the always exhausted coffers of the Camera Apostolica.

Between the end of the 1300s and the beginning of the 1400s, the *agro romano* was practically entirely devoted to pasture and cheese making. At mid-century, the registers of the Dogana dei pascoli record about 250,000 head of sheep in the Dominion of St. Peter. In 1629, the *agro romano* was home to 115,500 souls and 165,797 lambs! And, later, according to the evaluation of the agrarian condition of the *campagna romana* drafted by the French prefect De Tournon[69] between 1810 and 1815, for every three humans in the *agro* there lived four sheep. This explains why Rome had the highest consumption of fresh meat of all the great European cities. The most common types were lamb and *castrato*, pork, poultry, and water buffalo. Having become an important branch of the food business, the shepherds, in 1622, formed a *universitas*,[70] with headquarters in Rome at the Church of Santa Maria della Consolazione, in Piazza Campitelli, and in the city, next to the Annona dei grani, was formed the Grascia for the meat trade.[71]

The protagonist of all this enormous business was the shepherd, the figure with the solitary life, who spent his day leaning on his stick, watching the sheep, and contemplating the sky and the mountains, indifferent to rain or summer heat, dressed in a leather garment he himself had sewn. During the long solitary hours, he learned to read and read the adventure books of the moment, which, in the sixteenth century, might be epic poems, such as Ariosto's *Orlando furioso* or Tasso's *Gerusalemme liberata*. Many shepherds knew entire passages by heart and named their sheep for the main characters. The sheep dog, with his ruffly white coat, might thus bear a grandiose name such as Argante or Tancredi.

Many passed the time playing the *zampogna*, shepherds' bagpipes made of wood and sheepskin, and in the evening, after a supper of bread and ricotta, slept on straw mattresses made of wild fennel[72] inside small conical huts, much like those of their Neolithic ancestors around the Mediterranean. This type of accommodation survived in the *agro romano* until after World War II, when health regulations prohibited them.

Even in the 1800s, the incredible spectacle of hundreds of thousands of sheep leaving for the transhumance could be seen: They paraded in a great cloud of dust, and in their midst, riding a mule, the *vergaro* used his *verga* (staff) to set the pace of the flock, speeding them up or slowing them down as needed. Amid that sea of moving wool walked the shepherds, skin leathery from the sun despite their broad felt hats tied under the chin. After the flock came the so-called *vignarole*, a large cart where sick or lame sheep could ride, and, finally, the long string of laden mules, some with their loads balanced with cheese-making utensils.

Their march took place along *tratturi*, or "tracks," which are the oldest roads in the world. For centuries, the flocks always traveled the same route, across Tuscany, Abruzzo, Puglia, Lucania (Basilicata), and Campania. A census of *tratturi* conducted at the beginning of the 1900s counted a total of 3,050 kilometers (1,895 miles).

The flocks traveled at night, to avoid the heat of the day, but in the darkness it was necessary to keep the eyes wide open, because the brigand, who could already taste the roast lamb, hid behind the hedges, grabbed the legs of the last sheep in the line, and gagged its mouth to keep it from crying out. During the day, the shepherds hunted *terragni*,[73] or they gathered field greens. The shepherd had a trained eye and was able to fill his bag quickly with *lattughella di maggese,* chicories, radishes, and rampions, which ended up in a good soup in the evening. No clocks were needed to tell the time: when Venus—which they called *gallinella*—appeared in the sky, it was midnight.

Roads and Taverns

The great roads that radiated from the Urbs like the spokes of a wheel had once been one of the strengths of the Roman expansion. But over the centuries they deteriorated into small lanes, some wiped out by scrub, some reconstructed with a different route of greater local interest. Even the Via Francigena[74] was shifted to different routes, of which the only certain one is the end of the Via Cassia, roughly from the Baccano valley[75] to the entrance to Rome.

The ancient roads measured their distances from the gates in the Servian walls[76] and were named either for the city toward which they led or the political authority who had had them built. Thus the Via Nomentana led to Nomentum, today Mentana; the Via Tiburtina to Tibur, present-day Tivoli; while the Via Flaminia was called by the name of the censor Gaius Flaminius and went to Ariminum (Rimini), start of the Via Aemilia, built in the consulate of Marcus Aemilius Lepidus.

The most beautiful and important road was the Via Appia, built, says Livy,[77] in 312 B.C. It led to Capua[78] and was the first Roman road to be paved in the manner of the Carthaginian roads, that is, with basalt stones. By that time Rome was a major power. The roads of the early republican period were simple tracks, difficult to transit for merchants and armies. That must have been why the central government felt the need to speed up the traffic of the armies. Its surface was perfectly smooth, and two vehicles coming from opposite directions could pass each other. Along its route were numerous stages: Right after the Porta Capena was Ad Novum; there followed Bovillae (Boville, near Frattocchie), Aricias (Ariccia), Ad Sponsas (perhaps Cisterna), Tres Tabernae (still not identified), and Forum Appii (whose tavern was known for having mosquitoes as large as elephants). Then came Ad Medias (Mesa), Feronia, Tarracina (Terracina), Fundi (Fondi), Formiae (Formia), Minturnae (Minturno), Ad Pontem campanum, Urbanas (Urbana), Casilinum (present-day Capua), and finally Capua.

But there were other roads toward different points south, such as the Ostiensis, the Laurentina, the Campana, and the Ardeatina. Toward the east ran the

Latina, the Tusculana, the Asinaria, the Labicana, the Praenestina or Gabina, the Collatina, and the Tiberina or Valeria. The roads leading north were the Nomentana, the Salaria, the Flaminia, and the Cassia.

Besides the Appia, the richest and most ornate roads were the Flaminia, the Latina, and the Cassia. The first stretch, just outside the walls, was lined with tombs and mausoleums. In later centuries, shepherds and peasants of the *agro* used their ruins as shelter for the night.

Settlements gradually formed at the stopping places along the roads and grew into villages, towns, and cities. They were designated *municipium, civitas,* or *vicus,* but there were also small agglomerations, very important for the nomenclature of the roads, such as *mansio, positio,* and *mutatio.* A *mansio* was a simple cluster of houses that included one or more taverns for staying overnight. The *positio* was a *mansio* located on the seashore. And a *mutatio* was a place where horses could be changed.

With the centuries, the ancient Roman stations took the name of *stazioni di posta*[79] and added other services, such as a church and a grocery shop, especially for rural workers. Many of these villages were also fortified with sturdy walls; one entered through one gate and left through the other. A number of these stations became known as an *osteria della posta* and remained in operation for many centuries. Some are remembered for the illustrious names that passed through them: the osteria of Grotta Rossa, outside the Porta del Popolo, already existed in Cicero's day;[80] the emperor Vespasian camped in the neighborhood when getting ready to give battle to Vitellius in 69, and it was still standing during the Battle of the Milvian Bridge, between Constantine and Maxentius, in October 312. Tradition has it that, in the twelfth century, the concordat between Pope Paschal II and Henry V on the question of the investiture[81] was signed at an osteria near Sutri; much later, an osteria witnessed the retreat of Garibaldi in 1849. Montaigne and later Shelley and Byron stayed at Castelnuovo di Porto, since the sixteenth century a property of the Vatican, which gave it in concession for use as an inn for periods of nine years. From 1700 on, this station displayed the image of a peacock on its sign.

The population of these osterias along the great arteries grew over time. Other artisans joined the blacksmith, the tavern keeper, and the priest who said mass to provide needed services: shoemakers who made bags and purses, tinsmiths who made kitchen utensils. Little by little the villages grew into the large and small towns that today still line the major highways. One of the most important was certainly the Osteria della Storta on the Via Cassia, at a strategic point on the Via Francigena, 9 miles (14.5 kilometers) from Rome. There were actually five osterias here, given the importance of the interchange. Already in the Roman period there was an osteria for the postal service and to this end was built a *stabulum* for the post. According to tradition, Saint Ignatius of Loyola had a vision when he stopped here on his way to Rome. The Osteria dei Cacciatori (of the hunters), at the foot of Monte Sacro, was still standing, when, on August 15, 1805, Simón Bolívar swore he would liberate South America from Spanish domination; and the Osteria dei Francesi in Marino, near Frascati, in the Castelli Romani, took its name from Alberico da Barbiano, the great *condottiero* in the service of the papacy, in memory of his victory over the French in 1379.

One of the osterias on the Tiber Island belonged to a man named Grappasonne. In 1908, Queen Margherita's car broke down in front of it. Later the owner hung on a hook the chair on which Her Majesty rested while the problem was being dealt with. From that day on, the sign on the osteria bore this inscription: "Osteria with choice wines from the forest of Marino. In this wretched osteria, on the 17th day of October 1908, the automobile of Her Majesty the Queen broke down, and she sat in this humble chair. The owner, Abele Grappasonne, moved by such an honor, placed this commemoration."

Prices were already regulated in 1529, when in the absence of Pope Clement VII (1523–34), the legate Antonio del Monte published a "table of prices" for the osterias and the suburban taverns, from which we deduce that the price of bread in the osterias must have been one and a half bolognino per libbra, wine four bolognini the *boccale*, and the "evening," which included lodging for the night and the meal for the traveler and his horse, should not exceed twenty-five bolognini. A ration of fodder, or, as they called it then, *provenna,* cost five bolognini. In the city things were changing, because the rates varied according to the level and reputation of the establishments.

As the centuries passed, many of the suburban osterias disappeared with the vicissitudes of the territory, but vestiges of a number of them remain, and a careful eye today can still spot them, especially along the consular roads. Many were converted into something else and their former use lost from memory. But in their time, they had an importance we would find hard to believe nowadays, with duties that today are unthinkable. For example, a 1675 edict stated that *caporali*[82] must take peasants who fell ill,[83] with all their belongings, to the nearest osteria that was not a hut but was instead built of masonry and had bedrooms. The landlord was to be given a form with the patient's name and other information and was to provide the first treatment—something to eat. Often the main problem was hunger, for which the stock cure was a hearty bowl of soup, fresh eggs, and lemon balm (*melissa*), an herb with antipyretic properties. If the patient grew worse, the landlord was to take him personally to a hospital in Rome. The expenses of board and transport were reimbursed by the Elemosiniere di S.S.[84] This edict had to be displayed outside the osteria. But malaria was fierce, and too often the dead were buried in the countryside by the peasants themselves, or by the landlord near the osteria.

In the *agro,* the larders of the osterias were especially precious during the growing season: here the *caporali* got supplies for the peasants' meals; and when the osteria was near the fields, the workers would often go in person for supplies.

The hospitality situation in Rome was different. As the capital of Christianity, Rome has always been thronged by pilgrims, which explains why there have been so many taverns and osterias ever since the Middle Ages.

The historian Giovanni Villani, in his *Croniche,* tells that on the occasion of the jubilee year decreed by Pope Boniface VIII in 1300, some two million pilgrims came to Rome: "A large number of the Christians who were then living made the pilgrimage, both women and men, from distant and different countries, far and near. And it was the most marvelous thing ever seen, that all the year round in Rome, in addition to the Roman people, two hundred thousand pilgrims, not counting those who were on the road going and returning, all were supplied and content with their victuals . . . both the horses and the people."

Even if we cannot verify the number of travelers, it is easy enough to imagine how, on occasions of the kind, the city turned into one immense tavern, particularly since the less well-off Romans took the opportunity to rent their own beds and their own spaces.

Until the eighteenth century, no distinction was made between a tavern and an osteria, since the place of refreshment coincided with the place in which one could eat, drink, sleep, and lodge one's horses.

Since the number of taverns and osterias fluctuated, depending on a given year's feasts and holy days, this may be why Rome remained—from the fifteenth century nearly through the nineteenth—the city with the best hotel service and at competitive prices. In the middle of the sixteenth century, a room rented for two scudi a month, equal to about seven euros today.

A 1526 census of the crafts and trades practiced in the city documents 236 hoteliers and innkeepers, 134 bakery shops, 100 salami shops (which also sold dairy products and dried meats), 90 spice sellers (who also served as pharmacists), 88 butchers, 76 gardeners and vineyardists, and 58 water sellers.

Inns and osterias, like all other commercial establishments, had signs outside, or pictures painted on the walls or doors, so that potential customers, most of whom were illiterate, could recognize the place. Thus we have the osteria of the Bear (near Piazza Navona and still in business today as one of Rome's most elegant restaurants, Hostaria dell'Orso), the osteria of the Golden Dragon, the Elephant, the Helmet, the Two Swords, the Two Towers—all names corre-

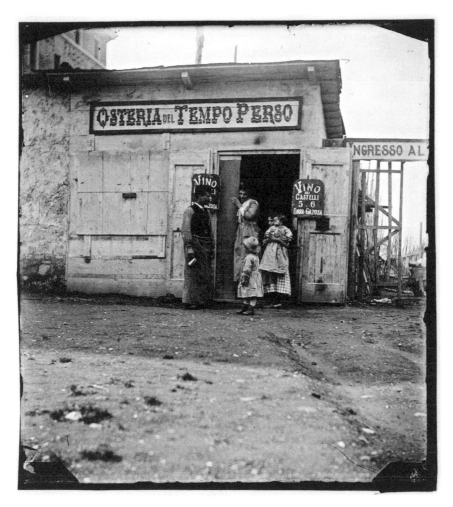

Osteria del Tempo Perso (literally, "wineshop of wasted time"), Via Ardeatina, Rome
(Fondazione Primoli, Rome)

sponding to easily recognizable emblems. These were the so-called talking signs for those who could not read.

The specialty of the osteria of the Falcon, in Piazza Sant'Eustachio, was a rice and giblet *timballo*. The trattoria of the Rooster, near present-day Via del Tritone, gave credit and served a special pot roast[85] of turkey.

Montaigne, who made his "journey to Italy" in 1580–81, stopped at the Orso. Extending his stay, he rented an apartment in the city center consisting of four luxuriously appointed rooms, with kitchen and pantry. The price of twenty scudi per month (about eighty euros today) included linens, wood for heating, cook, and stable service.[86]

Well-off pilgrims usually lodged with prominent families, since they were unlikely to venture to Rome without a letter of introduction to some acquaintance or religious order. Those who did not have introductions, friends in the city, or the money to sleep in a tavern found shelter in the porticoes of churches or palaces, where they often slept with plenty of company.

Pilgrims were not the only travelers to Rome. There were always emissaries of princes and rulers coming and going, especially during papal elections, not to mention merchants, businessmen, adventurers, writers and artists in search of patrons, and courtesans. Tourists, in the modern sense of the term, began to arrive around the beginning of the sixteenth century.

Until the end of the eighteenth century, single rooms in taverns were extremely rare, and people slept in crowded and mixed-gender conditions. The travelers' servants slept where they could, in the corridors, under the stairs, in the stable with the horses, or on guard in front of the master's door.

A census in the middle of the nineteenth century counted 217 osterias, 29 trattorias, 217 cafés, 37 inns, and 40 hotels in Rome.

Until the first decades of the twentieth century, the taverns and osterias offered simple and genuine home cooking, consisting exclusively of typical dishes of the Latian tradition. A carafe of common table wine always accompanied the meal. The city's vineyards provided plenty of wine, and one of the best was produced by the vineyards on the Via Nomentana adjacent to the basilica of Sant'Agnese. Some of the wine people drank in the osterias came, however, from southern Italy, and was unloaded in large barrels at the ports of Ripa Grande. This full-bodied wine was also used for blending with other wines.

Most of what we would call table wine came to Rome from the Castelli Romani, transported on special horse-drawn carts that carried eight barrels of sixty liters (about fifteen gallons) each. They traveled at night in order to have enough time to restock all the osterias, and it was not uncommon in the darkness to encounter a cart parked along the side of the road, while the exhausted driver caught forty winks, in the company of his dog, who slept under the wagon.

Since antiquity, publicans and innkeepers, divided in separate corporations, or guilds, were regulated by their own statutes, which prohibited, for example, standing at the city gates to solicit customers. This practice was so widespread that some provident innkeepers sent their employees as far away as Formia and Gaeta, which were the first large towns at the gates of the Kingdom of Naples. The innkeeper was obliged to report the arrival and departure of guests, while a special Roman police force gave publicans and tavern operators licenses to do business.

The osterias had special hours, staying open into the night, which gave rise to legitimate protests by nearby citizens who were trying to sleep. This is documented by the historian Gregorovius, with a letter sent by the Romans to Pope John XXII, in Avignon, to protest against the young clerics who frequented the osterias at night and whose rackets and brawls disturbed the peace.

The custom of decorating the doors of osterias with wreaths and branches (*frasche,* in Italian, from which comes the name *frasca* or *fraschetta* for a place where wine is sold) dates back to the Middle Ages. The custom lasted until our own day, when just before World War II, it was still common for someone strolling through old Rome, and not just colorful Trastevere, to encounter a vegetal sign. The family still went to the osteria, toting its own meal tied up in a large tablecloth. The innkeeper served a fragrant wine from the Castelli. This service was called "bread and cover" and survives as the cover charge, *pane e coperto,* in Italian restaurants today.

Those who did not bring their food from home could buy a snack from the ambulant peddlers who wandered through the city shouting the name of their product. There were the *fusajari* (lupine bean producers and sellers) and the olive sellers, who, depending on the season, also sold baked dried fava beans, squash seeds, and the famous *coppiette* (sun-dried salted horsemeat), an excellent invitation to drink cool, slightly sparkling wine. Throughout the eighteenth century and into the next, the Roman osterias were frequented by a vast assortment of regulars, including also travelers, artists, and writers—famous and not so famous—who left records of their pleasant memories written or painted on the walls, some of which remained until quite recently.

Among the oddest customs associated with the Roman osterias was the drinking game known as *passatella.* The players all together ordered and paid for a certain quantity of wine, then proceeded to count off to see who would be "master" and who would be "under." Two of the players were named the "commandants" and they distributed the wine to the other players. If he wanted, and if he was able, the master could drink all the wine himself, while the "under," who had the right to at least one drink, dispensed the wine to the other regulars seated around the table. Those who had not managed to get a drink by the end of the game were called *olmi,* tricked. Not infrequently, the *passatella* ended in a fight, sometimes with knives. The papal government finally had to ban the game—which only meant that it continued behind closed doors.

The landlord often lived with his family in the same building and had a friendly, confidential relationship with his clientele. His wife served the customers the same simple dishes that she prepared for her own family. People socialized in the osterias and discussed arts and letters, yes, but also politics, often closely observed by the sharp-eyed papal police.

In the early years of the twentieth century, or more precisely, when the layout of the archaeological area around the Ara Pacis was finally decided, the Piazza degli Otto Cantoni, home to numerous papal osterias, still existed. It was where one could taste first-rate *maiale in agrodolce* (sweet-and-sour pork) and where the *aliciaro* (anchovy man) made the best anchovies in town. Patrons whiled away the time between bites playing cards or dice.

Today the fashion of the osteria or the *fraschetta* has decidedly passed, and slowly but inexorably the ax of fast food has fallen.

Fairs and Markets

Lazio's gastronomic *sagre*—fairs usually dedicated to one particular food—as we know them today, are a fairly recent phenomenon and a favorite of a public ever in search of typical foods and typical everything else. Nevertheless, some of these have their roots in the ancient fairs and markets that were periodically held up and down the Italian peninsula in front of temples, where people converged from far and wide. In Lazio, in fact, the archaeological evidence for such spots is plentiful.

At first, markets must have been held once a year, open just one or two days, almost always near monasteries or other places having to do with worship. Very probably in Italy, but also in France, England, and the non-Muslim part of Spain, fairs and markets and the numerous privileges (licenses to sell) granted beginning in the twelfth and thirteenth centuries must have been much more common than sources tell us.[87]

By the tenth century, the markets were already quite common, and that is when the religious and secular signories began to provide security for the areas where they were held. This was needed especially for agricultural commerce in territories that were scantily populated and far from the larger towns. Such was the case of the isolated Abbey of Grottaferrata, which for centuries was the center of a very important market fair, still on maps in the 1600s. And for security, the authorities considered that the fairs should last no longer than two or three days.[88]

One of the most important ancient fairs was held at Praeneste, present-day Palestrina, a sacred city in Roman times strategically positioned between the Etruscan and Greek civilizations. Destroyed by the Romans, who rebuilt it and dedicated it to the goddess Fortuna, Palestrina had a great temple (brought to light by the bombs of World War II), which received offerings and gifts for the goddess from the entire Mediterranean. It was Christianity that abolished this divinity and replaced her with Saint Agapitus, today patron saint of Palestrina, martyred in the city's amphitheater and celebrated now in the holidays of mid-August.

But by far the most important of the fairs of central Italy was the annual market held at Farfa, in the province of Rieti. The great imperial abbey, *longa manus* of the emperor behind the papacy, had reached its maximum splendor in the sixth and seventh centuries. It survived for centuries and the beautiful sixteenth-century basilica and the medieval town center where the market was held, restored in the first decades of the twentieth century, can still be seen today.

The abbots of Farfa, who in the High Middle Ages extended the dominion of the abbey over the entire Sabina, had especially promoted the growing of olives. Farfa was served by a river port on the Tiber and managed directly by the abbots, who had their own fleet, which could trade with immunity from imperial taxes. The Farfa monks also made their abbey a splendid cultural center: In the valley nestled among the hills they built a church dedicated to the Blessed Virgin, rich in gold ornaments and gems. They surrounded it with five basilicas, an imperial palace, and numerous buildings, colonnades, and porticoes. It had all been protected by solid walls and towers that reached the top of the hill above—at least according to the description by one of its abbots of the time. The extremely wealthy abbey possessed territories not only in Sabina, but also in the Marca of Fermo in the Marche, and even in northern Italy. These were territories granted to vassals or managed directly by the abbots. Its already famous library grew richer with precious codices, today in the Vatican Library. Destroyed by the Saracens, but also by the so-called barbarians, the abbey was rebuilt several times, but by the year 1000 had already begun its decline. Nevertheless, the important annual market, a *fiera franca* (duty free, exempt from the taxes vendors owed the Camera Apostolica,[89] feudal lord, *comune,* or competent corporations), continued for centuries to attract the trade of the entire vast region.

Two other important fairs were held in the area of the Castelli Romani: the most famous was at Grottaferrata, held on the abbey walls, followed by that of the Madonna di Galloro in Ariccia.[90]

These crowded fairs could last as long as ten days. Not surprisingly, the temporary liberalization of trade attracted a huge number of people from beyond the surrounding territories to the fairs, which became crowded with a heterogeneous multitude of merchants (especially Jews);[91] convicts, who could not be arrested during the *fiere franche;* peasants; mountebanks; jugglers; and also brigands. Makeshift camps multiplied along the roads, in the piazzas, and in front of the doors of the churches to accommodate the crowds.

Often the fair and its related religious holiday was the occasion for a plenary indulgence, and thus the cathedral or abbey church managed to cover its annual quota of candles with the donations of the faithful. Goods were sold on the piazzas and side streets, set out on sawhorses and improvised boards or on the ground if they were farm products. The livestock market, however, was usually held outside the walls of the *abitato*.

The fairs were therefore also important opportunities for socialization that was normally prohibited elsewhere. Often the organization was in the hands of the local confraternities,[92] each of which took responsibility for the elaborate processions, always followed by fireworks. Every so often, races by men or animals were also organized. These were invariably followed by ruckus and disorder that frequently resulted in injuries, even though it was prohibited to carry knives or similar weapons at the fairs.

During the fairs, the roads were filled with the voices of hawkers and companies of players, while wine flowed like rivers in the wineshops. These and other public houses were filled to the maximum. After Pantagruelian eating and drinking came gambling and card games, such as *bassetta, biribissi,* and *zecchinetta,* which tradition says were brought to Rome by the Lanzichenecchi (imperial mercenaries) and remained very popular into the eighteenth century. But the games that interested the people most were the various contests borrowed from the Romans, among which the favorites were the race of the *barberi,* that of horses and donkeys, and the race of men and boys. A very popular contest that prompted general hilarity was the one in which women hoisted a large copper pot full of water onto their heads on a *coroglia*[93] and were supposed to carry it at a run without spilling. But the women could also participate in the spindle contest, in which the winner was the contestant who could spin the longest thread from raw wool without breaking it. The men could show off their skills in other contests, the most common of which was the *scifa,* wherein a large rectangular plate used for pasta (the *scifa*) was suspended from a cord attached to a ring. Riders would attempt to run through the ring at a gallop.

We find nothing of all this today in the modern small-town fairs in Lazio, even though many towns put on parades and games in costume in imitation of the old traditions, often organized by the local Pro Loco[94] or by local confraternities.[95] Until the 1960s, however, the *sagre* were mainly a market where the peasants sold their wares, even if very little money actually circulated and transactions were often by barter: salt for eggs, cheese for some other product needed for domestic subsistence.

Today *sagre* and fairs, their ancient peasant origins forgotten, along with the subsistence economy that made them necessary, are a Sunday outing for families, with tastings and with displays of typical products not always locally made. Many of these are dedicated to a single particular product that over time has been established in the area. Among the most famous is the strawberry festival in late May and early June at Nemi, in the Alban Hills just southeast of Rome. Today, the women and girls still wear the old costumes of the *fragolare,* or "strawberry women," and parade through the town's streets in a lively and beautiful procession. Finally, during the first days of October, Marino holds a *sagra* in honor of the god Bacchus, with the famous fountains of wine, which still today attract throngs of tourists and the curious from near and far.

Roman Carnival

If Carnival is an institution as old as the world, the Roman version must be as old as the city, and its celebration says a great deal about the nature of its lively party loving people.

It is difficult to establish the birthplace of this festival celebrated all over the world: it may have begun in India and been brought from there through Asia Minor to the Mediterranean. The handsome Greek god Dionysus became the flaccid, florid-faced, almost effeminate Roman Bacchus. His curly hair wreathed in vine leaves and ivy, he rode a wagon, accompanied by satyrs and bacchants, across the whole ancient world, the center of one of the most popular and enduring cults of antiquity. In his honor, the ancient Romans instituted the Saturnalia, celebrated between the end of December and the beginning of January. Tradition traces the Roman Carnival back to these raucous festivals, in which young and old, without caste or class distinction, abandoned themselves to merrymaking and banquets. The first masks appeared during the Saturnalia. Behind their shelter, people reveled in the streets and abandoned themselves to every sort of behavior, including the not strictly licit. Cart races, orgiastic dances, wild animal hunts—all outlived paganism and are documented, along with orgiastic banquets, as late as the Gothic domination.

The moving spirit behind Carnival came primarily from the wealthier classes, since the expenses one could run up in preparation for the masquerades and banquets could be enormous. The people participated mostly as spectators, but also actively in many games and races. Often the old documents provide resounding testimony of the contrasts of life even in the great civilizations, like the Italian Renaissance. The same people who had their palaces decorated with the works of Raphael and Michelangelo could find amusement in making Jews run races naked, like animals.

Beginning in the late Middle Ages, and for many centuries to come, even bishops and high churchmen participated officially in the Roman celebrations. They opened their sumptuous abodes, embellished for the occasion by famous architects and resplendent with gold and works of art, dances, theater, and banquets without end.

Carnival lasted a different amount of time every year, but always coincided, by definition, with the period just before the beginning of Lent. The word *carnevale* itself means farewell (*vale*) to meat (*carne*).

Among the best-attended celebrations were the festivals held in the piazza then known as Agone (reflecting its ancient use as a racetrack), now Piazza Navona, and in Testaccio, where races were run, followed by all-night feasting and carrying on. In the Middle Ages, these celebrations acquired a character of official solemnity, as well as great political importance, because they were largely regulated by statutes. They were often attended by the pope himself as well as any political bigwigs, ambassadors, and illustrious visitors who just happened to be passing through the Eternal City at that moment—a sort of modern Olympic Games. In fact, the opening day of Carnival was sometimes postponed to accommodate the imminent visit of some VIP. The people and the various corporations (trade guilds) were also enthusiastic participants in the organization of what was considered "the biggest party in the world."

A rare manuscript of the fourteenth century that recounts the organization of the Testaccio race describes how the leaders (known as *caporioni*), nominated by the Senate, went around to the various *rioni*, or city quarters, accompanied by a bull, to collect the offerings of food needed for the feast: "One saw nothing but hams, cakes, and pairs of *provature*, dry and fresh, good *fiaschi* of every sort of wine, reds and whites, and salamis and cheeses and pizzas of *pasta de provatura*, and tongues . . ."

The Roman Carnival achieved its maximum splendor in the Renaissance, thanks to the Venetian-born Pope Paul II (1464–71), who offered the people banquets that the chroniclers called *splendidissimi*. The tables were set up expressly for the occasion under pavilions constructed in the gardens next to the basilica of San Marco, decorated with precious vessels on which were served the most refined preparations of meats and fish and excellent wines. Important citizens and magistrates sat at numerous tables, while the abundant leftovers were thrown to the people who watched noisily and amusedly.

Often, after the races, it was the people themselves who sat at the papal table. During the Carnival of 1470, "His Holiness Pope Paul had races run, that is, those of the Jews, of men, of youths, of old men, and at Testaccio the other usual contests—both asses and water buffalo through the street of Santa Maria del Popolo to San Marco—and made lunch for the citizens in his Garden the Monday of Carnival."

Contemporary accounts describe sumptuous triumphal carts and masquerades that crossed the city. They also detail magnificent banquets, including long lists of the foods that were served, and the "parade dishes" that cooks, true artists of culinary ephemera, created to celebrate the greatness of the hosts.

The "parade dishes," already in vogue in the great medieval banquets, were the gaudiest manifestation of Renaissance cuisine. They were enormous constructions of food, cooked and mounted only to be displayed: for example, a cooked sow, dressed in her skin and surrounded by sucking piglets, or a peacock, again cooked, dressed in his plumage, displaying an imposing and extremely colorful wheel, while a flame emerged from his beak.

Beginning in the eighteenth century, theater became the great event of Carnival. But the parties and banquets did not give up their privileged position, even if customs gradually changed. At balls, the fashionable drink, the exotic chocolate, was served with pastries, and barrels of wine were distributed to the people stationed under the front door, though sometimes, to the laughter and the amusement of the guests, the wine was poured directly from the windows.

This is the moment when the most beautiful Roman palazzi opened up to parties and balls. Here is one account of the details of a ball at Palazzo Farnese held during the carnival of 1751:

At five o'clock was distributed the first sumptuous refreshment of every sort of water and fruit ices, cakes, biscuits, and other pastries in superior abundance to the numerous company and to the great contest of the masks; the ball continued and at eight o'clock were brought into the middle of the room various small tables laden with precious cold foods and various foreign wines, with a prodigious quantity of various pastries, whence those Princes and knights could generously serve the Princesses and Ladies. Nor was such generosity restricted only to the nobility, but passed to satiate the large number of the masks divided through the Gran Sala and in the Loggia. At the same time was opened a grandiose apparatus of a table, with Credenza,[96] raised on several steps, full to overflowing with an infinity of precious cold dishes with equal abundance of wines. . . . Meanwhile, the ball continued both in the noble Hall and in all the other rooms, and at 11 o'clock was carried in the third, similarly generous refreshment and, however, satiated both by the magnificence of the feast and the splendor of the refreshments, the masks began to make freer the step for the Apartment, where it was possible also to pleasurably enjoy rich playing tables and finally, at 12 o'clock, came the fourth generous distribution of chocolate, cookies, and other sweets, ending the great feast at daybreak, with the greatest and most sincere applause that could express the Nobility and the Masks assembled there.

The palace had been so sumptuously adorned for the occasion that for some days after the pope himself went to admire the decorations.

In the streets, bull races had long been replaced by *barberi,* famous riderless racehorses owned by the noble Roman families. The starting point of the race was Piazza del Popolo, where the stallions, cared for by special grooms called *barbareschi,* were paraded. At the signal, the horses were let out and ran down the Via Lata (the medieval name of the Via del Corso) to Piazza Venezia, between two wings of people who urged them on, while the nobles watched from the windows of the palazzi on either side of the street. The 1751 prize, won by the *barbero* of the Rospigliosi family, consisted of a gold brocade cloth in the fashion of the time.

At midcentury, the race was on among the noble families for possession of the best *barberi* to run during Carnival. And the victory in the race almost always preceded a distribution of wine and food to the people by the victor. The Rospigliosi won again in 1764, which was a year of great hunger, and the prince distributed large quantities of bread, in addition to the irreplaceable barrels of wine, for the occasion.

Outdoor games almost always ended with grandiose displays of fireworks, which the people watched from the osterias, where they were eating *la tonnina con la cipolla* (pickled tuna with onion), washed down with Castelli wine.

In the great palazzi, in addition to attending balls, participants played games of chance, such as *bassetta, goffo, faraone, zecchinetta,* and many others. These were the ruin of many nobles, who recklessly bet their ancestral palazzi and estates. The matter became so serious that the pope, Benedict XIV, was obliged to intervene with severe measures to keep the players, often high-ranking members of the clergy, from total ruin.

The Roman Carnival now makes us think of the flower of the European aristocracy, in whose honor parties and banquets multiplied, palazzi and courtyards were embellished in ever more costly and magnificent ways, transformed by contemporary painters, as fashion dictated, into idyllic scenes of Mount Parnassus.

From an issue of *Cracas,* the newspaper of the day, we learn that during the Carnival of 1784, in the course of a dinner hosted by the Venetian ambassador in honor of King Gustavus Adolphus of Sweden and Archduchess Anne Marie of Austria, the guests, "so as not to waste time changing the 124 dishes, [were] invited . . . to move to another room where there was another table." This flabbergasted the guests, since the table was laden with serving dishes of gold and precious stones and with splendid antiques.

Private parties, banquets, and theatrical representations multiplied. Banquets were held in the boxes at the theater, while on the stage playwrights and musicians, from Goldoni, Metastasio, Ariosto, and Monti[97] to Cherubini, Paisiello, and Piccinni,[98] in whose operas women's voices, finally, were heard, triumphed.

Feasts and "wardrobe" (*alla guardarobba*) parties—those at which only cold dishes and sweets were served—were held in the foyers of the theaters as well, most notably in the long-gone Alibert. Sumptuous meals were also served in the Piazza del Campidoglio, as had been the custom since the Renaissance, and it was a race to find the most prized ingredients to put on the menu, such as the trout from Lake Garda, which weighed twenty-six *libbre,* served at a meal at the Campidoglio offered by Don Abbondio Rezzonico.

The winds of revolution toned down the more garish aspects of the Roman Carnival. The horse races stayed, and those families who could afford it, even in a minor key, continued to organize banquets.

Then came Napoléon to threaten the papal throne. The citizenry waited with bated breath, and the Vatican diplomatic corps was even more nervous. it was impossible to think of stopping the wave of blows of the Napoleonic victories advancing on Rome. And when the French army, during Carnival of 1798, under the command of Joseph Bonaparte, took up quarters at Monte Mario, the pope, before ordering the clearing out of the fortress of Castel Sant'Angelo, thought to sweeten the enemy by sending him a gift of "40 bottles of wine, a milk-fed calf, and a sturgeon."

But the temporal power of the Church was over. The Jews of the Ghetto, right in the middle of Carnival, in front of the synagogue, raised the tree of liberty accompanied with a generous distribution of free wine and refreshments.

The Jacobin feasts that were to follow moved from the houses of the aristocracy to those of the emerging bourgeoisie. Despite the introduction of new customs, however, the banquets were no less rich. During Carnival of 1802, Count Bolognetti hosted a banquet in his home to which, as a Carnival game, each guest was invited to bring a dish. This game was almost certainly the origin of the modern custom by which each person brings a different dish to dinner with friends. The dinner at the Bolognetti house enjoyed such success that it was later repeated and copied.

Money for masks flowed like water. The masquerade of 1805 made it into the annals: its theme was "the banquet of the gods," painted and directed by Antonio Canova.

With the arrival of the French in Rome, and following a moment of stasis, Carnival resumed its old splendor, visited by ever more famous guests: there was not a king or emperor in Europe or the New World who did not travel to Rome in this period; and this time the doors of the great noble houses were open to the haute bourgeoisie as well. *Barberi* races and banquets were no longer restricted to Carnival, and on June 8, 1811, on the occasion of the birth of Napoléon's son, proclaimed the king of Rome in his cradle, the French general Miollis, in charge of Rome, organized a *barberi* race and a banquet on the Campidoglio for 150 persons, chosen from among both the nobility and the bourgeoisie. In the evening, the dome, facade, and colonnade of Saint Peter's were resplendent with thousands of torches, while a huge, luminous Catherine wheel lit up Castel Sant'Angelo.

No longer were the social classes rigidly separated and isolated to banquet in their respective palazzi. Rather, the nobles dined increasingly frequently in trattorias. Chigi wrote in his diary of a dinner held at the "trattoria of the Armellino, at the arch of Carbognano, 21 guests, 1 scudo and 65 bajocchi a head, including the women."[99]

The Carnival of 1816 was enlivened by the passionate performance of *Il Barbiere di Siviglia* commissioned by Duke Sforza Cesarini from the twenty-four-year-old Gioacchino Rossini, rising star of music. Success came at the second performance, as we learn from a letter of Rossini to the soprano Isabella Colbrand:

> My *Barbiere* gains from day to day. In the evening all you hear in the streets is Almaviva's serenade. Figaro's aria "Largo al factotum della città" is every baritone's warhorse. Girls go to sleep sighing "Una voce poco fa" and wake up with "Lindoro mio sarà." But what interests me a good deal more than the music is the discovery I've made of a new salad, the recipe for which I hasten to send you. I take oil from Provence, English mustard, French vinegar, a little lemon, pepper, and salt: beat everything together well and add some truffles cut up into small pieces. These truffles give the dressing a fragrance that sends a gourmand into ecstasy. The Cardinal Secretary of State, whose acquaintance I have made in the last few days, gave me his apostolic blessing for this discovery.

The Roman Carnival took place increasingly in the theaters and music halls, where Rossini launched *Tancredi* and *La Cenerentola*. After the theater, the old patrician families, ruined by gambling and no longer in any position to afford the parties they used to give, could enjoy the banquets offered by Principe Torlonia, the wealthy banker who had financed the needy scions of the great houses.

It was in those years that the governor of Rome banned the throwing of plaster stones in the streets, replacing them with coriander seeds covered with flour and sugar.

Political anticlericalism, which arose with the Roman Republic, was transferred to the table, and in trattorias the rage was a type of pasta that is still known today as *strozzapreti*.[100]

With the coming of the Kingdom of Italy, old papal Rome disappeared, the number of inhabitants increased disproportionately, and new quarters were built on the lands of the great archaeological parks that had made Rome one of the most prestigious gardens in the world, encouraged by a building-boom bureaucracy insensitive to the charm of the old city. The races run at Carnival became increasingly dangerous because of the enormous influx of spectators, and fatal accidents multiplied, including one witnessed by Principessa Margherita di Savoia, the future queen of Italy, from the windows of Palazzo Fiano on the Corso.

In 1884, the races were abolished, and the old Roman Carnival passed into history.

The Jewish Kitchen of the Roman Ghetto

Jewish food, in Rome as elsewhere, means kosher food, ancient food, food prepared according to principles laid down in the Bible, and food that still respects ancient laws regulating diet and hygiene.

Locked in the Ghetto from the sixteenth century until the middle of the nineteenth, the Jews of Rome, isolated and forced to be self-sufficient, including for food, were the most faithful keepers of the popular gastronomic tradition, which remained completely untouched by foreign influences or fashions. In fact, many recipes thought of today as typically Roman are actually of Jewish origin.

From the tenth century, after the struggle between empire and papacy, the Roman Jews were forced to live in the Trastevere quarter, around the Ponte Fabricio, which came to be called Pons judaeorum, and later crossed the river to the *rioni*[101] of Sant'Angelo and Regola, where they built their synagogue. In 1555, a papal bull turned what had been (and is now) the Jewish quarter into a true ghetto. Jews were restricted to the area bounded by the Ponte dei Quattro Capi, the Portico d'Ottavia, Piazza Giudia (no longer in existence), and the Tiber. The territory at their disposal was a rabbit warren of little streets and alleys overlooked by insalubrious dwellings, without light and often invaded by the floodwaters of the Tiber. The quarter was locked at sunset and reopened at dawn; transit was permitted through eight gates, one of which opened opposite the church of San Gregorio della Divina Pietà. And yet, it is precisely in this ambiance, in these poor, ill-equipped kitchens, that the Roman Jewish cuisine developed. It was poor, to be sure, but rich in flavors. In it, the loving hand of the housewife, who worked the humblest ingredients into something downright appetizing, is always evident.[102]

Outdoor cobbler's shop in the Jewish Ghetto in Rome (Biblioteca Clementina, Anzio)

When Rome became capital of a united Italy, the gates of the Ghetto were unlocked, but only the wealthier Jews sought to live elsewhere. The others stayed in the Ghetto, which became the Jewish quarter as we know it today. Those osterias and *fraschette* that kept alive the gastronomic tradition of the forefathers of today's Roman Jews are now smart restaurants where one can taste the best products of the Roman Jewish kitchen.

In the Bible, there is everything, says the Jewish cook. Kosher cooking excludes the flesh of animals considered "unclean," such as the pig, the hare, the rabbit, and shellfish, that is, animals that do not chew a cud and have neither hooves nor cloven hooves and fish without fins and scales. In Exodus 12 it is written, "Do not cook the kid in its mother's milk," so meat and dairy products must never be served at the same time, and different dishes must be used. This explains why in Jewish cooking, and Roman Jewish in particular, the use of fats is limited to oil or, in part, bone marrow. Meat is butchered according to ancient laws, by specialized butchers who must kill the animal without making it suffer and so that it loses all its blood. Only in this way can the meat be considered kosher, which is to say pure.

Like other cuisines, Roman Jewish cooking is closely keyed to religious holidays. Yom Kippur (Day of Atonement) is celebrated with sweet-and-sour red mullet and turkey meat loaf. Shavuot, the harvest feast, has sumptuous stuffed cabbage. For Hanukkah, the Festival of Lights, when one candle is lit on the

Boys taking turkeys to "pasture" through the streets of Rome
(Fondazione Primoli, Rome)

menorah each day, spinach and ricotta ravioli and fried chicken are eaten. Children in particular celebrate Purim (the Festival of Deliverance) with almond sweets and *struffoli* (small fried dough balls coated in honey), while the traditional dish for Sukkot (Festival of the First Fruits and Vegetables) is *gnocchi alla romana*. Each festival has, in addition to its own menu, its own special sweets, often based on ground almonds, which, with their high oil content, can partially replace butter.

The Papal Table

Like that of the other Italian courts, the kitchen at the papal court was in the hands of able *scalchi* (high-ranking food-specialist butlers). It was elaborate and costly, completely unrelated to what the general population was eating at the time. Rich and sumptuous or specialized as it might be, it changed not only with the times but also with the tastes of individual popes. Many chroniclers have given us an account of food habits at the papal court, beginning with the rigid ceremonial that regulated the meals of the cardinals when they met in conclave to elect a new pope.

In the Renaissance, a cardinal who attended the conclave[103] was followed into his own little room by a large trunk, called a *cornuta,* which contained the dishes for his meals,[104] and by a *borsa di credenza,* a large bag bearing his family's coat of arms, which contained various other objects for the cardinal's table. His seclusion was not exactly golden if the election went on for a long time. Whether it was held in the Sistine Chapel or, later, in the Quirinal Palace, or in some other place, the only means of contact with the outside world was a special passageway for the food, made of two large, revolving doors mounted on a partition. (A kitchen was not installed in the apostolic palaces until the end of the 1700s. Before that, meals were brought, in a colorful procession, directly from the home of each cardinal.)

Just outside the *clausura* (cloister), a committee of bishops, called the *Reveditori* (Reviewers), sat behind a long table and carefully checked the bags of food before letting them through. Silver utensils, on which messages could easily be engraved, had recently been prohibited, and so were certain foods, such as *pasticci in crosta,* or "pies in a crust," which made perfect hiding places for documents that might influence the nomination of the pontiff.

An army of cooks, *scalchi, credenzieri* (in charge of the inventory of tableware), and wine stewards was on duty to prepare the meals and serve the fine wines that each cardinal had brought, sometimes from very distant parts.

On occasion, the elections went on too long. Gregory X, elected after three years of balloting, later issued a provision to prevent such a thing from ever happening again. According to these measures, three days after the cardinals entered into the conclave, their meals would be drastically reduced to a single course; and if five days passed without the hoped-for white smoke, a draconian regime of bread and water would go into effect until a successful election took place. Later the rule was eased, but frugality became ritualized.

Once elected to the papal throne, each pope put his particular stamp on his kitchen. Innocent III, for example, who reigned from 1198 to 1216, had very frugal habits and ordered that only one course should appear at his table. Benedict X, on the other hand, owed the brevity of his pontificate (1303–04) to his passion for figs. On a visit to the Dominican monastery in Perugia, some conspirators took advantage of this weakness and served His Holiness a basket of beautiful fresh figs—filled with so much poison that he died within a few hours.

Martin IV (1281–85) was a glutton for eels, especially the tasty fat ones from Lake Bolsena,[105] north of Rome. According to a legend reported by more than one historian, he had them brought to his personal apartments, where there was a special tank in which the unfortunate eels were drowned in Vernaccia wine and then roasted. Not satisfied, evidently, to devote himself to affairs of state, this pope saw personally to the preparation of his favorite dish. Dante put him in Purgatory and stigmatized him with the famous lines:

> Ebbe la Santa Chiesa in su le braccia;
> dal Torso fu, e purga per digiuno
> le anguille di Bolsena in la vernaccia.

(He held the Holy Church up in his arms; he was from Tours, and purged by fasting the eels of Lake Bolsena in Vernaccia.)

We do not know how many people mourned Martin IV when he left this world, but certainly the community of eels in Lake Bolsena must have celebrated (see page 186 for a recipe).

Boniface IX (1389–1404), in civilian life Pietro Tomacelli, is believed to owe his name to an epicurean preparation known as *tomaselle* (spelled variously in the ancient texts), consisting of liver meatballs wrapped in caul fat, well seasoned, and cooked over coals.

The Venetian Paul II (1417–71), a great lover of antiquity and collector of ancient gemstones and cameos, ordered his meals to be served in precious ancient vessels.

Outside the Vatican citadel, certain popes' sins of gluttony were often blown up beyond all possibility, as though the popes were almost not human beings, and became the basis for malicious gossip. They were at any rate not a good example for the high-ranking clergy, willing and frequent guests at the Pantagruelian banquets.

So just to set the record straight, not all popes were gluttons. For example, Eugene IV (1431–47), a strict teetotaler, always had some cleric observe his meals to bear witness to his frugality.

The most grandiose banquet in the annals took place during the pontificate of Sixtus IV (1471–84). It was given in June 1473 by Cardinal Pietro Riario, the pope's nephew, in his sumptuous residence in Piazza Santi Apostoli, on the occasion of the visit to Rome of Eleonora of Aragon (the beautiful wife of Ercole I d'Este, duke of Ferrara). The chronicler Corvisieri gives us an account of it.

The muggy weather of the Roman summer obliged the organizers to cover the entire piazza with an immense tent

> made of Genoese sails, held up by ropes which departed from an extremely high antenna erected in the middle, and below that was a delightful fountain that flowed from above. The roof of the long portico of Palazzo Riario was removed and above it was placed a magnificent loggia of antique style partitioned with columns decorated with leaves and flowers. The loggia was divided into three rooms hung with tapestries.

The largest, the banquet room, was covered with a "blue sky, against whose pale color stood out a white cross in the middle." To refresh the air further,

> some bellows [were] hidden above, and for the same purpose had been set up [a] fountain of perfumed water, the extremely fine spray of which must have been regulated for the delight of the guests. . . . On the other side of the piazza, against the lower palazzo, rose the stage for dances and pantomimes. A chosen company of players had been brought from distant countries to entertain the tables with the most celebrated singers. The event lasted from the chiming of XII o'clock until XVIII, served with order and abundance that could not have been better.

The much-talked-about Alexander VI (1492–1503), Rodrigo Borgia, overindulged in the pleasures of the table, which was often attended personally by his daughter Lucrezia, who well knew the tastes of her gourmand father, especially for certain sweetmeats.

Julius II (1503–13), the great pope who commissioned Michelangelo to paint the Sistine Chapel, did not disdain the pleasures of the table, for which he seems to have spent the significant figure of 2,300 ducats a month. He especially loved wine, which, he maintained, cured every sort of indisposition. His doctors were often not of the same opinion, but the pope took advantage of his authority against them and even threatened to lock the doctors up in the dungeons of Castel Sant'Angelo if they did not let him choose his own medicine. It seems, however, that one time, almost moribund, he was brought back to the living by a glass of excellent Malvasia.

His successor, Leo X (1513–21), was the first Medici to ascend the papal throne. As was to be expected, he brought to Rome not only the artistic taste of that refined Florentine court but also its gastronomic culture. Under his pontificate, in fact, in addition to arts and letters, the taste for sumptuous and refined feasts also brought fame to his court. Banquets were held at any time and in any place. This might mean in the Vatican palaces or at the beautiful villa in the Magliana area on the outskirts of Rome, favorite refuge of the pope, who had planted a vineyard there that supplied a prized wine. Or it might mean the opulent villa that his friend and banker Agostino Chigi had just finished building on the bank of the Tiber, or one of the most splendid palazzi of the prelates. Life passed happily among country outings, balls, and hunts in the rich estates on the outskirts of Rome.

We have a charming account of one banquet in particular, held in the pope's honor at Chigi's villa (today known as the Villa Farnesina). The banquet was served

> to the Pope and the Cardinals in a loggia above the Tiber, built expressly from its foundations, with infinite ornaments and beautiful paintings in a single night, with so much sumptuousness and largesse that anything more beautiful would be impossible. In addition to there being the meat of all the four-footed animals, both domestic and wild, and birds of the air, water, and land that can be found, there were still all the sorts of fish, brought in infinite quantity alive from Spain, France, Flanders, Constantinople, and diverse distant parts. . . . [There were also] cheeses, fruits and other things to eat that are found or that can be made with art and that could never be described, with such a quantity of vases and dishes of silver and of gold, that once placed on the table, removing them they threw them in the river and they no more appeared.

In actual fact, the provident banker had had a net stretched next to the scaffolding, hidden beneath the surface of the water, into which the precious dishes fell and were later collected.

Leo X was not so much a gourmand as a gourmet. He did not eat to excess, but he enjoyed seeing others eat and have fun. And so he surrounded himself with a gang of jesters who liked practical jokes, including gastronomic ones, as when he served a rope made up like a lamprey that the guests proceeded to chew to the general hilarity of all.

Gifts of food arrived from the whole world for the kitchens of this pleasure-loving pope: the marquis of Mantua sent him wines from Lake Garda and marinated fish, accompanied by his personal *scalco* (steward). The cellars were also supplied with claret from France and a robust Portuguese wine of which the pontiff was inordinately fond.

The expenses for the feasts and banquets managed little by little to drain the coffers of the state, so that the austere Flemish pope who followed was obliged to repair the damage.

Hadrian VI (1522–23), in fact, proved to have very frugal habits: his meals consisted of a small dish of meat. Often he made do with a light soup, and on the eve of holy days, he ate fish or even fasted, eating only an apple. One chronicler tells us that he did not spend more than a ducat for his food, which he would take from his pocket and hand personally to the *scalco*. Naturally, he abolished feasts and banquets.

But the wheel of history turns, and the next pope was another Medici and another big eater. Of Clement VII (1523–1534), the contemporary humorous poet Francesco Berni wrote:

> The Pope does nothing but eat;
> The Pope does nothing but sleep;
> That's what they say, and
> that's what you can tell anyone who asks.

Julius III (1550–55), the great pope who did much to beautify the city (he built, for example, the Villa Medici and the Villa Giulia), was another *buongustaio* who loved stuffed roasted peacock and adored red onions from Gaeta. His successor, Paul IV (1555–59), so appreciated the good table that he sometimes took three hours over a meal, just time enough to taste twenty or so courses washed down with strong and generous wine brought expressly from the Kingdom of Naples.

The future Saint Pius V (1566–72) was an ascetic pope, but his famous cook, Bartolomeo Scappi, became the author of one of the most successful treatises on cooking that have come down to our own day. The first edition, published in Venice by Tramezzino in 1570, was to be followed by many, and often rare, subsequent editions.

From Scappi's famous *Opera dell'arte del cucinare,* we learn how at the pontifical table was often served the fish of Lake Garda, marinated, or the bogue of the Ligurian Riviera, wrapped in myrtle leaves and probably smoked. The great cook ordered caviar from Alexandria, in Egypt, since he considered the caviar taken from the sturgeons of the Tiber of inferior quality.

At the end of the century, Sixtus V (1585–90) rose to the papal throne. Eager to give a new look to the capital of Christendom,[106] this pope did not have the habit of wasting time at table. In fact, he ordered kitchen expenses drastically reduced to five giuli a day and required simply prepared, genuine foods.

Not long after him, and lasting for only three months, came an equally frugal pope: Innocent IX (1591) ate only once a day. His successor, Clement VIII (1592–1605), observed a strict fast of bread and water on Wednesdays and Saturdays. Urban VIII (1623–44), however, seems to have been a glutton for figs, as was an earlier predecessor, Benedict X. A malicious court anecdote tells how the pontifical chief physician advised him against their abuse, although he, personally, was very much of a glutton for them himself. Asked for an explanation, the chief physician supposedly replied frankly that while the life of a chief physician is of little importance, that of the pope is worth some sacrifice.

Clement IX (1667–69), on the other hand, fasted often, and when he did eat, he did not wish to be served more than three courses.

Pius VI (1755–99) was very sensitive to the problems of agriculture. His papacy is associated with important food-related measures, as well as an unsuccessful attempt to drain the marshes of the Pontina.

A successor, Leo XII (1823–1829), earned his place in gastronomic history—and the wrath of Pasquino and Marforio (Rome's satirical "talking" statues on which statements of political protest were affixed, and so they "spoke" in the name of the frustrated population)—as the pope who had gates put on the osterias.

In the nineteenth century, Gregory XVI (1831–46) became one of the popes who did the greatest honor to the table, even if the worshippers of Bacchus had it in for him when he imposed a new tax on wine.

We have more detailed information on his successor, Pius IX (1846–78). He lunched at two in the afternoon; his table was always very well set and his menu varied little: in general he ordered a risotto, a *fritto misto* (already a status dish in the popular cuisine), a roasted meat, a side dish of cooked green vegetables, and a great deal of fruit. He finished the meal invariably with sweet *bignè* or a *crostata di visciole,* a "sour cherry tart" (this too already typically Roman; a recipe is on page 258). He drank a few glasses of good Bordeaux and finished with coffee. In the evening, he made do with a soup and vegetables and a little glass of white Bordeaux, with which the French made sure his cellar was always stocked.

The *credenziere* Saraceni was charged with serving the first meal to the newly elected pope Leo XIII (1878–1903). Against etiquette, the pope invited Cardinal Foschi to his table for a meal served on dishes of gilded silver. De Cesare, careful chronicler of the events, tells us that the new pontiff was so excited that he ate very little and said even less. As for the other cardinals, they were served "a soup, boiled meat, two main courses and abundant dessert, excellent red and white wine."

With the twentieth century, the era of papal haute cuisine comes to an end. The popes who followed were very frugal; they ordered their meals brought in from outside and the papal kitchens were dismantled. The modern popes loved, rather, to keep their regional traditions. Thus Pius X asked for food cooked Veneto style, Benedict XV favored the cuisine of his native Genoa, and Pius XI dined on the fare of Lombardy. And so they continued. The simple and frugal table of the Pope John Paul II was attended by Polish nuns. His successor, Benedict XVI, started his pontificate with a taste for his native Bavarian cooking, but, on advice from his physicians, eventually switched to a blander diet.

Giuseppe Gioacchino Belli,
Poet of the Roman Kitchen

Mo 'ssenti er pranzo mio: ris' e piselli,
allesso de vaccina e gallinaccio,
garofolato, trippa stufataccio,
e uno spiedo de sarsicce e fegatelli.

Poi fritto de carciofori e granelli,
certi gnocchi da facce er peccataccio,
'na pizza aricresciuta de lo spaccio
e un agrodorce de cignale e ucelli.

(Now listen to what I'm having for lunch: rice and peas, boiled meat and fowl, clove-scented pot roast, stewed tripe, and a skewer of sausages and pork livers. Then deep-fried artichokes and testicles, and gnocchi so good it's a sin, and a yeasty pizza, and a sweet-and-sour stew of wild boar and game birds.)

The most important moment for popular Roman cooking, in which it crystallizes and becomes "modern" as we know it today, coincides with the life of the poet who perhaps, more than any historian, has left us in his sonnets a lively fresco of Roman life, from the social, economic, and—why not?—gastronomic point of view. Giuseppe Gioacchino Belli was born in Rome in 1791 and died there in 1863. He was an odd character, a misanthrope, insecure, a complainer, a bigoted supporter of the power of the pope-king, though he did not hesitate to make fun of his extravagant appetites and rich food, in contrast to the simple and fragrant popular cuisine.

Anyone who could have had a bird's-eye view of Belli's Rome would have flown over a sleepy little city of about one hundred and twenty thousand inhabitants, subdivided into fourteen *rioni,* confined by the old walls and the Tiber, immersed in the green of its great parks, gardens, vineyards, and flax fields that covered four-fifths of its area. The population on which the curmudgeonly lens of the poet was focused consisted of a more or less well-off bourgeoisie and a rich sampling of common people. All lived very simply on the proceeds from grazing, small businesses, and service activities, in the small houses built on top of one another in dusty alleys and among the ruins, where sheep grazed and turkeys fed.

Shopping was done with the bajocco[107] and the grosso (a copper coin worth five bajocchi). But if the shopping was more substantial, one needed a testone, a large silver coin worth thirty bajocchi. The other coins in circulation were the carlino, worth fifteen bajocchi, the paolo worth ten bajocchi, and the papetto worth twenty bajocchi. The most renowned food shops were found near the Pantheon and competed, especially around religious holidays, in displaying the products in the most captivating and imaginative ways. Among the most famous was that of "Biagio alla Rotonda," whose shop filled up on certain occasions with columns of cheeses and necklaces of sausages, among which could be admired a Moses of lard, armed with a stick like a policeman, sitting atop a mountain of prosciutti. And . . .

> sott'a lui, per stuzzicà la fame,
> c'è un Cristo e una Madonna de butirro
> dentro a una bella grotta de salame.

(Beneath him, to whet the appetite, there is a Christ and a Madonna of butter in a beautiful cave of salami.)

Rome in these same days was home to the crusty Madame Letizia, mother of Napoléon Bonaparte. After his exile to Saint Helena, she had retired to Rome under the protection of the pope. She led an austere and withdrawn life, but appreciated good food and had a weakness for *pasticcio di maccheroni* (baked macaroni).

Madame Letizia spent her days on the verandah of her palazzo on Piazza Venezia, the one at the corner of Via del Corso, and from up there watched the comings and goings in the street. She observed the parades with bands, principal among which was that of the Ospizio degli Orfani (orphanage), and she was amused by the horse races during Carnival. She recognized the carriages of all the grand Roman families and knew who went out and who came in; she admired the ladies' dresses and the gentlemen's fine clothes, until the canonical hour for going to sleep.

Cassandrino[108] reigned in the marionette theaters, and at the theater of Tor di Nona the ballerina Clara Piglia was queen. Belli took note of everything and wrote about it, especially the cooking. From his pages comes forth, as from a handbook for gourmands, a subtle aroma of *stufato* (stew) with celery, while he tells us with great precision what were the most common dishes on the Roman tables in those years: mostly boiled meats or stews, rarely roasts, and often grilled fish, which the fishmongers of the Portico d'Ottavia, where for centuries there had been a fish market, sold at a high price. Belli's verses are redolent of the bitter salad greens *ruchetta* (arugula) and *caccialepre,*[109] of home-baked bread fresh from the oven, of *gnocchi al sugo* "so good they're a sin" (*da facce er peccataccio*).

The food of the poor, yes, but also the food of the rising bourgeoisie, which could afford to spend a few bajocchi more at the butcher shop. Here then are some popular dishes, but richer and more elaborate.

When Belli died, dark clouds were already on the horizon heralding political changes the poet would certainly not have approved—the new monarchy and the end of the papacy's temporal power—but that would deeply affect the life and cooking of that fat, noisy, and extroverted world that, with all its faults, he loved deeply.

Hollywood on the Tiber

In the 1950s and 1960s, Rome and its food underwent profound changes owing to altered economic conditions in general and prosperity in particular. People migrated to the city from all over Italy, not just the surrounding countryside, and these new arrivals brought with them different eating habits and new products, thanks to a rapid transportation system that the construction of new roads had made possible.

Transportation! That was a decisive factor in the transformation of Roman cooking. It brought a good deal more than new foodstuffs. The 1950s and 1960s brought crowds of tourists to the city, an elitist sort of tourism, perhaps, the stuff of gossip columns. Hollywood discovered Rome and its cinema, but also its cooking. And the photographs of Tyrone Power and Ava Gardner seated before a plate of spaghetti were the scoop of the photo agencies of the whole world. Italian stars held up their end, too. This was the heyday of Rome's own actor-chef, Aldo Fabrizi.

Fabrizi was a sensitive poet who acted and sang his cuisine—based on hearty pastas—in verse.[110] His pleasure-loving rhymes remain an important point of reference in the evolution of Roman food in those years.

The grandmother in the kitchen gradually disappeared, and a new class of restaurants began to emerge. These new restaurateurs were numerous, and they were skilled professionals. They turned their venerable trattorias into modern restaurants in more than just the decor. They rose from the ranks and gave Roman cooking a new direction. They elaborated poor, popular recipes into dishes of great class that, in the new version, would girdle the globe. These were the days when stars, politicians, and celebrities from around the world had their photograph taken eating the rich and famous *fettuccine al triplo burro*, known today as Alfredo.

No less famous (in Italy) is *fettuccine alla papalina*—the pope's noodles (recipe on page 100)—a variant of the homely *spaghetti alla carbonara* prepared by a Roman restaurateur for a certain obscure cardinal named Pacelli, who ate the dish with some regularity. When Cardinal Pacelli became Pope Pius XII, it was renamed in his honor. Then there is the *timballo di mezze zite* dedicated to the well-known journalist and expert in all things Roman, Giuseppe Ceccarelli, known as Ceccarius.[111]

Many of the best-known pasta dishes, pride of the Roman and Latian gastronomic tradition, are the elaborations of this generation of restaurateurs. Their versions of the traditional recipes are the ones made at home today because, in those years of plenty, people ate out quite often, and the mothers found it easy to memorize the simple recipe for, say, *spaghetti alla boscaiola,* in which the great discovery was to mix porcini mushrooms with tuna in a tasty tomato sauce (recipe on page 117).

There is no doubt that the 1950s and 1960s will pass into the history of Roman food as one of its richest and most fertile periods.

Traditional Sweets

Sweets were originally made for feasts dedicated to a saint or to the Blessed Virgin or for such religious holidays as All Souls' Day or Carnival. Only much, much later, when prosperity had come to everyone, were sweets for family feasts such as confirmations, communions, and weddings common. These customs are still alive in the small towns of the *campagna romana,* where, when spring comes, in the steep, shady streets, one is enveloped in the strong fragrance of vanilla and cinnamon wafting from the homes of the children about to be confirmed or make their first communion. The housewives take their assembled sweets, neatly lined up on large wooden boards and covered by clean linen towels, to the town oven to bake. The religious celebrations of families are taken much more seriously in the country than in the city. In some towns, the family of the bride or communicant sends enormous trays full of little colored sweets to the guests' homes. To make them, the family had had to call in the help of the neighbor women, with the pleasure of returning the favor when needed.

But the most precise and specialized kitchen work is that dedicated to the ritual Christian feasts and to the patron saints—from Saint Anthony and Saint Blaise to Saint Joseph, it seems that the ranks of gourmet saints in heaven are well fed. The origin of these traditions, though obscured by time, is related to the pagan past. And once the propitiatory purpose was gone, the sweets themselves became the reason for the feast. Many became customary outside the strictly religious aspect of the tradition, such as that of celebrating Saint Valentine, martyred in the fourth century A.D. and called on to protect lovers. Modern sweet are dedicated to him, but especially the custom of exchanging gifts.

Life in the *campagna romana,* and, for that matter, throughout the Italian countryside, was very difficult not so long ago. Pay levels and working conditions would be unimaginable today, and the very rare occasions for celebrating were circumscribed solely by religious feast days. A feast day, in times of great poverty, meant only a feast, not a day off. Sometimes the indulgence of a roast was permitted, sometimes not, but at least sweets, made of a simple paste of water, flour, and honey, were never missing.

Even when we speak of sweets, it is difficult to resist the temptation not to speak of ancient Roman culture. Much is said and has been said about the fact that the cooking of that distant period of our history is today neither conceivable nor reproducible, but sweets are a different story. As different as the flours of today are from those of the past, surely the honey cannot be much different, and olive oil, though theirs was more acidic and robust, has always been pressed from the same fruit. These few, simple elements were the main ingredients of Roman confectionery, from the austere days of the republic to the rich and luxury-loving times of the empire. Of course, the terminology changed over time, and even cake fashions evolved, but in general, given the simplicity of their preparation and the poverty of the ingredients, the biscuits Cato could have found in the second century B.C. must not have been very different from the ones Pliny the Elder might have enjoyed in the first century A.D.

In ancient Rome, the *pistores dulciarii,* or "bakers of sweets," were differentiated by name according to the type of sweet they made. For example, the *crustularii* made *crustuli,* and the *crustulum sabellicum,* made in Sabina, were famous, no doubt, because the oil there was superb even then.[112]

The *pistores dulciarii* of ancient Rome used mainly honey for sweetening. Sugar, which the Romans imported from Egypt, was very expensive, rare, and certainly not used for making cookies.[113] But even today, the sweets of the *agro romano* are sweetened with honey.

Like the foodies of today, the old Romans distinguished the various types of honey according to the seasons and the different floral essences. They particularly liked the honey that was redolent of thyme, savory, or elder flower; less prized was a honey that tasted of smoke, owing to the systems of extraction that involved smoking the hive to force the bees to keep their distance during the harvest.

The production of honey was an enormous source of earnings for the bee-keepers, and because what the hinterland could produce was not enough, honey was imported from all over Italy: from Noricum (more or less modern Austria) to Calabria and Sicily, tons of the precious nectar traveled the road to Rome. Even though the bitter arbutus honey from Sardinia and Corsica was not highly prized, many tons of it a year flooded the Roman market. Anyone—rich or poor, gentlemen or slaves—could buy it in the shop of the *mellarius*. Its main use was in the preparation of soups and sauces, though a honey of superior quality was more often consumed plain or in clotted milk.

One substitute for honey was a sort of date honey still used in Eastern cook-ing, but another, easier to make and keep, was a fig syrup, which is still used in some sweets in southern Italy. Finely chopped fruit was yet another option.

The Roman sweets of the past have strong similarities to the simple ones still made in the towns of the *agro romano*. For example, the *globus*, a ball of dough fried in oil and dipped in honey, is much like the contemporary *castagnole* (sort of doughnut holes); and the ancestors of today's *frappe* (fried strips of dough served for Carnival; see recipe on page 261) may well be what the Greek philoso-pher Chrysippus called *catillus ornatus*, which were small pieces cut from a thin sheet of dough and briefly cooked in boiling oil. Another popular sweet—and children today still like this one—was a thin crepe spread with honey and eaten warm. It was called *placenta* and was bought at the shop of the *placentarii*.

The flours used to make sweets were made by grinding different grains, espe-cially wheat, but also millet and *farro*. But the wheat used by the *pistores* to make bread found limited use by the makers of sweets, at least in comparison with the substantial quantities of flour obtained by grinding aged cheese. This custom must have been borrowed from Greece, where already the Cretans were using *colostrum*, from cow's milk, for a special focaccia that would be offered to the goddess of fertility. Today, a main ingredient of the typical sweets of the *cam-pagna romana* is excellent sheep's milk ricotta.

With the arrival of the year 1000, sugar, albeit in limited quantities, entered the kitchens of the privileged classes and the convents. In the thirteenth century, a variety of sweets appeared in Rome: small fruit gelatins; *pinocchiate*, made by kneading pulverized pine nuts or almonds with honey and other ingredients; fruit *crostate* (tarts); little almond cakes; and the first candied fruits, introduced to the countries of the Mediterranean by the more highly developed Arab kitchen.

The Roman pastry repertory of the next two centuries expanded with elder flower fritters, sweet junket, candied fruits, and fruit in syrup. In the sixteenth century, with the greater diffusion of the still-costly sugar, the variety of sweets multiplied to include *zeppole alla romanesca* and blancmange fritters. Jams and fruit preserves were perfected and flavored with numerous agents used especially for wine, such as musk, cinnamon, cardamom, juniper, and others.

In the first cookbooks, *pangiallo* contained more spices than that of today (recipe on page 267). The sixteenth century also marked the arrival of marzipan in Rome. Both art and pastry are treated to the elaborate flourishes of the baroque period: Hence we have *pizze sfogliate,* true ancestors of the *millefoglie* (millefeuille), rolled in numerous paper-thin layers, each of which is dressed with butter, sugar, spices, and cheeses. Here, too, are the first custards baked in the oven in cases of a special *pâte brisée* up to two inches (five centimeters) thick. And since the sweet and the savory, as in life, were pleasantly mingled, *pandispagna* (sponge cake) was also served in soups.[114]

Fruit was the essential ingredient for cakes: the rich orchards of the *campagna* supplied the markets of Rome daily and abundantly. Until the nineteenth century, Rome celebrated the "triumph of the strawberries" on June 13, the feast of Saint Anthony. On that day, a parade of people in costume would leave Campo de' Fiori, bearing on their heads enormous baskets overflowing with the fragrant fruits, in the middle of which towered a statue of Saint Anthony. They traversed the main streets of the city singing popular songs to the accompaniment of tambourines, mandolins, castanets, and guitars, and this lasted probably until traffic problems brought the annual custom to a halt.

In Rome, as elsewhere in Italy, there were no *pasticcerie* (pastry shops) for much of the eighteenth century. Sweets were either made at home or ordered from nuns, and every convent had its specialties. The production of sweets fell to the convents largely because they were related to religious festivities. In Rome, throughout the eighteenth century, the convents turned out *ciambellette* (ring-shaped cookies), *castagnole* (something like doughnut holes), puddings, gelatins, sorbets, *pizze cedrate* (with citron), *cucuzzate* sweets (made with squash), *biscottini,* and *maritozzi* (buns, recipe on page 266). The seventeenth and eighteenth centuries brought the use of yeast dough to Rome, and thus began the making of the celebrated *pizza ricresciuta,* a ring-shaped bread similar to a very yeasty pizza, which in the nineteenth century, first the bread bakers and then the pastry cooks would sell in great numbers. The *maritozzo* became a feature of the Roman Lent, even giving its name in the nineteenth century to a poem by Adone Finardi. And the almond cake, which originated in the Jewish quarter, reached the tables of everyone.

Then, with the arrival of coffee and chocolate, came the habit of going to cafés, which, following English and French fashion, opened in considerable numbers in somnolent Rome.

The Roman *pasticceria* does not know the meaning of recession. Until a few decades ago, after mass on Sunday, people would stop at the best *pasticceria* in the neighborhood for a small or large tray of *pastarelle* (small pastries) to take home. Today people seem to prefer the rich *tiramisù*.

And in the countryside? In the *campagna,* people made small cookies for the feasts connected with farmwork, source of life and food. Thus, we have the spring feast for the sowing, followed by feasts for the harvest and the beating of the wheat, the harvest and the pressing of the grape, the killing and butchering of the pig and the working of its meat, and, in certain areas, the arrival and departure of the transhumance and the *merca*[115] of the animals. Propitiatory rites were naturally connected to these recurring events of a good harvest, of a favorable season, because the gods above were always in charge! From seasonal cycle to seasonal cycle, the rite of life on the land is repeated and with it the propitiatory rites: first to the gods and goddesses and then to the saints and to the Heavenly Father. Thus, the illuminated shrines at the corners of the roads in ancient Rome dedicated to the *lares compitales,* the tutelary gods of the public roads, became shrines with the image of the Blessed Virgin, which, now as then, are adorned with votive flowers.

The propitiatory procession of a good harvest, which long ago was held on the feast of Saint Mark (April 25) and left from Ponte Milvio and turned across the fields toward Saint Peter's, almost traces the route of the ancient pagan procession that left for the countryside from the same bridge headed toward a sacred wood located at the fifth mile of the Via Clodia, where participants made sacrifices to the god of the frost, Robigo (whence the name Robigalia for the celebration). And, again, the pagan calendar marks December 25 as the *Natalis invicti,* that is, the day of Mithras, the sun god. It is by analogy with this important pagan feast that Christianity established the same date for the birth of Christ, true sun and true light of the world.

They are feasts that have crossed the millennia and that, softened around the edges and in their rites, have reached our own day. Philosopher and historian G. B. Vico called them "wrecks of antiquity," but they are among the few things in this world that turns ever faster that give a sense to our "roots."

Olives

If you could fly like a bird over the *campagna romana* where it fades toward the hills, you would see it clothed in a broad, silvery gray cloak of olive leaves. Those trees are the pride of all Italy's oil production.

For the ancient Italic peoples, the olive tree symbolized not only the fertility of humans and of the earth but also peace and a serene life. Thus, it easy to understand why this plant has traveled the centuries clothed in an aura of sacredness. The oil produced by its fruit was an essential food on poor tables, ever since the time of republican Rome; its oil served to light the lamps, its dregs were a good fertilizer, and its wood, considered precious, could be burned only on the altar of the gods. And the olive tree is indissolubly linked to the advance of Mediterranean civilization.

In the imperial period, the tables of the Roman gourmands made a distinction between the sapid oils of Sabina and the lighter oils of Liguria.[116] The strong, heavy oils from Spain and North Africa were primarily used to fill lamps.

Beginning in the late empire (fourth century A.D.), olive culture declined along with agriculture. The great abbeys, such as Farfa and Subiaco,[117] had charge, sometimes together, of the large holdings of agricultural lands, rich also with olive orchards. Thanks to them, the region's olive culture survived until the economic upturn between the eleventh and thirteenth centuries.

During the fourteenth century, the olive tree became a leading player in the region's agriculture and appeared frequently in art. It was depicted clothed in the ancient symbolism and the pregnant meanings in the splendid iconography of the time. In the Renaissance, it was, together with the grapevine, the great protagonist of Italian agriculture. But in the *agro romano,* olive culture was to languish for a long time to come. Until the end of the eighteenth century, the old trees, neglected and unfertilized, had become significantly reduced in number, and almost no new cultivation had been started, either because of the cost of planting or because the olive tree became productive on average only after ten years and no peasant had the means to obtain a long-term rental contract. Finally, a bull of Pius VI (1775–99) awarded cash for every olive tree planted, and subsequent initiatives by the French occupiers also attempted to get things moving. Despite these actions, the oil supply in the papal states continued to depend almost entirely on imports.

At the time, there were twenty-seven olive oil mills in Tivoli and its hinterland, fifty-three in the territory of Frosinone; eight in that of Viterbo, and thirty in Rieti. Most of these were located on the consular roads, which made it easier to get the oil to Rome. The tiny number of mills on so great an expense of land gives some idea of the gravity of the situation. Many of the mills were water powered, some were horse driven, and typically only four to six men operated in each mill.

De Tournon, named prefect of Rome by the French from 1810 to 1814 (see page 281, note 69), was a careful agronomist, sensitive to the problems of the territory, and his study is still one of the most serious and in-depth. As he himself suggests, it ignores the often superficial observations of travelers. He realistically divides the territory of the *agro* into healthy and sick, the latter all the part near the sea marred by marshes and swamps. The olive orchards were found only in the healthy part and covered the lower region of the Monti Cimini, of Albano, of Sabina, and of the Monti Lepini,[118] often scattered among other crops, and were always present up to an altitude of 1,640 to 1,970 feet (500 to 600 meters) above sea level.

The important operation of pruning was done by specialists, many of whom came from Lucchesia, the area around Lucca, in Tuscany, while the operation known as *rincalzo ai piedi*[119] was entrusted to local hands, who fertilized the trees by this method every three or four years. The oil produced, says De Tournon, was as good as that produced in the rest of Italy, and the production methods certainly did not improve the final product, which was already quite good. Nevertheless, at that moment, already in the areas of Tivoli and of Aspra in Sabina, the olive growers were managing, with careful methods, to produce a better oil. And also at that time, production increased significantly, especially along the Via Tiburtina and Via Appia. De Tournon estimated there were about four hundred oil mills in all of Lazio, providing employment for fifteen hundred people. In 1813, the residue from the milling was used to produce a black soap that though not of good quality was sufficient for local needs. Some 60 percent of the oil produced was consumed in the place of production, in part because it also constituted the pay for the day's work on the harvest. The rest of the oil traveled the road to Rome.

This situation remained almost unchanged until the eve of World War II. The harvest workers were mostly women and children, most of whom came from the areas on the border with Abruzzo. They worked from dawn to sunset and, like the farmworkers, slept in temporary shelters or in scattered farmhouses. The meal was bread and oil, supplemented, depending on the season, with wild chicory or tomatoes. In the evening, after the local farmworkers had walked the long distance from the orchards scattered on the hills to the town, they were greeted with a *caldarello*—a cauldron—on the hearth in which a hot soup or a good polenta was slowly cooking.

The old people of the olive-growing areas in Sabina still remember with nostalgia the festivals and dances that, weather permitting, took place every evening after work, accompanied by the accordion and concertina.

The years after World War II are those of the rebirth of olive culture in Lazio, especially after the distribution of new lands to the farmers, which encouraged new planting. In Sabina at that time, when a child was born, an olive seed was planted in a pot. "It will be your dowry," mothers used to tell their daughters. It would be ready to plant in the ground when she married.

Today the olive tree is one of the main crops in the hilly area of the region. The old system of harvesting the olives only when they have fallen to the ground has almost disappeared. The olives are now harvested by hand and milled quickly. Most of the old stone mills have been abandoned. Specialized machines now produce far better oils, in terms of both the flavor and the almost nonexistent acidity, and they can withstand comparison with their more popular Tuscan cousins. The few stone mills that remain produce the cold-pressed oil so much in demand by gourmets for their salads, but also for the ancient, poor soups of days gone by.

Etruscan Lands: Viterbo and Tuscia

The Via Cassia, one of the great so-called consular roads, still travels north from Rome, past the marshes, now drained, of Lake Baccano, and then winds almost immediately into a particularly fertile and green countryside. In a relatively short time, the traveler, whether on a Roman *biga* (two-horse chariot) or a nineteenth-century stagecoach, was soon in the heart of Etruria.

It is impossible to start a discussion of the food of this region without first talking about the Etruscans. They inhabited a land in which, in the late Bronze Age and early Iron Age, blossomed the first flurry of life associated, thanks to the discovery of iron, with technical advancement. From the eleventh and tenth centuries B.C., one would have witnessed a new ferment of life in the vast area that extended from Samnium in the south to Liguria in the north and encompasses today's Lazio, Umbria, Tuscany, and Liguria regions.

The people spoke a non-Indo-European language. They occupied the hills and plains made fertile by the numerous watercourses. They grew grains and certainly also relied on sheep raising and hunting on the immense wooded hills and fishing in the numerous lakes and elsewhere. The Etruscans were also great traders and navigators;[120] along the coast, they placed large settlements at Civitavecchia, Castrum Novum, Pyrgi, Cerveteri, Caere, Alsium, and Fregene.[121] According to the same ancient sources, the city of Caere and its port, Pyrgi, which stood more or less on the spot where the Castello di Santa Severa is today, enjoyed great wealth, owed in large part to the geographical position, with the metal-rich Tolfa Mountains at their back. The three inscribed gold sheets[122] found in 1964 at Pyrgi finally provided evidence of the close contacts between Caere and Carthage, which the nimble Etruscan ships could reach easily.

It was the dawn of one of the most fascinating civilizations in the history of the world, and it would endure until when, already in decline, it would be engulfed by the new power, Rome.

More closely tied to nature and the land than other civilizations, the Etruscan was eminently agricultural, to the point of being considered a parasite of the land: the Etruscans were canny farmers. To read the Greek historians, the terrains of Etruria had notable resources, thanks not only to the fertility of the soil but also to the water that the farmers had learned to regiment. The Etruscans introduced the idea of fallow fields, as well, that is, of allowing fields that had previously been abandoned after the first harvest to go unseeded for a period of time. In certain cases, they used the fallow land for pasture or minor crops.

The historian M. Terentius Varro, who lived in the first century B.C., maintains that seed-to-harvest ratio in Etruria was one to fifteen.[123] Even if recent archaeological investigations reduce this to a maximum of one to five, it still means that Etruscan lands managed three times the yield found in the rest of archaic Italy. The Etruscans were able to stockpile and sell the surplus around the Mediterranean[124] and, in times of famine, even to Rome. The farmer at the same time sharpened his knowledge, created infrastructures, and perfected his tools. The discovery of iron was a great help: Farm implements, whose shapes had already greatly developed at the end of the Bronze Age, were further perfected in the Iron Age. The plow, conceived in a surprisingly modern form, was made of wood with an iron blade and hitched for traction to a pair of oxen.

From the seventh century, contact with Greek civilization intensified, and the Etruscans learned to cultivate the vine and the olive tree, which was also a cash crop. Oil was also widely used as a protective unguent, for anointing the dead, and also for athletes and warriors.

The tufaceous terrains of southern Etruria were particularly well suited to the vine. Wine of excellent quality was produced in quantity and was traded.[125] To read the "gossip column" of the first-century-B.C. historian Diodorus Siculus,[126] it was an Etruscan who, tired of his wife's complaining and of her lover, one fine day loaded his belongings onto a wagon, with a few amphorae of good wine, and betook himself to Gaul, where the precious nectar enjoyed such success that the Gauls decided to go down to Italy. Legend aside, that actually happened at the beginning of the sixth century B.C.

If therefore the territory was the earthly paradise that it was held to be, it is no wonder that the Etruscans were the happy people the historians unanimously depict. The pen of those Greeks is often caustic and severe in their regard, since they filter the Etruscan reality through the lens of Hellenistic civilization. Today the historian would certainly be more objective.

So, yes, the Etruscans possessed a fortunate, fertile, and rich land, lived in beautiful houses, and set the table twice a day (highly unusual in antiquity). The women had a role of almost modern equality and dined with the men, under the same blanket, as Aristotle was said to have noted disparagingly and as can be admired on some magnificent sarcophagi.[127] Their kitchens were well equipped, with plenty of utensils and tableware, since the banquet was one of the essential activities of the society, as numerous tomb paintings attest.

In the wealthy families, slaves did the kitchen work, often under the direction of a woman. Presumably, as was later the case with the Romans, free cooks, probably freed men, might be hired for special occasions, such as funeral banquets (those depicted in the tomb paintings). But while the rich grave goods have provided us with an enormous wealth of vases, cups, amphorae, jars, braziers, and skewers,[128] in other words, everything that was needed for the preparation of a banquet, we know nothing of how the food was prepared. What we can infer about the preparation is drawn almost entirely from the funeral banquet, as represented in the tombs. Much meat was consumed on these occasions: pork, sheep, wild boar, hare, venison, fowl. It was sometimes boiled in enormous cauldrons, but more often was first parboiled and then roasted, as the large number of skewers discovered confirms.

The products of their flourishing agriculture were certainly on their tables and must have constituted the bulk of the daily diet: *farro*, barley, vetch, wheat, and fava beans were without doubt the base for soups and bread making. Bread, in the form of a large unleavened focaccia, likely doubled as a plate on which to rest the flavorful roasts. This practice was also well established among other peoples of the Mediterranean area. Even Aeneas, tired and hungry and moored at Lavinium on the banks of the Tiber with his bold companions, greatly appreciated this rustic and flavorful food. It was his son, little Iulus, who reminded him of the prophecy of the Harpy Celaeno,[129] perhaps precisely while he watched him enjoy a plate imbued with the juices of a fine roast.

Over the centuries, the unleavened focaccia, made with different flours, is always present in the *cucina povera* of Tuscia (an area that roughly corresponds to today's Viterbo Province). In the 1400s, cooks made a focaccia of combined wheat and chestnut flours, drizzled with oil and sprinkled with rosemary, which must have been used in place of bread.

The tufaceous terrain must have been hard to work. Already in the Renaissance, the food-distribution policy of the towns, foremost Viterbo, was founded on the distribution of the so-called "bread" lands. But the people were farmers and, over the centuries that followed, exploited the land well. By the 1400s, wheat was widely grown, while millet and foxtail millet were used primarily as fodder for cattle, pigs, and especially sheep.[130]

Every house, even in the towns, had a garden for growing fava beans, cabbages, leeks, onions, turnips, romaine lettuce, fennel, spinach, radishes, shallots, carrots, purslane, squashes, melons, cucumbers, and saffron (used especially to dye cloth).

Among the most common herbs were arugula, mustard, parsley, caraway, and coriander.

The city of Viterbo and its hinterland have plentiful water, and this explains the abundance of vegetables in both its old and its new cooking. The statutes of the vegetable men of Viterbo, already in place in 1481, minutely regulated the use of water inside the city. The city's water was supervised by the *balivio dell'acqua,* which ensured that the creation of new trenches or moats did not cause damage to roads or adjacent property. Lands for gardeners were monitored even when they were rented out: documents as early as 1336 obliged owners of rented gardens to supply half of the manure needed to fertilize the land, and it was recommended to use the hoe rather than the plow. This also suggests that the city's gardens could not have been tiny.

The city's gardens also typically contained olive and fruit trees. And in the countryside, within the vineyards, there were often rows of fruit and olive trees, which were used both for their yield and to delimit the boundaries of the property.

The vineyard became all-pervading around Orvieto, with 14½ percent of the garden lands planted to grapevines and viticulture the only source of sustenance for many locals. Lake Bolsena was surrounded by beautiful vineyards that sloped down toward the water and produced a very popular wine, and the wine for the banquets hosted by the rector of Orvieto was supplied from nearby Montefiascone.

Customary regulations and statutes regulated the vinification, the date of which was established each year according to the weather. Among other things, this prevented premature harvesting of the grapes and the theft of grapes on the vine. It also established a rigid set of rules for the production of the *vino novello,* or "new wine," which was among the most in demand on the Roman market.

The grapes were crushed in tufa vats, often in the large caves on the edges of the holdings. Or, if the wine was made at the castle, the grapes were gathered in large vats, taken to their destination, and crushed there by paid workers. The must was then transferred to barrels to ferment. If the season had been particularly favorable, vats and casks could also be rented, but the prices were decidedly high.

A 1365 document that describes the cellar of the bishop of Orvieto mentions numerous barrels in which wines of different types and origins were aging. Among others, there was *unus barilis vini cocti pro mostarda.*[131] Also in northern Lazio, as in other areas, a special kind of grape, called *uva* (grape) *di pergola,* was harvested while still tart to make the famous *agresto* (verjuice) widely used in cooking and not only for sweet-and-sour *(agrodolce)* dishes.

The wine trade in the *agro romano* was strictly regulated by statutes that tended to protect the exceptional quality of the wine produced there. Thus, it was prohibited to cut the local wine with one from outside the area. Even citizens of Viterbo who possessed vineyards outside the designated zone could, yes, consume their own wine at their own table, but they had to swear that they would not sell it. Northern Lazio produced an excellent Vernaccia, Trebbiano, and Moscato, absorbed almost totally by the Roman market.

Along with the vines, the Viterbo area still produces a special olive oil. Already in the fifteenth century, the quality of the area's oil was so famous that many peasants paid their rent in wine and oil. Olive culture was highly specialized: many types of olives were grown, but the most renowned was Canino, which takes its name from the town that today still produces one of the best Italian oils, which received, together with the oil of Sabina, the first Italian DOP (Protected Denomination of Origin). The traditional slice of country bread toasted over the fire, rubbed vigorously with garlic, and held beneath the oil that poured from the *frantoio* (the press)—a simple way of tasting the new oil—has evolved, greatly embellished, into what we today know and love as *bruschetta*.

The woods of Tolfa and of northern Lazio in general were among the richest in game and were the favorite hunting grounds of the Roman nobles, including Popes Leo X and Paul III.[132] Among the animals hunted were many wild pigs, which, roasted with the rustic herbs of the *macchia* (maquis), constituted a true gourmet item. We can consider it the ancestor of today's famous *porchetta* of Viterbo, redolent of wild fennel.

The *porchettari* of contemporary Viterbo cook *porchetta* in much the same way as it was cooked in the past and sell the meat from roadside stands. They use large animals, weighing well over two hundred pounds (one hundred kilograms), which they roast in special ovens, either wood burning or electric, according to timing they have mastered with experience.

Today the woods practically no longer exist: most were cut down in the nineteenth century to make charcoal, and as a result the land is now covered with *macchia mediterranea,* which offers no shelter from the wind and lets the waters run free. The scant remaining woods can hardly be considered a hunter's paradise, but game is still certainly important in the local cooking.

Lakes and watercourses of Tuscia were rich in fish. The catch contributed substantially to the diet of the rich and poor, especially during the periods of abstinence from meat, which amounted to 130 days a year. For centuries, however, freshwater fish was considered more valuable than fish from the sea, and the lakes of Tuscia have always been the largest suppliers of the Roman markets.

Fishing, which was also carried out along the Fiora River, in the northwestern Viterbese, was done with the *nassa,* a large basket made of willow branches that was placed in an artificial narrowing of the watercourse, thereby forcing the fish into the trap. It appears that something similar was used in the Mesolithic period on the shores of the Baltic for catching salmon. But fishing was also done with particular grasses, whose roots, when crushed and put in the water, asphyxiated the fish.

By the Middle Ages, the Marta River, which flows out of Lake Bolsena, was home to one of the largest aquaculture operations of the time. In fact, it appears that the pike, tench, and especially the eels of this lake, thanks to the particular food they were fed, had unequaled flesh. The "Marta fishery" included hatcheries whose enormous size can be deduced from archival documents relating to expenses of upkeep. They were equipped for the capture of the fish, since the Marta offered particularly favorable conditions. The fishery was the obligatory point of passage for the eels on their way to lay their eggs in the sea. Then, in spring, the young eels swam back up the same route, where they were captured and held in the hatcheries until they were grown. From here they were sent to the main markets, as far away as Avignon, where the pope resided.[133]

The complex of establishments, on the southern shore of the lake, employed almost the entire local population. The largest establishment was on the island of Martana, in the middle of the lake, where the fishermen lived who had a regular work contract with the Camera Apostolica. The fishery is well documented. We know, for example, that in 1341, it supplied, for the banquet at Montefiascone in honor of the new rector, 150 eels, 85 pike, 450 nase, and 148 tenches. A later document (1363) gives an account of a shipment of 1,120 eels to the papal court at Avignon. Freshwater fish are still the pride of the local gastronomy.

The long strip of flat land that runs from the sea to the volcanic hills around Viterbo is commonly called the Maremma Laziale. The low part used to belong to the Marittima[134] and, as in the Pontina area, the marshy terrain was the ideal habitat for malaria-bearing mosquitoes, which meant that it had been almost uninhabited for centuries. But even after the drainage, the countryside, covered with *macchia mediterranea* and grazed by bovines and ovines, remained uncultivated, because pasturage, as everywhere in the *agro romano,* was more profitable than crops.

Toward the end of the nineteenth century, the Maremma Laziale raised oxen for work, cows for milk, and calves for meat to send to the bordering provinces of Umbria and Tuscany, and it was only then that beef found its way onto the tables of ordinary people. The Maremma Laziale began to be cultivated in the 1950s, but not all if it. Part of it still preserves that evocative and uncontaminated landscape on which *butteri* (cowboys) and herds lived their rustic and solitary life in the *macchia* redolent of myrtle and lentisk, resting in the shade of centuries-old ilexes.

The meats used in Viterbese cooking are lamb, poultry, and, to a lesser extent, beef and veal. The preparations are simple and poor and much like those of other parts of the region, but here they are flavored with particular herbs, the most characteristic of which is wild fennel. The extreme simplicity of the cooking of Tuscia is perhaps best illustrated by its famous *acquacotta,* or "cooked water": the name says that the soup is almost nothing, yet by mixing together herbs and a few vegetables and providing consistency with the addition of bread, local cooks have created incredibly tasty dishes in line with modern dietary guidelines. The *acquecotte* made in the province of Viterbo are numerous. They might be flavored with tomatoes, or, as in the case of the one called *bagnone* (big bath), with wild herbs, such as *crespigno,*[135] or with parsnips or horseradish leaves. These bread soups might also be made with turnips; with broccoli; often with potatoes and onions; or with cress, hops, squash shoots, or wild cardoons. The soup, which was a whole meal for poor families, when possible was enriched with an egg cooked right in the soup or with a few little pieces of salt cod.

Among the most highly prized and abundant crops of Tuscia is hazelnuts, which contribute the characteristic flavor to many of the area's typical sweets. These are mainly "dry sweets" (as opposed to "spoon sweets"), that is, biscotti, and some are associated with religious holidays, such as the famous *maccheroni* with walnuts (recipe on page 265).

Sabina, Land of Olive Trees and Hill Towns

It would be easy to think the Sabine country of northeastern Lazio was a land forgotten by time. The view, yesterday and today, is sketched by the soft profiles of the hills against which stood, and still stand, castles among the green, carefully drawn rows of olive trees.

Even now, the countryside must be much like what the Roman legions saw, and later the pilgrims, and still later the travelers on the Grand Tour. It must be what the prefect De Tournon saw when the French government, after the Jacobin interlude, charged him with drafting a report on the economic situation of the papal states.

During the Roman period and in the High Middle Ages, the habitat was scattered with farms and farmhouses, and hamlets stood along the watercourses and on the Via Quinzia and Via Salaria. The lands were in the hands of the great families: Marsi, Mareri, and Brancaleone, and later the Orsini, the Savelli, and the Borghese.

The tenth century brought the spread of the agricultural concentrations of the very powerful Abbey of Farfa. These concentrations were surrounded by defensive walls against the Hungarian and Saracen invasions. The rural populations too took to more easily defended elevated positions and surrounded themselves with walls: these are the fortified castles of Ornaro, Aspra, Longone, Amatrice, and Roccasinibalda.[136]

The Middle Ages were important in Sabina, because it is the period in which food habits still alive today got started. The farm life in the territory was regulated by the sound of the horn and, from the thirteenth century, by the bells.

Olive culture and agriculture, lynchpins of the kitchen, began to feel the changes of the times only with the arrival of mechanization: the medieval peasant and the farmer of the 1940s differed little in the methods and tools they used.

The olive tree flourished in the area toward the fifth century, and the cultivars were—and it seems almost incredible—the same as today: Carboncella, Leccina, and Rosciola, all of them favored by Cato, Horace, and Varro, who considered "the liquid gold of Sabina" the best. The cooks in the kitchens of wealthy Romans got their supplies from these trees, and it is here that the producers of the twentieth century would receive the first DOP for their magnificent olive oil.

Thanks to the area's mild climate, between the eighth and thirteenth centuries, the olive tree was planted all over, even on the rocky ridges of the Alta Sabina, or northern Sabina (today the province of Rieti), beaten by the west wind and exposed to the south.

The vegetable crops were distributed in the plains of the Tiber and in that of Rieti, where drainage projects carried out mainly by the great abbeys had gradually freed the lands from the waters. The Velino mingled its waters for a goodly stretch with the lake, and locals traveled by boat from Rieti to Terni. The abbeys promoted the rebirth of the countryside. In addition to the drainage systems, they provided the incentive to trade in farm products, and under them the markets at Vescovio, Vacone, Granica, and especially Farfa flourished. Trade was carried out at the ports and warehouses of Magliano, Stimigliano, Cerri, and Corese, as well as along the more perilous Via Quinzia and Via Salaria.

The main cash commodities were grains, oil, and wine. Salt from Ostia was bartered for iron. Sea salt was too expensive, so the Abbey of Farfa built a number of salt flats, which gathered water in caves of saline sand and then let it flow into vats and evaporate. Nothing—the peasant sages used to say—is more useful than sun and salt.

Grain and oil mills were numerous on the valley floors and along the streams and rivers: the Velino, the Salto, the Corese, the Turano, the Tiber, and the Farfa. Still today it is easy to see their ruined remains, and they give the name to many Sabine localities known as *le mole* (the mills). In the towns and villages, there was one mill for every fifty families, and the Abbey of Farfa possessed more than one hundred. The harvesting technique has not changed over time: the olives are *piluccate*[137] on the tree, so as not to damage the precious fruit.

Sabine cooking is practically inseparable from olive oil. The soups of yesterday, which constituted a single-dish meal irreplaceable in the people's diet, were imaginatively constructed in the kitchen by the farmwives from herbs they found along the ditches and streams as they returned from work: *caccialepre, indiviola* (wild endive), chicory, beans, fava beans, the almost extinct (and recently revived) *cicerchia* (chickling vetch). Everything went into the *paiolo,* a large copper pot hung over the fire, where the wild scents blended slowly. A stream of oil transformed—and still does today—the simple soup into a meal fit for a king. If available, an egg, some snails, or some fish caught in the brook could be added to the pot. Fishing was widespread and an economic source of great importance. Almost all the numerous watercourses were dammed by fisheries, and fisheries punctuated all the estates of the *agro romano* in general. The fish were copious but free only in the brooks.

In the last decades of the twentieth century, crabs were still being caught in great numbers in the brooks and imparted an unforgettable flavor to local soups. Fish, it was said, placates lust, while hunting stimulates it. Perfect for the refectory table of Farfa!

The garden was an integral part of the houses and farms. During the thirteenth century in the Bassa Sabina, or southern Sabina (today the province of Rome), the cultivation of the fields was strictly regulated in some towns, and every family with a male over fourteen years of age had to cultivate a garden with at least one row of vegetable plants and a certain quantity of onions and legumes.[138]

Many plants were also grown for their aphrodisiac powers, among them all those that we today call *odori:* parsley, basil, rosemary, and lemon balm. But the gardens always had cabbages, chickpeas, onions, cucumbers, beans, lettuces, fava beans, and turnips. Sabine families still make *cococciata: cocozze* are zucchini, and the flavorful soup is made with zucchini enhanced with onions, tomato, and olive oil (recipe on page 130).

The most commonly grown grains were rye, sorghum, emmer, millet, and spelt, as well as wheat. They were all used for bread: the better-off families had wheat and rye breads on their tables; the poor made bread from spelt, barley, fava beans, hazelnut flowers, fern roots, and chestnuts, with only the smallest amount of flour to ensure that the bread was somewhat softer than a brick. A delicious soup is still made today with chestnuts and lentils.

Meat was rarely found on the tables of the middle and lower classes. For special occasions, there were chickens, rabbits, ducks, and geese, but often someone would bring a porcupine or badger in from the countryside. Good trappers could also catch a wild dove, so common in the area that the name occurs in place names: Fonte Colombo, Contrada Palomba, and others. Hunting was reserved for the nobles. On the lands surrounding the Abbey of Farfa, people could hunt freely, as long as the quarry was delivered to the kitchens of the monastery.

The ox was eaten only when it could no longer pull a plow. The Abbey of Farfa engaged in a very important cattle-raising activity: calfskin, especially of stillborn animals, was used to make precious parchment.

But the most important animal for the food economy, and not just of Sabina, was the pig. Eighty percent of the Sabine territory was made up of woods, and the value of the terrain was determined by the number of pigs that fed there and that paid, in the Middle Ages, the *Decima porcorum*. Pigs, which at the time were crossed with wild boars, were numerous; rare, however, were those that had a white band on their coat and the highly sensitive sense of smell needed for hunting truffles. The operations of killing, salting, and preserving the pig today do not differ much from those of yesterday and even longer ago. Modern times have brought the freezer, but only a few decades ago, families still preserved both sausages and precooked pork cutlets immersed in oil in glass jars.

Then and now the killing of the pig was followed by the feast of the *padellaccia,* which called for browning pancetta, *guanciale,* liver, and various bits of the animal, scented with white wine and rosemary, in a *padella,* or large skillet (recipe on page 245).

Goats and sheep were common too: Sabina was a land of transhumance in the valleys of the Cicolano, in the plain of Leonessa and of Amatrice. Still today if you travel the peripheral roads or unpaved paths, it is easy to encounter the flocks coming from or going to pasture, all in an orderly line led by the so-called *guidarella,* a sheep trained by the shepherd to guide the flock, and followed by the shepherd with his ever-present staff. Also still common in Sabina are the isolated great oaks that were left to give shade to the flock under the beating sun of a summer's day.

Nowadays, lamb is the main dish on feast days. It is roasted, scented as long ago with herbs, today rosemary and sage; with fragrant garlic; and, of course, with Sabine olive oil. And in October, when boar-hunting season opens, families of the hunters still sit down to the area's famous wild boar sausages cooked on the grill.

A herd of goats being guided along Via Sistina (Fondazione Primoli, Rome)

Today, as long ago, fruit trees are cultivated in the Sabine hills: cherries, apples, pears, plums, and, from the fourteenth century, also peaches and apricots.

But the pride of Sabine gastronomy has to be pasta: until a few decades ago, no family used "store-bought pasta." Every day the women made *sagne, cecamariti, frigulozzi, frascarelli,* and the famous *fregnacce* (recipe on page 102).[139] These were poor pastas, some made with eggs, but more usually with just water and flour. Today, all summer long, numerous town fairs and *sagre* are dedicated to these local pastas.

The tastes of this land, far from the great thoroughfares, have remained miraculously intact. In the families, there is always a grandmother or mother who cooks, and in the winter, a copper *paiolo* is bubbling on the fire, just as it did one hundred, two hundred, five hundred, or even a thousand years ago.

From the Castelli to the Ciociaria

For the splendor of its monuments and importance of its route, the Via Appia is the most famous of the great Roman roads. It was heavily traveled, since it linked the capital with the south, including the Bay of Naples and the beautiful seaside residences that dotted the coast and islands, a haven for wealthy Roman society, emperors included. With the fall of the empire, the great road declined, and by the fourth century A.D., the adjacent Via Asinaria, which began at the Basilica of Maxentius, adjacent to the Roman Forum, and left the city at the present-day Porta San Giovanni, was preferred. Today, the urban sprawl around the Via Asinaria, now known as the Via Appia Nuova, with its unattractive modern buildings, makes it difficult to picture. But less than a century ago, the people who used it, could, even before the road began to snake through the hills, smell the fruity bouquet of *cannellino* wine and the musky odor of certain caves,[140] where they would drink it, seated on rustic benches with *porchetta* sandwiches. It is the same wine, fresh, fragile, and light, whose fame has remained unchanged over the centuries.

The Castelli were already famous as a zone designated for wine production in Roman times; and even in the Middle Ages, the lands, registered elsewhere in the cadastral documents as farms, here were counted in vineyards. Most of the vineyards of the Castelli were the property of the Roman monasteries or abbeys; they were rationally and intensely cultivated. Some medieval acts recording the sale and purchase of landholdings often specify that the vineyard was also registered as plowed land, at that time assigned to kitchen gardens or the growing of other crops.

Vineyards, as far as the eye could see, covered the area all the way to Velletri. In the Valle di Ariccia, called Valle Aricina in the old documents, some of them also contained olive trees and oil mills.

Andrea Bacci,[141] who lived in Rome in the sixteenth century and was one of the first historians of wine making and viticulture, wrote a treatise in which he gives an account of the wines produced and sold in Rome and its hinterland.

The already celebrated Abbey of Santa Maria di Grottaferrata, which possessed immense vineyards, supplied white, red, golden, tart, lightly aromatic, and flavored wines to Rome, and, says Bacci, they were in no way inferior to the more famous wine of Albano. The abbey was then under the supervision of the Roman Curia, and Cardinal Farnese stocked the cellars of his residences in Rome, Caprarola, and Palo with the abbey's production. According to the same source, the wines of Grottaferrata were by far the most common on the tables of prosperous Romans, since, perhaps because of the nature of the terrain, they were much more stable than those from Albano and could be kept for up to three or four years.

The wine of Albano, both white and red, was considered a perfect wine, albeit unstable, and the best was made from young vineyards. The "wine of the Riccia," similar to that of Albano, was greatly appreciated in the area but was unstable and traveled poorly, as well.

The celebrated Monterosso vineyard of Cardinal Farnese was also located in the Castelli. It had a single defect: given the quality of its wine, it was much too small! A summer table wine, as we would call it today, was produced in the vineyards that framed the Lake of Castelgandolfo, but this wine too absolutely had to be drunk on the spot.

We learn from a precious letter to Cardinal Guido Ascanio Sforza written by another famous oenologist of the sixteenth century that the vineyards of Rome produced the "Romano": the best was made at Porta San Pancrazio, at the beginning of the Via Aurelia, or outside the gate of Sant'Agnese, on the Via Nomentana, "above the hill in the vineyard of Cardinal Paggio and at present all the vineyards of Casa de' Monti." This was a light, thin table wine traditionally drunk during Lent. It was often aromatized with sulfur, cypress, cinnamon, carnations, or elder flowers.

In the same letter, the author, Sante Lancerio, says marvelous things about the wine produced in the vineyards planted by Leo X on his Magliana estate, just south of Rome. But at the date of the manuscript, around midcentury, these vineyards were already completely abandoned.

The viticultural picture of the zone did not change in the centuries that followed. The proximity of Rome and its slightly elevated position made it an area of great prestige. Nobles and the rich built summer villas and palaces. The woods were a favorite destination for hunting, one of high society's favorite pastimes. Game was plentiful enough to satisfy the Roman market and was one of the favorite subjects of the local gastronomy.

(facing page) The old bar of Grottaferrata, founded in 1808 (Fondazione Primoli, Rome)

BAR GREGORIO DI TVSCOLO

GRANDE
ASSORTIMENTO
DI
CARTOLINE
ILLUSTRATE
DELLA BADIA
E
DEL PAESE
CARTOLERIA
E OGGETTI DI
CANCELLERIA

13 SALE + TABACCHI 13

DROGHE
E
CONFETTURE
COLORI
PENNELLI
E
VERNICI

DEPOSITO
DI
VETRI

Grottaferrata – Il più antico negorio fondato nel 1808.

At the end of the eighteenth century, the Castelli became, and remained, a favorite destination for Sunday outings, at first only for the wealthier classes. For their convenience, a number of famous osterias sprouted on the Via Appia. With their festive and relaxed atmosphere, they became a favorite subject for painters, especially in the nineteenth century. One of the most celebrated was dei Francesi in Marino. Then, halfway between Rome and Frascati, there were Tor di Mezzavia, Finocchio, Torrenova, Pittanella, and Malagrotta, which, because of their relative nearness to the city, were visited also by shepherds, peasants, and, at the beginning of this century, by a new category of road users, cyclists.

In the period between the two wars, but especially after the second, the Castelli underwent a real boom, becoming an obligatory stop for visitors to Rome: an outing to the Castelli or a dinner in the famous osterias could not be left out of any itinerary. And on Sunday, especially in the hottest months, a good part of the population of Rome invaded the woods and restaurants, which began to proliferate. There people always enjoyed the same light, fruity wine and simple food that they ate in the osterias of Rome. In addition, one went to Genzano to see its famous *infiorata* (flower festival) and to Frascati to buy—as today—an odd bread in the form of a three-breasted doll: two for milk and one for wine, a curious visual reminder of the goddess of plenty. At the end of winter, when the vines were pruned, people traveled to Velletri to taste the famed *carciofi* (artichokes) *alla matticella*.[142]

Where the hills of the Castelli go down toward the plain, the vineyards gently give way to plowed fields and vegetable gardens: this is the entry to the Ciociaria, the old Roman *campagna*.

It is difficult to think of any place in which more lively folk traditions exist than in the Ciociaria. The festivals, singing, and ceremonies that take place in some small villages have stayed unchanged for generations. The women and men proudly wear the splendid and colorful traditional garb, and they sing and dance to the same folk music as their great-grandparents did. In some towns, the religious or family festivals are celebrated with rites that mirror those of long ago. At Campoli Appennino, as late as a few decades ago, the bridal procession after the wedding ceremony would begin at the groom's father's house, where the wedding luncheon took place. There the bride, in a loud, clear voice, called to her mother-in-law, who was supposed to come to the door and ask her what she wanted. The bride then asked whether her joining her new family was welcome, and receiving an affirmative answer, the bride and groom with all the retinue could enter and sit down to the feast.

During the festival of the *cantamesse* at Ceprano, the women parade through the streets in their multicolored costumes, balancing on their heads enormous baskets filled with giant loaves of bread decorated with flowers and bows. The loaves, which have been blessed on August 15, will later be distributed to the people. The next day, at Villa Santo Stefano, the venerable ceremony of the *pan-arda* takes place in celebration of the feast of San Rocco. Twenty enormous cauldrons containing three quintals (six hundred pounds) of previously soaked chickpeas are placed in the town square. The head cook adds oil, salt, pepper, rosemary, and water to cover, lights the fires under the cauldrons, and starts to cook this Pantagruelian chickpea soup. The fires are tended and poked all night. The next day, after the solemn procession during which the benediction of the legumes takes place, an ad hoc committee distributes the soup, first to the town authorities, then to the persons who contributed most to the success of the *pan-arda,* and finally to all the others.

The Ciociari (the people of the Ciociaria) have enriched Roman popular cooking with the products of their gardens and their farms and with their succulent lambs. Until a few decades ago, they would come down to Rome on set days to engage in bargaining. They met at Piazza Colonna to contract for the sale of products of the Roman countryside, as well as for the buying and selling of land and the acquisition of estates and farms. At Piazza della Rotonda (where the Pantheon is), affairs related to sheep, shepherds, and sheep farms were negotiated. Agricultural workers in search of employment stationed themselves in Piazza della Consolazione.

The Ciociari who came to Rome every week on business took the opportunity to make the rounds of the shops. They were easily recognized in the street because both men and women wore old military uniforms, complete with badges. They had bought them from junk dealers just because, as everyone knows, military clothes are sturdy and warm.

The countryside of the Ciociaria was largely dedicated to pasture, and beginning in the nineteenth century, when the consumption of bovine meats began to spread, a type of farm called *procojo* began to develop. These flourishing establishments employed a large part of the local manpower, albeit with wages that would be ridiculous today. Almost as in a ministry, the *procojo* had its hierarchy. The high-level personnel had, in addition to a salary, the right to a horse (like a company car): the steward ran the farm on behalf of the owner; the *portaspesa,* who wore the livery of the family of noble proprietors because he operated outside the farm's borders, had the responsibility of taking the calves to slaughter; the *capoccetta* controlled the *cavalcanti,* that is, those who had the right to a horse; and the *cavallaro* tamed the colts.

The lower hierarchies included the *coratino,* head of the cow men; the *vaccari,* who did the milking; the *appressataro,* who, with the right to a horse, herded the cows to pasture and brought them back to the barn for milking; the *capoccia delle mucche,* who watched the cows in the barn and sometimes helped with the milking; the *gnuccaro,* who cleaned up the cows and the barns; and the *lattarolo,* who took the milk to town.

A similar hierarchy existed on sheep farms. The *vergaro* ran the farm; the *buttero* took the kids, lambs, and fresh cheese to town; the *agaglione* or *sogliardo* gathered firewood and did odd jobs; the *pecoraro* tended and milked the sheep; and the *biscino* was a boy responsible for the transport of water and the changing of the fences of the sheep pen. The whole staff of the farm, had, in addition to wages, the right to divide among themselves the skins of sheep that died of illness and to a certain quantity of cheese.

Like modern pets, the oxen of the Ciociaria had names, some quite important, sometimes borrowed from history (including the annals of crime; some were named for famous brigands) and sometimes merely fanciful. The most recurrent names, those that most struck the popular fancy, were Gasparone, Murfatore, Malandrino, Macchiarolo, and Spadolino, but also Rubacuori (heart stealer), Belviso (nice face), Bellicapelli (nice hair), Occhineri (black eyes), as well as Caporale (corporal), Generale, Re di Francia (king of France), Nerone (Nero), Gradasso, Garibaldi, Cardinale, Passeretto, Serpente (serpent), and Cardellino.

As noted earlier, in addition to work in the fields, cattle were now raised for their meat, which began to appear in the popular cooking of Rome and the Ciociaria, but always in the form of second-choice cuts or offal. Like the rest of Lazio, chicken, rabbit, and pork were the most commonly consumed meats. Garden vegetables and legumes were used to round out the meal, as were game and fish.

Travelers over the centuries who have crossed its valleys and mountains agree that the Ciociaria is pleasant country—mild climate, good air, good food. But until the beginning of the twentieth century, it was extremely poor. Most rural people were illiterate and farmwork was calculated with the *staglio,* a stick cut lengthwise, one side of which went to the boss and the other to the worker. When the halves were joined, a day's work was scored on the stick.

In this sort of cultural environment curious beliefs and superstitions can take root, including some of a gastronomic nature. A pain in the legs, it was said, could be cured with earthworms fried in oil. If you find a fava pod with nine beans, hold onto it: it keeps bad luck away. Two grains of wheat, two grains of salt, and two leaves from olive branches blessed on Palm Sunday are the best amulet against the evil eye. To cure hemorrhoids, nothing is better than ivy fried in oil.

In such a poor economy, everything is homemade, beginning with the famous *ciocie,* the shoes that had the honor of giving the area its name. Here is how they were described by Gregorovius, who traveled through the Ciociaria in the second half of the nineteenth century:

> Ciociari: men and women of the country of the *ciocie* . . . it is a country of savage beauty and mountainous, which extends from Ferentino to the Neapolitan border. It is there that the people wear the *ciocie*, a very simple kind of footwear that has given the country its name. Starting in Anagni already I saw these special sandals in use. I could not imagine a system more primitive and at the same time more comfortable; at least I sincerely envied the Ciociari them: the *ciocia* is made with a square piece of skin of ass or horse, in the holes is threaded a lace that wraps the foot in such a way that the sandal becomes thinner toward the toe and ends in a curve; the leg is wrapped to the knee with rough, gray canvas, tied with many laces of cord or thread, so that the Ciociaro moves freely in the field where he hoes the earth or on the rocks tending the sheep and the goats, wrapped in a cloak or a short jacket of gray hair, always with his *zampogna* [bagpipe].

It is the shepherds of the Ciociaria who come down into the streets of Rome in the days before Christmas to play their *zampogne* (bagpipes). Until a few years ago, they arrived in groups of three, singing their beautiful Christmas melodies and accompanying them with the bagpipes. They can still occasionally be seen in Rome.

The pastures that extended over the mountains and hills made sheep raising one of the main occupations of the rural population. The best lambs on the Roman market were the ones from the Ciociaria, and this is why lamb and sheep's milk cheeses are common in popular cooking. Today parmigiano has largely replaced the stronger pecorino, but parmigiano used to be rare in the houses of the Ciociaria.

The old Ciociaria, called Campagna e Marittima, which extended south from the mouth of the Tiber, the Alban Hills, and the Aniene River, was bordered by the sea as far as Fondi and on the other side was, as it were, protected by the bulwark of the Apennines, from Subiaco as far as Sora. From here the border followed the Liri River to Ceprano. Of course, the borders of the Ciociaria have shifted over the centuries; around the twelfth century it even included a part of present-day Sabina.

The political seesawing between the Kingdom of Naples and the papal states left its mark on the culture of the Ciociaria. Although historians continue to argue over the political borders of this land, we can agree that its food—taken as an index of valuation—does not vary between Velletri and Anagni, or between Ferentino and Tivoli. The simple preparations, made with the same type of ingredients, are identical in bordering zones. The now-famous *gnocchi alla ciociara* can be also tasted in zones that administratively do not belong to the Ciociaria.

There is a lovely legend to explain their origin: they were used as projectiles against the Saracen invaders during the siege of Acquafondata. In memory of the event, the eagerly awaited *sagra degli gnocchi* is still held there every summer.

The country, still very poor even in the 1920s, had practically no roads: one went from town to town on foot or on the back of a mule. The highways, such as they were—unpaved and dusty—linked only the major towns with one another and with Rome. The traveler who undertook the difficult and long trip from Frosinone to Rome could take the stagecoach, which usually traveled with an escort. If there was no escort, one could be hired for an extra charge. The post stations on the way were Ferentino, Anagni, Valmontone, and Colonna. In the latter was one of the most famous post osterias, run by a certain De Mattheis.

Isola Liri, for example, was reached only by mule, as was Veroli. In compensation, the traveler who made it to the latter could eat a famous *fritto* of *ciammaruche,* the snails collected in the woods after it rains.

From the small town of Santopadre, the writer Cesare Pascarella, traveling in the region for work, left a lovely description of a food shop.

> Inside the little town, to rest, we went into a shop, where they sold everything. On tightly packed shelves, the cheeses were piled up on a few meters of rolled up cloth and among the faded ribbons, and here and there loaves of rough bread on the writing paper and packets of tobacco on the clay pots, and higgledy-piggledy clay pipes, salt cod, buckets, ropes, strings, and images of saints, and at the back, in a counter of worm-eaten and filthy walnut, a rusty scale rose among a quantity of measures, and in the middle of the counter, on a piece of tin that served as a tray, a footless glass leaned on the belly of a black bottle in which there was some brandy. . . . I looked for a chair, but there were no chairs. I looked for the shopkeeper, but the shopkeeper had gone to Mass . . . and when the shopkeeper goes to Mass, business is suspended in the little piazza of Santopadre.

Both for its geographical position and for the mildness of the climate and its medicinal waters, the Ciociaria has been a vacation destination since antiquity. Cicero's family had a villa there, and the great orator himself went to Isola Liri when he was tired of the noisy city life. The poet Horace suggested stopping, for unforgettable *otia (dolce far niente)*, at the lovely town of Ferentinum; the emperors Marcus Aurelius, Commodus, Septimius Severus, and Caracalla stayed there too. In later centuries, the game-filled woods were a favorite destination for aristocratic hunters and the Curia, and even popes. Innocent III, Gregory IX, Alexander IV, and Boniface VIII all sojourned at Anagni, where the latter received the notorious "slap of Anagni."[143] But in gastronomic history, the town is better known for a famous *pasticcio di maccheroni in crosta* (pasta baked in a pastry crust).

Buffalo Country: The Pontine Marshes

Before we can talk about the food of the area known as the Pontina, the southernmost part of Lazio, we must take a look at the geography of a region that was only recently united under a single administration. This combined diverse and heterogeneous cultural areas that have, even over time, maintained their physiognomy, including the gastronomic. Lazio, in fact, was formed only after 1860, from Sabina, which belonged to the cultural sphere of the Abruzzo; the area of Viterbo, which belongs to Tuscia; and finally the provinces of Frosinone and Latina, many towns of which belonged to the Kingdom of Naples and had infrequent relations with the papal states.

Before the Kingdom of Italy existed, the southern border of the papal states (including today's southern Lazio) was at Terracina. There, in the ancient zone of Portella, one crossed the great gate, the ruins of which are still visible today, which gave access to the Kingdom of Naples.

Until the beginning of this century, four-fifths of the territory that extended from the Roman littoral to Terracina, occupying the present-day Pontine plain, was a wasteland of malarial marshes. The fetid air was unbreathable. Only one-eighth of the territory was inhabited—the high ground of the Monti Lepini.

The fish-rich seas off the coast between Anzio and Circeo—according to old accounts—beckoned the fishermen of the nearby Kingdom of Naples, who, however, ventured to fish in the marshes as well. These were full of eels, but they could be fished only during the winter, because the mephitic summer air made access impossible.

Over the centuries, numerous attempts were made to drain the marshes and thus acquire fertile lands for farming. The Romans had tried and failed. Pope Sixtus V tried in the sixteenth century, and other, later attempts were disappointing. Finally, in the 1930s, the problem was solved in a radical fashion.

The first records of the difficult conditions of life there come from the classical writers. Horace's account of his trip on the Via Appia from Rome to Brundisium in 37 B.C. contains his unpleasant memory of the stretch between Rome and Forum Appium (possibly present-day Fossanova), the first main stop. The poet recounts how it was impossible to sleep because of the noise made by sailors, innkeepers, and frogs and the torment of mosquitoes.

For centuries to come, the Pontine area remained the uncontested kingdom of marsh game, both migratory and not. Even after the marshland was drained, some lakes remained for the joy of hunters, so that dishes using this special game can still be found in the local cuisine. Moorhens (*folaghe*), for example, were numerous in Lake Fogliano, and still in the 1950s it was not hard to find them on sale in poultry shops.

With the draining of the marshes, the fertile lands that emerged were distributed to peasants from the areas of Ravenna and Ferrara, in Romagna, and especially from the Veneto, as payment for their work in recovering the land. That is why Pontine food today embraces two diverse cultural spheres: that of the Monti Lepini and that of the plain, recently acquired, representing a hybrid of the foods and recipes brought by the first settlers, especially from Veneto and Tuscany. With these were mixed the fish-based recipes of its coasts, and what came out was a particular cuisine, redolent of the wild herbs of its hills, enriched by the cheeses of its pastures, and one that has full right to a place with Lazio's best.

In the Pontine area, as in the rest of the region, an economy of poverty meant that meat appeared on the table only rarely, on special occasions, and was almost exclusively poultry and rabbits or lamb, or, more rarely, game. The pig was the most important of all meats and was called for in all the recipes, from soups to sweets (made, of course, with lard).

Terracina was the gateway to the Kingdom of Naples and the Terra di Lavoro (Land of Work), so-called until our own day. It extended as far as Caserta and corresponded to the famous Campania Felix of antiquity.[144] Even today the stretch of coast to the south of Terracina seems distinctly more Neapolitan than Latian: the dialect changes and becomes more lilting, seafood is used more, and the dominant flavorings are capers, oregano, and sweet and sour.

Today Lazio extends as far as Minturno and has adopted the recipes of the fishermen of the coast, which was rich in fish until quite recently. The waters around the island of Ponza were famous for their tuna and also for oysters and spiny lobster.

The local fishermen, whose cooking began on the fishing boats known as *paranze,* still in use today, found a way to give their soup the taste of the sea without actually using fish—which were to be sold, not eaten. Instead of using seaweed to flavor their soups, fishermen would boil one of the spongy rocks they collected on the sea bottom in the soup water. If fish were plentiful, they might toss waste fish from their boat or stuck in their nets into the pot. Today, *acqua-pazza* (crazy water), in step with the general concern for health, has become more nutritious, and cooks add, as their fancy strikes, mantis shrimp, conger eel, octopus, a few little cuttlefish, or whatever fresh fish is at hand. The broth in which the fish has been cooked is strained, poured over bread, and then garnished with the just-drained fish (recipe on page 127).

The sea helps fill all kinds of *torte rustiche* (savory pies), including the cele-brated *tiella di Gaeta* (recipe on page 249), flavored with anchovies and olives according to the most traditional recipe but now found in numerous variations in which the filling is enriched with octopus, small squid, or cuttlefish. One famous version is filled with onions and *scamorza* cheese, another has a filling of escarole and salt cod, and still another, simpler recipe calls for ricotta and spinach. On the tables of the poor it was a one-dish meal of exceptional nutri-tional value. The name *tiella* refers to the round, shallow pan in which the pie is baked.

Everyone in Minturno has an opinion on how to catch and cook fish. Here, Roman history tells us, lived a famous gourmand who even fitted out a ship to go fishing off the coast of Africa, where, it was said, he could catch larger shrimp than those already notable ones caught on the coast.[145] He went, he verified, he returned disappointed. The Roman poet Martial had sung the praises of the area's shellfish and the particular fish that were caught at Formia, and even then the hills behind Fondi were largely planted to low vineyards.

The countryside at the foot of the Monti Lepini was and is very fertile. Graz-ing alternated with cropping where buffalo were raised. For centuries, water buffalo were the only livestock raised in the area and must have been quite prof-itable. One document attests that the *procojo* of the cow buffalo of Fondi was rented from 1606 to 1614 for the enormous sum of 3,528 ducats.

The vast agricultural holdings, subdivided into *fondi,* were inhabited by farm-ers joined in so-called *fuochi* (literally "fires").[146] A document from Pastorano dated 1541 gives a precise picture of what was meant by a *fuoco.* This one con-sisted of a family head thirty-seven years of age, his wife, age twenty-five, and their son age ten. With him lived the mother, a married brother with three chil-dren, and three families, called, generically, farmhands. They lived in a house of four rooms, with oven, courtyard, and hayloft; they owned six oxen, two cows, a donkey, a mare, and six sows with seventeen piglets. He managed thirty-seven *tomoli*[147] of land divided into eleven small parcels, often separated one from the other. He cultivated two small gardens, and his land produced a small surplus to sell in order to pay the taxes and rent.

The *fuochi* lived grouped together in villages. Mostly wheat, hemp, and vines were grown on the plain; but by the end of the 1600s, the cultivation of maize, known as "wheat of India," was already documented. Among the agricultural jobs to do in April was hunting down mice, which damaged the crops.

Allowing fields to lie fallow was widely practiced. The farms produced wheat, legumes, hemp, straw, wood, and wine for sale; vegetables for their own consumption; and for both sale and consumption, oats, barley, corn, foxtail millet, fava beans, vinegar, salamis, and cheeses. A fair income was also made from the woods and from grazing, since cheeses were a substantial source of income. Dairy products and especially vegetables were the basic ingredients of the Pontine kitchen.

As in the rest of the region, choice meats came only with prosperity. The cooking was simple: if the meats were roasted, they were perfumed with the fragrant herbs that grow throughout the area, including rosemary, sage, marjoram, oregano, and parsley. Garlic and onion were and are found everywhere. It follows, not surprisingly, that roast lamb, lamb *alla cacciatora,* and chicken with bell peppers (recipe on page 171) are made more or less the same way in Sabina, Tuscia, and the Pontina.

The Pontina is home to some specialty sausages, the most famous of which are made with liver and are seasoned with garlic and with orange and lemon rind, fruits that grow in this mild climate. The local pork sausages are often flavored with coriander seeds and have a wonderful taste when roasted.

The popular Pontine sweets are also common to all of Lazio: they are mostly dry, that is, cookies or cookielike, often made with honey, walnuts, and hazelnuts and flavored with anise, coriander, cinnamon, and cloves, following a very old tradition.

Coastal Lazio and the Sea

Mare Nostrum, this sea of ours, the Mediterranean—it has been the protagonist of the economy and of the cultural development of the territory! By the second millennium B.C., it was already plowed by boats that practiced local coastal navigation in search of profitable trade. For one thing, the sea was safer than the land, and for another, numerous watercourses from the hills made it possible to penetrate the interior by boat. The daring sailors had to travel along the coast only by day, exploiting the moorages on the sandy shoreline because boats with shallow draft could easily moor in the mouths of the rivers. Scholars attribute the first profitable trading posts to the outlets into the Tyrrhenian Sea of the numerous rivers between Civitavecchia and Nettuno. The topography has changed since then, and the ancient river mouths were likely much farther back from the sea than they are today. Some archaeologists have even identified the first maritime moorings at the mouths of the Marta and the Fiora.[148]

The main goods for trade were iron (especially from the hills behind Populonia); salt, essential for food preservation and the tanning of leather; and surplus grains, which the fertile area produced in quantity. Salt, especially in later centuries, would constitute a considerable source of income for the Vatican.

With the fall of the empire began the slow transformation of the agrarian landscape on which fallow or pasturage was imposed. The invasions of the migrant peoples, starting with Alaric and his Visigoths in the fifth century A.D. and continuing up to the Saracens in the ninth and tenth centuries, contributed to the degradation of the landscape, not only on the Roman littoral,[149] but, terrifyingly, on the whole peninsula. The villages along the Latian coast slowly became depopulated as their inhabitants moved to hidden localities in the interior.

The situation south of Rome, from Ostia toward Nettuno, was not very different; here too reigned the *latifundium* with the uncontested dominion of pasturage. Gregorovius[150] writes about the Anzio area:

> Here there are neither vineyards nor olive orchards, only flocks that pasture on the coast; the foodstuffs come from the interior: Nettuno sends wine and daily even fresh bread; Genzano sends oil and fruit, and from the mountains of the Volsci, from Cori, come even cherries and figs.

The various popes had repeatedly called for the reclamation of the territory so that they could fell trees and recover land to cultivate. But it was only with the large drainage works of the twentieth century that the problem would be solved at the root.

Since antiquity, the sea along the Roman littoral has been famous for its abundance of fish, and still today the fish caught off Anzio and Nettuno are considered excellent. Scholars maintain that fishing methods saw little change from Etruscan times until the technological advances of the twentieth century. Simple, double, and triple hooks; *folgori* (tridents); nets on curved frames; terracotta fish pots; large and small nets for special fish; grandiose chamber nets for tuna fishing; hatcheries for fish farming; and tanks of fresh- and saltwater were all in use in maritime Etruria. It is possible that some techniques reached Italy from the Phoenician world, and the so-called *lavoriero*[151] seems even to be a pre-Roman invention.

Tuna fishing was very well organized, and in fact always was, from Roman times until the twentieth century: at the high points on the coast where watchtowers would be built in later centuries, trained slaves stood watch for the arrival of the school of tuna, detectable from the slight undulation of the surface of the water or from changes in its color. In time, the slaves would be replaced by trained sailors who would continue the tuna fishing from these stations over the centuries. In ancient times, the Tyrrhenian coast, especially along the Latian littoral, was already considered among the most fish rich in Italy, in part thanks to the wealth of aquatic plants. The toponym Algae, present-day Valdaliga, suggests that the characteristic must already have been known to the Etruscans and Romans.

At Santa Marinella, between the two wars when beach tourism was just beginning, doctors were already suggesting that children be taken to the seaside to get the benefit of the iodine. Moreover, the Roman littoral, which alternates sandy beaches with low coastal rocks, with many little inlets at the mouths of the Rivers Fiora, Arrone, Marta, and Mignone, is washed by a current of warm water from Sicily that favors the quantity of fish in the waters and the consequent wealth and variety of the catch.

Different fishing methods were practiced along the entire coast. For example, to catch an octopus among the rocks, a small amount of oil was poured into the water to prevent the ripples of small waves and thus see the bottom better. The octopus was then captured with a *lanzatore,* a large hook with a barbed end that was thrown at it. Fishing with the *coppo* (convex roof tile) was also common. A fisherman, half naked or protected by a suit called a *palombara,* would partially immerse himself in an area of shallow water particularly rich in fish and fill his basket with cuttlefish, small shrimp, and small fish. *Arselle* and *vongole,* types of small clams, were fished *a schiari,* by searching in the sand with fingers. The *tellinari* who walked along the beach, barelegged and wielding a sort of rake, gathering the *telline* (tiny clams) could still be encountered a few decades ago. Sea urchins were captured with specially prepared reeds whose tops were split in four and held open by a cork. The *lenza a traina,* a trolling line up to 165 feet (50 meters) long, was baited and spread on the surface of the water to catch *spigole* (sea bass), *dentici,* and *occhiate* (the latter two both breams). A slightly different method called for using the *lenza da traina da fondo,* which was 330 feet (100 meters) long and weighted with olive-shaped plumb bobs to keep it on the sea floor (*fondo*). A very similar fishing method used the *bolentino,* which consisted of a *lenza libera da fondo,* it too weighted. When the moon was full during the winter, and the squid (calamari) came close to the coast, they were caught by a method called *alle callamare* (that is, calamari). Tuna fishing was done, as in Sicily, with deer antlers baited with squid, of which tuna are very fond.

Seafood was a late arrival in the gastronomic tradition of Rome and the Latian interior. It expanded beyond the coastal towns only in the last few decades, and now even the most isolated towns of Sabina or the Ciociaria have learned to cook sole and red mullet in a tasty fashion, often using their own local flavorings and cooking methods. Fish-based cooking is a new branch of Latian cooking. It fully respects the spirit of the region's gastronomic tradition in general, which is to make simple, unadorned dishes that bring out the fresh taste of the foods. Tomatoes are sometimes used, but fish is more typically roasted or grilled, and the obligatory herbs are marjoram, garlic, parsley, basil, and sometimes thyme. Olive oil is omnipresent as a condiment, and its fruitiness harmonizes perfectly with fish for a most Mediterranean marriage of flavors.

(previous page) Giovanni Fanei, a group of women harvesting hay in the *campagna romana*
(Biblioteca Clementina, Anzio)

Recipes

THOUGHTS ON THE INTERPRETATION
OF ITALIAN RECIPES

In the individualistic and imaginative world of Italian cooking, the metric system always strikes me as discordant. It sounds so precise and scientific. Our antiquated American system of measurement, with its fractions and its dashes and pinches, seems better suited to the freewheeling Italian cook who measures by look and feel, experience and instinct. In most of the recipes in this book, I have rounded the English equivalent of the original metric measurement to something credible and manageable and have tried to render the metric equivalent equally friendly, without straying too far from what the author wrote. Both sets of measurements are to be taken as meaning "about what you would use if (ha ha) you actually measured." The amount and direction of rounding may vary from ingredient to ingredient and recipe to recipe: these are traditional recipes, not conversion tables. Measurements for baking are held to a higher standard, of course, and here the metric original has been respected or altered only with the author's permission. And speaking of the author, no amount of asking, badgering, or cajoling has had any effect on Oretta's refusal, for most recipes, to give amounts of salt. Evidently, if we have to ask, we're probably not ready to be alone in the kitchen. In any case, she cannot possibly know how salty our particular capers (or whatever) will taste and thus declines to offer an opinion when we can perfectly well taste the dish for ourselves.

For a number of ingredients for which American cooks measure volume while Italians use weight, I have stuck with weight and urge readers to get the habit of using the handy kitchen scale. It is, for example, much more logical to weigh out a piece of cheese and grate it (or weigh the piece from which it is grated before and after to see how much has been used) than to wonder how much cheese, when grated, is needed to fill a half cup or how many almonds to buy to fill a cup.

The recipes come from different parts of the region, different social groups, different seasons of the year. Therefore, we can't ask for similar ingredients always to be handled in a similar way. If beans are cooked by method A in one recipe and method B in another, that's not inconsistency, it's tradition. Sometimes a recipe calls for a white onion, sometimes a yellow, sometimes just an onion, in which case it doesn't matter what color you use.

The verbs of Italian recipes can be delightful—you accommodate the fish in a pan, you moisten or bathe with wine—but, after a flirtation with this colorful vocabulary, I reverted to the prosaic "put" and "add." I felt enough was being left to the imagination without my having to worry about making the fish comfortable. One Italian verb needs explanation, *insaporire,* literally "enflavor." It is the final phase of many recipes, wherein the ingredients exchange their flavors. That is what is meant in the recipes by "let the flavors blend." It usually takes place over low heat but may also be the purpose of the off-heat final rest period.

Pan dimensions, even ballpark, are rarely given because all Italians (we must believe) know what is meant: in most cases, a shallow, straight-sided pot with two short handles. A deep skillet will be ideal when a small saucepan or large soup pot are clearly not the thing.

Oretta is very concerned that readers understand about substitutions. This is not a modern cookbook, which would do its best to accommodate what the readers' local shops and kitchens might be expected to contain. The recipes in this book represent the home cooking of a particular area over generations. If you are unable to find ingredients that are a close approximation of those called for, then you have two choices: make something else or do the best you can with what you have and understand that you are not making the traditional recipe. Occasionally Oretta has vouchsafed alternatives that will make a very tasty dish, but in using them you may forfeit your right to use the original name of the dish. For example, *zuppa di telline* (recipe on page 148) by definition includes *telline,* tiny wedge-shell clams. If you use any other clams, your soup will surely be delicious, but it will no longer be *zuppa di telline.* Another thing: while it is easy to be flippant about Italian measurements, it is also important to bear in mind that these recipes have been made over a long, and indeterminate, expanse of time; variation—say, for pasta sizes or quantity of protein—is to be expected. Today they are written in ink, but they have never been written in stone.

Some of these recipes are not for the fainthearted (decapitate the frogs? skin the spinal cord?), but fortunately that is not a translation problem. What is a problem is the Italian reliance on the reader's experience vis-à-vis the Anglo-American expectation that a well-written recipe will contain all essential information. Oretta was a good sport and provided answers to a great many methodological questions, but readers will still find they are expected to need little more than a reminder of how to boil beans, make a risotto, or fill and seal ravioli, as well as to know when to turn on their own oven. Just roll with it.

—*M.B.F.*

PRIMI PIATTI · FIRST COURSES

Paste asciutte · Pastas and their sauces

Fettuccine all'ammiraglia · Fettuccine with seafood
Makes 4 servings

about 2 pounds (1 kg) *telline* (see page 275) or other small clams
2 cups (500 ml) fish broth (or meat broth made with a bouillon cube)
7 ounces (200 g) jumbo shrimp in their shells
7 ounces (200 g) small shrimp in their shells
2 garlic cloves
2 tablespoons lightly fruity extra-virgin olive oil
1½ pounds (700 g) sauce tomatoes, preferably San Marzano
1 small white onion
4½ tablespoons (70 g) butter
salt
freshly ground pepper
14 ounces (400 g) fresh egg fettuccine

Soak the *telline* for a few hours in lightly salted water to purge them. Put the broth in a pot and bring it to a boil. Add the jumbo shrimp and small shrimp and boil them over medium heat for 5 or 6 minutes. Drain the shrimp, reserving the broth. Peel the shrimp and dice the flesh, reserving it along with the broth and the shells.

Crush 1 garlic clove and put it in a skillet with the oil. Drain and rinse the *telline* carefully, add them to the pan, cover, and cook them over low heat just until they open. Remove the *telline* and set aside, discarding any that failed to open, then strain their liquid and add it to the reserved shrimp broth. Pour a few tablespoons of this broth into a food processor, add the shrimp shells, and process until the mixture is smooth. Pour the mixture into a pot, add the remaining broth, and cook over medium heat for about 20 minutes. Strain the liquid through a fine-mesh sieve.

While the broth is simmering, peel the tomatoes and cut them into strips. Chop together finely the remaining garlic clove and the onion, place them in a saucepan with half the butter, and sauté over medium heat for 7 to 8 minutes. Then add the tomatoes, one-fourth of the strained broth, some salt, and a grinding of pepper. Continue cooking over medium heat until the sauce is quite smooth and well blended. Remove from the heat and add all the diced shrimp and the reserved mollusks.

Drop the fettuccine into about 4 quarts (4 liters) boiling salted water. Drain when al dente and transfer to a warmed serving bowl. Toss first with the remaining butter and then with the sauce. Serve immediately.

Fettuccine alla papalina · The pope's fettuccine
Makes 4 servings

1 white onion
3½ ounces (100 g) sliced prosciutto
5½ tablespoons (80 g) butter
3 eggs
3 heaping tablespoons grated *parmigiano-reggiano*
2 tablespoons heavy cream
salt
14 ounces (400 g) fresh egg fettuccine
pepper

Finely chop the onion and cut the prosciutto into narrow strips. Put the onion and prosciutto in a deep skillet with half the butter and sauté over medium heat for about 4 minutes, or until golden brown. Meanwhile, break the eggs into a food processor, add 2 tablespoons of the parmigiano, the cream, and some salt, and process until smooth.

Drop the fettuccine into about 4 quarts (4 liters) boiling salted water. While it cooks, melt the rest of the butter in a small pan over low heat, then pour it into a warmed serving bowl. Add the egg mixture and mix rapidly to warm it up without scrambling the eggs from the heat of the butter. Next add the onion and prosciutto mixture. Drain the fettuccine when al dente and add to the bowl. Toss for a few seconds, then sprinkle with the remaining parmigiano and a little pepper. Serve immediately.

Fettuccine alla romana · Fettuccine with giblets and tomatoes
Makes 4 servings

9 ounces (250 g) chicken giblets
¼ (20 g) dried porcini mushrooms
1 pound (450 g) sauce tomatoes
1 small white onion
1¾ ounces (50 g) prosciutto fat
1 garlic clove
2 tablespoons medium-fruity extra-virgin olive oil
4 tablespoons dry white table wine
salt
scant 1 cup (200 ml) meat or vegetable broth, heated
2 or 3 tablespoons *sugo d'umido* (recipe on page 253)
14 ounces (400 g) fresh egg fettuccine
2 heaping tablespoons grated *parmigiano-reggiano*

Trim the giblets, eliminating the green bile ducts from the livers. Rinse them for a good, long time, then dice. Soak the dried mushrooms for 20 minutes in at least two changes of warm water. Drain, rinse, and squeeze well, then cut them into small pieces. Peel, halve, and seed the tomatoes, then cut into small pieces.

Chop together finely the onion and the prosciutto fat and crush the garlic clove. Put the onion mixture and garlic in a saucepan with the oil and sauté over medium heat for about 5 minutes. As soon as the onion and fat become translucent, add the mushrooms and the giblets, raise the heat, and sauté until the mushrooms and meat have wilted. Add the wine, then add the tomatoes, sprinkle with salt, cover, and continue cooking over low heat for about 20 minutes, adding the hot broth from time to time. Shortly before you remove it from the heat, stir in the *sugo*.

Drop the fettuccine into about 4 quarts (4 liters) boiling salted water. Drain when al dente and transfer to a warmed serving bowl. Toss first with the parmigiano and then with the sauce. Serve immediately.

*Fregnacce alla reatina · Handmade flour-and-water pasta
with tomato sauce*
Makes 4 servings

FOR THE FREGNACCE
7 ounces (200 g) durum flour
salt

FOR THE SAUCE
11 ounces (300 g) ripe tomatoes
1¾ ounces (50 g) *lardo* or pancetta
9 ounces (250 g) onion
9 ounces (250 g) celery
4 tablespoons medium-fruity extra-virgin olive oil,
   preferably from Sabina
small piece dried chile

TO FINISH
2 very heaping tablespoons grated pecorino, preferably
   pecorino romano

To make the *fregnacce:* Knead the flour with a pinch of salt and ½ cup (120 ml)
water to make a rather firm dough. Let it rest, covered, for 30 minutes. Roll out
the dough into a sheet, not too thin, and cut into irregular rhombuses about ¾
inch (2 cm) on a side.

To make the sauce: Cut the tomatoes into small pieces. Chop together finely
the *lardo,* onion, and celery. Sauté the *lardo* mixture in the oil in a deep skillet
until golden brown, then add the tomatoes and chile and cook the sauce for
about 20 minutes.

Cook the pasta in about 4 quarts (4 liters) boiling salted water and drain it
as soon as it floats to the surface. Transfer to a warmed serving bowl, toss with
the sauce, and sprinkle with the pecorino.

Maccheroni con la ricotta · Pasta with ricotta

Ricotta romana owes its particular sweetness to the grass on which the sheep of the *campagna romana* graze. Nevertheless, for this dish, other kinds of ricotta will do, including that made with cow's milk.

Makes 4 servings

14 ounces (400 g) *maccheroni,* broken up
9 ounces (250 g) ricotta, preferably *ricotta romana*
   (see page 275)
1 teaspoon confectioners' sugar
ground cinnamon
salt

Drop the pasta into about 4 quarts (4 liters) boiling salted water.

While it is cooking, put the ricotta in a large warmed serving bowl and add the sugar and a pinch each of cinnamon and salt. When the pasta is about half done, add a few tablespoons of the pasta cooking water to the ricotta mixture and mix well until smooth.

Drain the pasta when al dente, add to the ricotta mixture, toss well, and serve immediately.

Panzerotti di maiale · Pork turnovers

Pâte brisée, typical pastry of classic cuisine, is common in Roman gastronomy. Use your favorite recipe.

Makes 6 servings

1¾ ounces (50 g) crustless bread, soaked in milk
7 ounces (200 g) boneless pork
scant ½ cup (100 ml) béchamel sauce
1 heaping tablespoon grated *parmigiano-reggiano*
2 whole eggs plus 1 egg yolk
salt
pepper
nutmeg
1¾ pounds (800 g) *pâte brisée*

Squeeze the bread well. Chop the pork into small pieces and put in a food processor. Add the béchamel and process until smooth. Transfer to a small bowl and add the bread, parmigiano, 2 whole eggs, a little salt, a grinding of pepper, and a generous grating of nutmeg. Mix thoroughly.

Roll out the *pâte brisée* into a sheet about ¼ inch (6 mm) thick. Cut the sheet into disks about 5 inches (12 cm) in diameter. Put a tablespoon of the pork filling in the center of each disk. Fold over and seal the edges, pressing firmly with fingertips.

Arrange the *panzerotti* on a rimmed sheet pan. Lightly beat the egg yolk and brush the tops of the *panzerotti*. Bake in an oven preheated to 375°F (190°C) for about 20 minutes, or until golden brown.

Serve hot or at room temperature.

Pappardelle con le rigaglie · Pappardelle with giblets
Makes 4 servings

11 ounces (300 g) chicken giblets

1 ounce (30 g) dried porcini mushrooms

1 white onion

1 tablespoon lard, or 3 tablespoons intensely fruity extra-virgin olive oil

2 tablespoons dry Marsala

salt

pepper

14 ounces (400 g) fresh egg *pappardelle*

1¼ cups (300 ml) *sugo d'umido* (recipe on page 253)

2 heaping tablespoons grated *parmigiano-reggiano*

Trim the giblets, eliminating the green bile ducts from the livers. Rinse them for a good, long time, then chop them, not too finely. Soak the dried mushrooms for 20 minutes in at least two changes of warm water. Drain, rinse, and squeeze well, then chop.

Chop the onion finely and put it in a deep skillet with the lard. Sauté over medium heat for 7 to 8 minutes. Add the giblets and mushrooms and cook for about 5 minutes longer. When the giblets are perfectly browned, moisten with the Marsala, season with salt and pepper, and continue cooking for another few minutes over medium heat.

Meanwhile, cook the *pappardelle* in about 4 quarts (4 liters) boiling salted water. Heat the *sugo*. When the pasta is al dente, drain and transfer to a large warmed platter. Toss with the *sugo* and the parmigiano, then add the *ragù* of giblets and mushrooms, toss again, and serve.

*Pasticcio di maccheroni con la ricotta · Baked pasta
with meat and cheese*
Makes 8 servings

1 yellow onion
1 carrot
1 celery rib
1 pound (450 g) boneless beef or pork, in one piece
5 tablespoons intensely fruity extra-virgin olive oil
salt
pepper
scant 1 cup (200 ml) light red table wine
11 ounces (300 g) tomato purée
1⅓ pounds (600 g) *ziti* (long, tubular pasta)
7 ounces (200 g) *caciotta* or other semihard cheese
1 pound (450 g) ricotta, preferably *ricotta romana*
   (see page 275)
3½ ounces (100 g) grated *parmigiano-reggiano*

Chop together finely the onion, carrot, and celery. Tie the meat with kitchen string so it will keep its shape. Put it in a saucepan with 3 tablespoons of the oil and brown uniformly over medium heat for about 5 minutes. When a crust has formed on the surface, add the chopped vegetables and sauté for a couple of minutes. Season with salt and pepper, pour in the wine, and reduce over medium heat until the odor of the alcohol has disappeared. Add the tomato purée, lower the heat, cover, and finish cooking, about 40 minutes.

Remove the pan from the heat and lift out the meat. Snip the string and cut the meat into small dice. Set aside in a good-size bowl. Reserve the pan with its contents.

Break up the *ziti* and drop into about 6 quarts (6 liters) boiling salted water. While the pasta is cooking, dice the *caciotta*. Put the ricotta in a bowl and soften it with a ladleful of the pasta cooking water. Add the *caciotta* and parmigiano to the reserved pork and mix well, then add the reserved contents of the pan.

Drain the *ziti* when it is very al dente, transfer to a bowl, and toss with some of the *ragù* and half the parmigiano. Grease the bottom of a baking dish with the remaining oil. Now make layers of *ziti*, a few tablespoons of *ragù*, and a little parmigiano until all the ingredients are used up. Bake in an oven preheated to 425°F (220°C) for about 7 minutes, or until piping hot. Let the *pasticcio* rest for 5 minutes before serving.

Penne all'arrabbiata · *Penne with spicy tomato sauce*

The presence of porcini mushrooms in this authentic traditional recipe will shock those who have seen the dish only on modern trattoria menus, where it contains just tomatoes, garlic, and chile. Today an expensive treat, fresh porcini used to be employed with great frequency in popular cooking, thanks to the extensive oak forests around the city.

Makes 4 servings

9 ounces (250 g) fresh porcini mushrooms
3½ ounces (100 g) lean pancetta
6 tablespoons (90 ml) intensely fruity extra-virgin olive oil
2 garlic cloves
¾-inch (2-cm) piece dried chile
1 pound (450 g) tomato purée
4 or 5 basil leaves
salt
14 ounces (400 g) penne
3½ ounces (100 g) mixed grated cheese, equal amounts
    pecorino, preferably *pecorino romano,* and
    parmigiano-reggiano

Separate the stems of the porcini from the caps and scrape the caps and stems gently with a small knife to remove any clinging dirt, then wipe with a damp cloth. Slice the stems and caps.

Dice the pancetta finely, put in a deep skillet with the oil, and sauté for 5 to 6 minutes. Remove the pancetta with a slotted spoon to a bowl and keep warm. Cook the mushrooms for a few minutes in the same pan (in the pancetta fat). Remove with the slotted spoon and add them to the reserved pancetta. Reserve the pan with its contents.

Crush the garlic cloves and add them and the chile to the fat remaining in the skillet. Cook over medium heat for a couple of minutes. Discard the garlic and chile and add the tomato purée, basil leaves, and a little salt. Cook for about 20 minutes. A few minutes before the sauce is ready, add the reserved pancetta and mushrooms.

Drop the pasta into about 4 quarts (4 liters) boiling salted water. Drain when al dente and transfer to a warmed serving bowl. First toss with the cheeses and then with the sauce. Serve immediately.

Ravioli di carne · *Meat-filled ravioli*

These meat-filled ravioli are usually served with *sugo d'umido*
(recipe on page 253) and grated parmigiano.

Makes 8 servings

FOR THE FILLING

4 ounces (100 g) spinach

salt

1 ounce (30 g) sliced prosciutto

7 ounces (200 g) boneless pork (or veal or beef), in a
single piece

4 teaspoons (20 g) butter

1 heaping tablespoon grated *parmigiano-reggiano*

1 egg yolk

nutmeg

1 tablespoon dry Marsala

pepper

FOR THE PASTA DOUGH

14 ounces (400 g) flour

4 eggs

salt

1 tablespoon lightly fruity extra-virgin olive oil

To make the filling: Trim and rinse the spinach. Put it in a pot, add a pinch of
salt, cover, and cook over medium heat in just the rinsing water clinging to the
leaves until wilted. Drain the spinach, squeeze well, and chop. Cut the prosciutto into small pieces.

Put the pork in a small saucepan just large enough to hold it, add the butter,
and sauté on all sides for 4 or 5 minutes, or until a brown crust has formed on
the surface. Transfer to a cutting board, reserving the juices in the pan, and cut
into small pieces.

Put the pork and the pan juices in a food processor along with the prosciutto
and spinach. Process until smooth and transfer to a small bowl. Add the parmigiano, egg yolk, a grating of nutmeg, the Marsala, a little salt, and a pinch of
pepper and mix thoroughly. Cover and let rest for about 2 hours in a cool place.

To make the dough: Sift the flour onto a wooden board, shape it into a mound,
and make a well in the center. Break the eggs into the well, add a pinch of salt
and the oil, and begin to incorporate the eggs into the flour with a fork. When
the mixture is too stiff to use a fork any longer, begin forming the dough with

your hands. Once it comes together in a fairly uniform ball, knead it energetically with your hands until you have a smooth, firm dough. Cover with a dish towel and let rest in a cool place for about 1 hour.

Divide the pasta dough in half, then roll out each half into a thin disk. Place teaspoons of the meat mixture on one disk, spacing the mounds about 1¼ inches (3 cm) apart. Lightly moisten the second disk and lay it on top of the first disk. With fingertips, press firmly around the little mounds of filling to seal the sheets together and remove any air pockets. Cut the ravioli apart with a fluted-edged pastry wheel.

Boil the ravioli in about 4 quarts (4 liters) salted water, then drain carefully when al dente and transfer to a warmed bowl. Dress as desired and serve immediately.

Ravioli quaresimali · Meatless ravioli for Lent
Makes 8 servings

Pasta dough for *ravioli di carne* (recipe on page 107)

FOR THE FILLING
9 ounces (250 g) ricotta, preferably *ricotta romana*
  (see page 275)
2 heaping tablespoons grated *parmigiano-reggiano*
2 eggs
salt
pepper
nutmeg

FOR THE SAUCE AND TO FINISH
5½ tablespoons (80 g) butter
4 or 5 sage leaves
5 ounces (140 g) grated *parmigiano-reggiano*

Make the pasta dough as directed and set aside to rest.

To make the filling, pass the ricotta through a sieve placed over a bowl. Add the parmigiano, eggs, a little salt, a grinding of pepper, and a grating of nutmeg. Mix thoroughly.

Divide the pasta dough in half, then roll out each half into a thin disk. Place teaspoons of the filling on one disk, spacing the mounds about 1¼ inches (3 cm) apart. Lightly moisten the second disk and lay it on top of the first disk. With fingertips, press firmly around the little mounds of filling to seal the sheets together and remove any air pockets. Cut the ravioli apart with a fluted-edged pastry wheel.

Boil the ravioli in about 4 quarts (4 liters) salted water. Meanwhile, to make the sauce, melt the butter in a small pan, add the sage leaves, and let them wilt, then discard the leaves. When the ravioli are al dente, drain carefully and transfer to a warmed serving bowl. Sprinkle with the parmigiano, pour on the sage butter, and mix gently. Serve immediately.

Rigatoni con la "pajata" · Rigatoni with veal intestines
Makes 6 servings

3¼ pounds (1.5 kg) *pajata* (see page 274)
3½ ounces (100 g) prosciutto fat
leaves from 1 small bunch flat-leaf parsley
needles from 1 sprig rosemary
salt
pepper
nutmeg
1 whole clove
1 garlic clove
scant ½ cup (100 ml) dry white table wine, preferably
   from the Castelli Romani
1½ pounds (700 g) tomato purée
1 pound (450 g) rigatoni
3½ ounces (100 g) grated pecorino, preferably
   pecorino romano

Cut the *pajata* into lengths of about 8 inches (20 cm), bend each length into a ring, and tie the two ends together with kitchen string.

Chop together finely the prosciutto fat, parsley leaves, and rosemary needles. Put everything in a pan (preferably earthenware) and sauté over medium heat for a few minutes, or until the fat has completely melted. Add the *pajata* rings and season with some salt, a grinding of pepper, and a grating of nutmeg. Sauté for 6 to 7 minutes.

Meanwhile, put the clove, the garlic clove, and the wine in a food processor and process until smooth. Pour this over the *pajata* rings and cook over medium heat until the liquid evaporates. Add the tomato purée, season with salt and pepper, reduce the heat to low, cover, and continue cooking for 2 hours. If the mixture begins to dry out, moisten with a few tablespoons boiling water.

Boil the rigatoni in about 5 quarts (5 liters) boiling salted water. Drain when al dente and transfer to a warmed serving bowl. Sprinkle on the pecorino, then add the sauce and toss well. Serve immediately.

Spaghetti aglio, olio e peperoncino · Spaghetti with garlic, oil, and chile
Makes 4 servings

14 ounces (400 g) spaghetti
leaves from 1 small bunch flat-leaf parsley
3 garlic cloves
6 tablespoons (90 ml) intensely fruity extra-virgin olive oil
¾-inch (2-cm) piece dried chile

Drop the spaghetti into about 4 quarts (4 liters) boiling salted water. While it is cooking, chop the parsley leaves and crush the garlic cloves. Put the oil in a small pan and add the garlic and chile. Sauté over medium heat for a couple of minutes, then discard the garlic and chile.

When the spaghetti is al dente, drain and transfer to a warmed serving bowl. Pour the flavored oil on top and mix well. Sprinkle with the parsley and serve immediately.

Spaghetti aglio, olio e pomodoro · Spaghetti with garlic, oil, and tomato
Makes 4 servings

leaves from 1 small bunch flat-leaf parsley
3 garlic cloves
4 tablespoons intensely fruity extra-virgin olive oil
¾-inch (2-cm) piece dried chile
1 pound (450 g) canned tomatoes
salt
14 ounces (400 g) spaghetti

Chop together finely the parsley leaves and garlic cloves. Put them in a pan with the oil and chile and sauté over medium heat for a couple of minutes. Add the tomatoes, season with salt, and cook the sauce for about 20 minutes over a lively flame, mashing the tomatoes with a fork as needed to break them up. Discard the garlic and chile.

Drop the spaghetti into about 4 quarts (4 liters) boiling salted water. When al dente, drain, transfer to a warmed serving bowl, and toss with the sauce. Serve immediately.

Spaghetti al pomodoro con le alici · Spaghetti with tomatoes and anchovies
Makes 4 servings

2 garlic cloves
¾-inch (2-cm) piece dried chile
4 tablespoons intensely fruity extra-virgin olive oil
4 salt-packed anchovies, prepared as described on
   page 273
9 ounces (250 g) canned tomatoes
14 ounces (400 g) spaghetti

Crush the garlic cloves and put them in a skillet with the chile and oil. Sauté over medium heat for a couple of minutes. Add the anchovies and cook until they are completely dissolved. Now add the tomatoes and cook the sauce over a lively flame for about 20 minutes, mashing the tomatoes with a fork as needed to break them up. Discard the garlic and chile.

Drop the spaghetti into about 4 quarts (4 liters) boiling salted water. When al dente, drain, transfer to a warmed serving bowl, and toss with the sauce. Serve immediately.

Spaghetti all'amatriciana · Spaghetti with tomato and guanciale
This dish is attributed to, and claimed by, Amatrice, a town in the northeast corner of Lazio, near the Abruzzo border. Purists would have it made simply with *guanciale* and pecorino, but nowadays, onion and tomato are usually added. If you can't get *guanciale,* use a very fatty pancetta.
Makes 4 servings

5 or 6 small sauce tomatoes
3½ ounces (100 g) *guanciale*
1 tablespoon intensely fruity extra-virgin olive oil

1 small white onion
piece dried chile, to taste
salt
14 ounces (400 g) spaghetti
2½ ounces (70 g) grated pecorino, preferably
   pecorino romano

Peel, halve, and seed the tomatoes, then cut into thin strips. Cut the *guanciale* into small pieces, put in a skillet with the oil, and sauté for 2 to 3 minutes, or until crisp. Remove the *guanciale* with a slotted spoon to a bowl and keep warm. Reserve the contents of the pan.

Chop the onion and put it in a saucepan with the chile and the contents of the *guanciale* pan. Add the tomatoes and a little salt and cook over medium heat for about 10 minutes, or until the tomatoes have broken down. Discard the chile, then add the reserved *guanciale*.

Drop the spaghetti into about 4 quarts (4 liters) boiling salted water. When al dente, drain and transfer to a warmed serving bowl. Toss first with the pecorino and then with the sauce. Serve immediately.

Spaghetti alla carbonara · Spaghetti with eggs and guanciale
Makes 4 servings

3½ ounces (100 g) lean *guanciale* or, only if necessary, very
   lean slab pancetta
1 tablespoon medium-fruity extra-virgin olive oil
14 ounces (400 g) spaghetti
3 eggs
3 ounces (80 g) mixed grated cheese, equal amounts *pecorino
   romano* and *parmigiano-reggiano*
salt
freshly ground pepper

Dice the *guanciale,* put in a skillet with the oil, and sauté over medium heat for a couple of minutes, or until crisp. Set aside in the skillet and keep warm. Drop the spaghetti into about 4 quarts (4 liters) boiling salted water. Meanwhile, break the eggs into a bowl, add the grated cheeses, a pinch of salt, and a grinding of pepper. Beat energetically with a fork until the mixture is smooth.

Drain the spaghetti and transfer to the skillet with the *guanciale;* toss gently over very low heat. Lift the pan straight up so it is over but not touching the burner (or the eggs will scramble), then pour in the egg mixture in a stream while flipping and tossing the pasta constantly by flicking the wrist holding the pan. (Or, remove from the heat and pour in the egg mixture while stirring constantly.) Be careful not to let the eggs scramble. Transfer to a warmed serving bowl and serve immediately.

Spaghetti alla carrettiera · *Spaghetti with tuna and mushrooms*
Makes 4 servings

11 ounces (300 g) fresh porcini mushrooms
1¾ ounces (50 g) lean *guanciale* or very lean slab pancetta
2½ ounces (70 g) oil-packed tuna (1 small can)
2 garlic cloves
4 tablespoons medium-fruity extra-virgin olive oil
salt
pepper
14 ounces (400 g) spaghetti
1⅔ cups (400 ml) *sugo d'umido* (recipe on page 253)
2 heaping tablespoons grated *parmigiano-reggiano*

Separate the stems of the porcini from the caps and scrape the caps and stems gently with a small knife to remove any clinging dirt, then wipe with a damp cloth. Slice the stems and caps. Cut the *guanciale* into small pieces. Drain the tuna and break it up with a fork.

Crush the garlic cloves and put in a saucepan with the oil. Sauté over medium heat for a couple of minutes, or until the garlic has colored. Discard the garlic, add the *guanciale,* and sauté over low heat for 3 to 4 minutes. Now add the mushrooms, season with salt and pepper, and continue cooking for about 3 minutes. Add the tuna to the pan, cover, and finish cooking the sauce over low heat for 15 to 20 minutes.

Drop the spaghetti into about 4 quarts (4 liters) boiling salted water. At the same time, heat the *sugo.* When the spaghetti is al dente, drain and transfer to a warmed serving bowl. First toss with the mushroom and tuna sauce, then add the *sugo.* Dust with the parmigiano and serve immediately.

Spaghetti alla checca · Spaghetti with raw tomatoes
Makes 4 servings

leaves from 1 small bunch flat-leaf parsley
2 ounces (60 g) pitted green olives
leaves from 1 small bunch basil
14 ounces (400 g) salad tomatoes (firm and not too ripe)
4 tablespoons medium-fruity extra-virgin olive oil
salt
pepper
1 teaspoon fennel seeds
14 ounces (400 g) spaghetti

Chop together the parsley leaves and olives. Chop the basil leaves. Halve and seed the tomatoes, then drain them for a few minutes. Slice the tomatoes, put them in a large bowl, and dress them with the oil and some salt and pepper. Stir and then add the parsley and olive mixture, the basil, and the fennel seeds. Let the flavors blend for about 20 minutes.

Meanwhile, cook the spaghetti in about 4 quarts (4 liters) boiling salted water. When al dente, drain and transfer to the bowl containing the tomato mixture. Toss without interruption until the pasta has cooled somewhat, then serve.

Spaghetti alla gricia · Spaghetti with guanciale and pecorino cheese
Makes 4 servings

12 ounces (350 g) spaghetti
3½ ounces (100 g) *guanciale*
2 garlic cloves
small piece dried chile
3 tablespoons extra-virgin olive oil
12 ounces (350 g) spaghetti
2 heaping tablespoons grated pecorino, preferably
  pecorino romano
salt

Cut the *guanciale* into strips. Chop together the garlic and chile. Put the *guanciale,* the garlic and chile, and the oil in a large skillet and brown everything over medium heat.

Meanwhile, drop the spaghetti into about 4 quarts (4 liters) boiling salt water. When al dente, drain, add to the skillet with the *guanciale,* and toss briefly over low heat. Transfer to a warmed serving dish, add the pecorino, and serve immediately.

Spaghetti alla bucaniera · Spaghetti with seafood
Makes 4 servings

4 ounces (100 g) Manila clams
4 ounces (100 g) octopi
4 ounces (100 g) small shrimp
6 tablespoons (90 ml) fruity extra-virgin olive oil
4 garlic cloves
leaves from 1 small bunch flat-leaf parsley
14 ounces (400 g) sauce tomatoes
salt
freshly ground pepper
14 ounces (400 g) spaghetti

Soak the clams for a few hours in lightly salted water to purge them. Rinse the octopi and dice them. Peel and dice the shrimp.

Drain and rinse the clams carefully and put them in a pan with 1 tablespoon of the oil. Crush 1 of the garlic cloves, add it to the pan, cover, and cook over a lively flame for about 5 minutes, or just until the clams open. Lift the clams out of the pan and remove them from their shells, discarding any that failed to open. Discard the garlic from the pan. Strain the liquid and reserve.

Chop the parsley leaves and set aside. Peel the tomatoes and cut them into strips. Crush the remaining 3 garlic cloves and put them in a saucepan with half the remaining oil. Add the tomatoes, some salt, and a grinding of pepper and cook over medium heat for about 20 minutes. Discard the garlic.

Meanwhile, heat the remaining oil in another pan, add the octopi, and cook over medium heat for about 3 minutes. Stir in the diced shrimp and shelled clams and continue to cook for 2 minutes longer. Remove from the heat, season with salt and pepper, and add to the tomato sauce along with the reserved clam liquid. Keep the sauce hot.

Drop the spaghetti into about 4 quarts (4 liters) boiling salted water. When al dente, drain and transfer to a warmed serving bowl. Toss with the sauce and sprinkle with the parsley. Serve immediately.

Spaghetti alla puttanesca · Spaghetti with tomatoes,
anchovies, capers, and olives
Makes 4 servings

5 or 6 sauce tomatoes, preferably San Marzano
5 ounces (150 g) pitted brine-packed olives,
  preferably Gaeta
4 oil-packed anchovy fillets
1 heaping tablespoon salt-packed capers, rinsed thoroughly
  to remove the salt
2 garlic cloves
6 tablespoons (90 ml) lightly fruity extra-virgin olive oil
leaves from 1 small bunch flat-leaf parsley
14 ounces (400 g) spaghetti

Peel the tomatoes and cut them into strips. Slice the olives thinly. Drain the anchovies and chop finely together with the capers and garlic cloves. Put the oil in a skillet, add the anchovy mixture, and cook over medium heat until the anchovies have dissolved. Add the tomatoes and olives and cook gently over medium heat for about 15 minutes, stirring occasionally. Meanwhile, chop the parsley leaves finely.

Drop the spaghetti into about 4 quarts (4 liters) boiling salted water. When al dente, drain and transfer to a warmed serving bowl. Dress with the sauce, sprinkle with the parsley, and serve immediately.

Spaghetti cacio e pepe · Spaghetti with pecorino romano
and black pepper
Makes 4 servings

1¾ ounces (50 g) black peppercorns
14 ounces (400 g) spaghetti
5 ounces (150 g) grated pecorino, preferably
  pecorino romano

Put the peppercorns in a mortar and crush, not too finely, with a pestle.

Drop the spaghetti into about 4 quarts (4 liters) boiling salted water. Using two large forks (so that some of the cooking water will remain), quickly transfer the spaghetti to a warmed serving bowl. Toss first with the pecorino and then the pepper. Mix until the cheese is completely melted. Serve immediately.

*Spaghetti alla boscaiola · Spaghetti with tuna
and mushrooms*

Precious *ovoli* mushrooms will not be easy to find, but ordinary button
mushrooms will give a satisfying result.

Makes 4 servings

7 ounces (200 g) fresh *ovoli* mushrooms
leaves from 1 small bunch flat-leaf parsley
2 garlic cloves
6 tablespoons (90 ml) intensely fruity extra-virgin
    olive oil
14 ounces (400 g) canned tomatoes
salt
freshly ground pepper
3½ ounces (100 g) oil-packed tuna
14 ounces (400 g) spaghetti

Using a small knife, gently scrape the surface of the *ovoli* to eliminate any clinging dirt. Wipe them with a damp cloth and then slice. Chop the parsley leaves.
Set the mushrooms and parsley aside.

Crush the garlic cloves and put them in a pan with half the oil. Sauté over
medium heat for a couple of minutes, or until the garlic has colored. Discard the
garlic, then add the tomatoes to the garlic-flavored oil along with some salt and
a grinding of pepper. Continue cooking over medium heat for about 15 minutes,
mashing the tomatoes with a fork as needed to break them up.

Warm the remaining oil in a second pan, add the *ovoli,* and sauté over medium heat for 3 to 4 minutes, stirring constantly. Drain the tuna, add to the
pan, and cook for 2 more minutes, crumbling it gently with a wooden spoon but
not too much. Combine the two sauces.

Drop the spaghetti into about 4 quarts (4 liters) boiling salted water. When
al dente, drain and transfer to a warmed serving bowl. Toss with the combined
sauces, then add the parsley. Serve immediately.

Spaghetti con il tonno · Spaghetti with tuna
Makes 4 servings

11 ounces (300 g) oil-packed tuna
leaves from 1 small bunch flat-leaf parsley
1 garlic clove
4 tablespoons intensely fruity extra-virgin olive oil
9 ounces (250 g) tomato purée
salt
pepper
14 ounces (400 g) spaghetti

Drain the tuna and break it up with a fork. Chop the parsley leaves finely.

Crush the garlic clove, put it in a saucepan with the oil, and cook over medium heat for a couple of minutes, or until it begins to brown. Add the tuna and the tomato purée, season generously with salt and pepper, and continue cooking the sauce over medium heat for about 20 minutes.

Meanwhile, drop the spaghetti into about 4 quarts (4 liters) boiling salted water. When al dente, drain and transfer to a warmed serving bowl. Toss with the tuna sauce, sprinkle with the parsley, and serve immediately.

Spaghetti con le vongole · Spaghetti with clams
Makes 4 servings

2½ pounds (1.2 kg) Manila clams
2 garlic cloves
4 tablespoons medium-fruity extra-virgin olive oil
scant ½ cup (100 ml) dry white table wine
leaves from 1 small bunch flat-leaf parsley
14 ounces (400 g) spaghetti
¾-inch (2-cm) piece dried chile

Soak the clams for a few hours in lightly salted water to purge them. Then drain and rinse carefully. Crush 1 of the garlic cloves.

Put the clams, the crushed garlic, 1 tablespoon of the oil, and the wine in a pan. Cover and cook over a lively flame for about 5 minutes, or just until the clams open. Lift the clams out of the pan and remove them from their shells, discarding any that failed to open. Set the clams aside. Strain the broth and reserve. Chop the parsley leaves finely and reserve.

Drop the spaghetti into about 4 quarts (4 liters) boiling salted water. Meanwhile, crush the remaining garlic clove and brown it in a large skillet with the remaining oil and the chile. Add the reserved broth and simmer for a few minutes. Remove the sauce from the fire, discard the garlic and chile, and add the clams. Stir carefully.

When the spaghetti is very al dente, drain, transfer to the skillet holding the sauce, and toss for not more than 1 minute over low heat. Remove from the heat, sprinkle with the parsley, and serve immediately.

Spaghetti in bianco con le alici · Spaghetti with anchovies
Makes 4 servings

> 4 salt-packed anchovies, prepared as described on
>   page 273
> 1 garlic clove
> leaves from 1 small bunch flat-leaf parsley
> 14 ounces (400 g) spaghetti
> ¾-inch (2-cm) piece dried chile
> 4 tablespoons intensely fruity extra-virgin olive oil

Chop the anchovies very finely. Crush the garlic clove. Chop the parsley leaves finely.

Drop the spaghetti into about 4 quarts (4 liters) boiling salted water. Meanwhile, put the garlic, chile, and oil in a skillet and sauté over medium heat for a few minutes, or until the garlic is golden brown. Add the anchovies and stir over low heat until dissolved.

When the spaghetti is very al dente, drain, add to the skillet holding the anchovy mixture, and sauté energetically over a lively flame for 1 minute. Discard the garlic and chile and transfer to a warmed serving bowl. Sprinkle with the parsley and serve immediately.

Tagliolini col sugo di agnello · Egg pasta with lamb sauce
Makes 4 servings

> 1 small onion
> 1 carrot
> leaves from 1 small bunch basil

3½ ounces (100 g) lean pancetta
2 tablespoons extra-virgin olive oil
1½ pounds (700 g) boneless lamb, in ¾-inch (2-cm) pieces
1 cup (250 ml) dry white table wine
12 ounces (350 g) canned tomatoes
salt
pepper
12 ounces (350 g) fresh egg *tagliolini*

Chop together finely the onion, carrot, basil, and pancetta. Put them in a pan with the oil over medium heat. When the pancetta fat has completely melted, add the lamb and brown, stirring. Add the wine and let it evaporate, then add the tomatoes and 4 cups (1 liter) boiling water. Season with salt and pepper and continue cooking until the meat is tender. Remove the lamb from the sauce with a slotted spoon and keep warm.

Add the *tagliolini* to the sauce, which should be quite liquid, and cook until al dente. Return the lamb to the pan and stir for a few minutes. Transfer to a warmed serving bowl and serve immediately.

Risi e risotti · Rice and Risotto

Riso e piselli · Rice and peas
Makes 4 servings

5 ounces (150 g) small sauce tomatoes
2 cups (500 ml) meat or vegetable broth
1 heaping tablespoon *battuto* (recipe on page 251)
salt
pepper
11 ounces (300 g) shelled peas
11 ounces (300 g) Vialone Nano or other rice for risotto
1 heaping tablespoon grated pecorino, preferably
    pecorino romano
1 heaping tablespoon grated *parmigiano-reggiano*

Peel the tomatoes and cut them into strips. Pour the broth into a pot and bring to a boil. Put the *battuto* in a pan (preferably earthenware) and cook over low heat for 4 to 5 minutes, or until the *lardo* has completely melted. Add the tomatoes, season with salt and pepper, and cook for about another 20 minutes. Then add the peas and rice and stir to coat evenly with the other ingredients. Add a little of the boiling broth, cover the pan, and finish cooking over low heat, moistening with the remaining broth a little at a time, until all of the broth has been absorbed. The dish will be ready in 13 to 15 minutes.

Sprinkle the rice with the cheeses and serve immediately.

Risotto alla ciociara · Risotto with vegetables

Dishes such as this one, which are usually associated with the far north of Italy, were brought to southern Lazio by migrant workers from the Veneto.

Makes 4 servings

1 medium onion
2 medium zucchini
2 tablespoons (30 g) butter
5 ounces (150 g) shelled fresh shelling beans such as borlotti (cranberry)
5 ounces (150 g) asparagus tips
5 ounces (150 g) shelled peas
12 ounces (350 g) canned tomatoes
pepper
4 cups (1 liter) vegetable broth, or more if needed
11 ounces (300 g) Carnaroli, Arborio, or other rice for risotto
1 heaping tablespoon minced flat-leaf parsley
2 heaping tablespoons grated *parmigiano-reggiano*

Finely chop the onion and dice the zucchini. Put the onion in a saucepan with the butter and sauté over medium heat for 3 to 4 minutes, or until translucent. Add the beans, asparagus, peas, and zucchini and let the flavors blend for a few minutes over low heat. Then add the tomatoes, season with pepper, and continue cooking for 10 minutes. Meanwhile, pour the broth into a pot and bring to a boil.

Add the rice and the boiling broth to the vegetable mixture, cover, and continue cooking over low heat for about 15 minutes. If the rice is not tender at this point, add a little more boiling broth. Sprinkle with the parsley and parmigiano and serve.

Risotto con le animelle alla romana · Risotto with lamb sweetbreads
Makes 4 servings

1¾ ounces (50 g) lamb sweetbreads
1¾ ounces (50 g) lamb liver
1¾ ounces (50 g) sliced prosciutto
2 cups (500 ml) meat broth
1 small white onion
2½ tablespoons (40 g) butter
salt
pepper
3 tablespoons dry Marsala
11 ounces (300 g) Vialone Nano or other rice for risotto
2 heaping tablespoons grated *parmigiano-reggiano*

Soak the sweetbreads in warm water to cover for about 30 minutes, then drain. Peel off and discard the membrane. Put the sweetbreads in a pot with about 2 quarts (2 liters) water and bring to a boil. As soon as the water begins to boil, drain the sweetbreads, let them cool, and then dice. Rinse the liver carefully in cold water, pat dry, and dice. Very finely chop the prosciutto. Pour the broth into a pot and bring to a boil.

Chop the onion. Put it in a saucepan with half the butter and cook over medium heat for 3 to 4 minutes, or until translucent. Add the prosciutto, sweetbreads, and liver and season with salt and pepper. Cook over low heat for about 2 minutes, stirring often. Add the Marsala and cook until it evaporates. Finally, add the rice and stir to coat evenly with the other ingredients. Add a little of the boiling broth, cover the pan, and finish cooking over low heat, moistening with the remaining broth a little at a time, until all of the broth has been absorbed. The dish will be ready in 13 to 15 minutes.

Stir in the remaining butter and the parmigiano. Serve immediately.

Risotto con le seppie · Risotto with cuttlefish
Makes 4 servings

1 pound (450 g) small cuttlefish
1 garlic clove
leaves from 1 small bunch flat-leaf parsley
1 salt-packed anchovy, prepared as described on page 273

3 tablespoons lightly fruity extra-virgin olive oil

pepper

4 cups (1 liter) fish broth

1 teaspoon tomato paste

12 ounces (350 g) Carnaroli, Arborio, or other rice
   for risotto

Clean the cuttlefish, reserving the small ink sacs. Wash and dry the cuttlefish. Cut the tentacles into small pieces and the bodies into small strips. Chop together the garlic clove, parsley leaves, and anchovy. Put the mixture in a saucepan with the oil and sauté over medium heat for a couple of minutes, or until the anchovy is completely dissolved. Add the cuttlefish and a grinding of pepper and sauté for 3 or 4 minutes, stirring often.

Meanwhile, pour the broth into a pot and bring it to a boil. Dissolve the tomato paste in the boiling broth. Add the rice to the cuttlefish and stir to coat completely with the other ingredients. Add 2 ladlefuls of the boiling broth, cover, and finish cooking over medium heat, adding the remaining broth 2 ladlefuls at a time only after the previous dose has been absorbed. The risotto will be ready in 13 to 15 minutes. Serve immediately.

Timballo di riso all'antica · Timballo of rice with sausage and organ meats
Makes 8 servings

4½ ounces (130 g) butter

1 pound (450 g) Carnaroli, Arborio, or other rice for
   risotto

6 cups (1.5 liters) light meat broth

3½ ounces (100 g) grated *parmigiano-reggiano*

1¼ cups (300 ml) *sugo d'umido* (recipe on page 253)

2 egg yolks

scant 1 ounce (25 g) dried porcini mushrooms

1¾ ounces (50 g) lamb sweetbreads

7 ounces (200 g) chicken giblets

1¾ ounces (50 g) prosciutto, in a single piece

1¾ ounces (50 g) fresh pork sausage

salt

pepper

3 whole eggs

4 teaspoons (20 g) lard, or 2 tablespoons lightly fruity
    extra-virgin olive oil
3½ ounces (100 g) dried bread crumbs

Make a very al dente risotto with 6½ tablespoons (100 g) of the butter, the rice, and the broth, by first sautéing the rice in the butter and then adding the boiling broth 2 ladlefuls at a time until the broth is used up. When the risotto is done, let it cool a bit, then add the parmigiano, half the *sugo,* and the egg yolks. Mix well and let cool completely.

Soak the dried mushrooms for 20 minutes in at least two changes of warm water. Drain, rinse, and squeeze well, then chop.

Soak the sweetbreads in warm water to cover for about 30 minutes, then drain. Peel off and discard the membrane. Put the sweetbreads in a pot with about 2 quarts (2 liters) water and bring to a boil. As soon as the water begins to boil, drain the sweetbreads, let them cool, and then dice. Trim the giblets, eliminating the green bile ducts from the livers. Rinse them for a good, long time, then dice. Finely dice the prosciutto and crumble the sausage.

Now make a *ragù.* Put the sweetbreads, giblets, prosciutto, sausage, and the remaining 2 tablespoons butter in a saucepan and sauté over low heat for 5 to 6 minutes, or until the fat has completely melted. Add the mushrooms, season with salt and pepper, and cook for about 3 minutes more. Pour in a bowl, add the remaining *sugo,* and mix thoroughly.

Break the whole eggs into another bowl and beat them with a fork until blended. Grease a large mold (at least 7-quart/7-liter capacity) with the lard. Sprinkle with the bread crumbs, coating evenly and abundantly, and then brush with the beaten eggs. Arrange half of the risotto in the mold, lining the bottom and the sides and leaving the center empty. Fill this center space with the *ragù.* Top with the remaining risotto, and then cover the mold with a lid or a sheet of aluminum foil.

Put the mold in an oven preheated to 375°F (190°C) and bake for about 30 minutes. Let the *timballo* rest for a few minutes, then turn it out onto a platter and serve.

Gnocchi e polenta · Gnocchi and Polenta

Gnocchi di patate al sugo · Potato gnocchi with tomato sauce
Makes 6 servings

3¼ pounds (1.5 kg) floury potatoes
7 ounces (200 g) flour
salt
2 cups (500 ml) *sugo d'umido* or *sugo finto* (recipes on
    pages 253 and 254)
3½ tablespoons (50 g) butter
2 ounces (60 g) grated *parmigiano-reggiano*

Pour 4 quarts (4 liters) water into a pot, add the potatoes, place over medium heat, and cook for about 20 minutes, or until tender. Drain the potatoes, peel them, and put them through a potato ricer while they are still very hot. Transfer to a wooden board, shape into a mound, and sift the flour onto the potatoes. Knead energetically with your hands until the dough is quite firm. With floured hands, pinch off pieces of the dough and roll them into ropes about 1 inch (2.5 cm) in diameter. Cut the ropes crosswise into small pieces about 1¼ inches (3 cm) long. Gently draw the tines of a fork or the back of a cheese grater across each piece to make little grooves. As the gnocchi are made, line them up on a floured dish towel, being careful not to let them touch.

Heat the *sugo*. Meanwhile, bring 4 quarts (4 liters) salted water to a boil. Drop the gnocchi, a few at a time, into the boiling water. As they bob to the surface, lift them out of the water with a slotted spoon, place them on a warmed large platter, and dot with the butter. When all the gnocchi are ready, dress them with the *sugo* and the parmigiano. Serve immediately.

Gnocchi di semolino alla romana ·
Semolina gnocchi
Makes 4 servings

3¼ cups (750 ml) milk
salt
7 ounces (200 g) semolina
6½ tablespoons (100 g) butter

5 ounces (150 g) grated *parmigiano-reggiano*
2 egg yolks

Pour the milk into a large saucepan and bring to a boil. Add ½ teaspoon salt and pour in the semolina in a shower. Cook over medium heat for about 10 minutes, stirring constantly with a wooden spoon. Remove from the heat, add 2 tablespoons (30 g) of the butter, 1 tablespoon of the parmigiano, and the egg yolks and mix well. Turn out the mixture onto a marble surface (or other cold surface) and level it to a thickness of ⅜ inch (1 cm), using the back of a wet tablespoon. Let cool completely, then cut into rhombuses (or into squares) about 1½ inches (4 cm) on a side.

Grease a 12-by-8-inch (30-by-20-cm) ovenproof dish with 1 tablespoon (15 g) of the butter. Arrange the dough scraps from cutting the rhombuses on the bottom and sprinkle with a little parmigiano. Begin arranging the rhombuses in layers, sprinkling each layer with plenty of parmigiano. Continue forming layers until all the rhombuses are used up; reserve a little parmigiano. At the end, you should have a sort of flattened dome. Gently heat the remaining 3½ tablespoons (50 g) butter in a saucepan until melted and pour it over the dome. Sprinkle with the remaining parmigiano.

Bake in an oven preheated to 400°F (200°C) for about 15 minutes, or until the gnocchi are golden brown. Serve directly from the dish.

Polenta con le cotiche e le salsicce · Polenta with pork rinds and sausages
Makes 4 servings

9 ounces (250 g) fresh pork rind
½ white onion
1 small carrot
1 small celery rib
leaves from 1 small bunch marjoram
1¾ ounces (50 g) prosciutto fat
1 tablespoon intensely fruity extra-virgin olive oil
8 fresh pork sausages, skinned and crumbled
scant 1 cup (200 ml) dry white table wine
1½ pounds (700 g) tomato purée
salt
pepper
11 ounces (300 g) finely ground corn flour (polenta)

2½ ounces (70 g) grated pecorino, preferably
  pecorino romano

Bring 4 cups (1 liter) lightly salted water to a boil. Drop in the rind, cover, and simmer over medium heat for 10 minutes, then drain. Scrape the rind carefully to remove any hairs and then cut into ¾-inch (2-cm) cubes.

Chop together finely the onion, carrot, celery, marjoram leaves, and prosciutto fat. Put everything in a saucepan with the oil and sauté over medium heat for about 5 minutes, or until the fat is almost translucent. Add the sausage meat and the rind, then pour in the wine and let it evaporate over medium heat until the odor of the alcohol has disappeared. Add the tomato purée, season with salt and pepper, cover, and cook over low heat for about 1 hour.

Bring 3 quarts (3 liters) lightly salted water to a boil and add the corn flour in a shower. Cook over low heat, stirring constantly, for about 30 minutes, or until the polenta pulls away from the sides of the pan. Meanwhile, reheat the sauce.

Pour the polenta onto a warmed wide platter and dress first with the sauce and then with the pecorino. Serve immediately.

Minestre e zuppe · Soups

L'acquapazza · Seaweed soup

Edible seaweeds found in the Tyrrhenian Sea include *Halimeda tuna*, or *fico d'India marino* in Italian ("sea prickly pear," so-called for its paddle-shaped leaves), and sea asparagus (genus *Salicornia*), named for its superficial resemblance to the terrestrial spears. The edible Sargasso seaweed (genus *Sargassum*) is common in the Mediterranean.

Makes 4 servings

2 garlic cloves
3 or 4 pieces seaweed, or 1 sprig Sargasso seaweed
small piece dried chile
7 ounces (200 g) small sauce tomatoes
8 slices *casereccio* bread (see page 273)
4 tablespoons extra-virgin olive oil
salt

Boil the garlic, seaweed, and chile in 4 cups (1 liter) salted water until the seaweed is tender. Meanwhile, dice the tomatoes.

Divide the bread among individual bowls, ladle the hot liquid over the top, and add the tomatoes. Garnish each serving with 1 tablespoon of oil and serve.

La bazzoffia · Spring vegetable soup
over poached eggs
Makes 4 servings

7 ounces (200 g) shelled peas
5 ounces (150 g) shelled fresh fava beans
    (not peeled)
juice of 1 lemon
3 medium artichokes
1 head romaine lettuce
1 onion
2 tablespoons extra-virgin olive oil
salt
pepper
4 slices stale *casereccio* bread (see page 273)
4 eggs
2 heaping tablespoons grated pecorino, preferably
    pecorino romano

Ready the peas and fava beans. Fill a bowl with water and add the lemon juice. One at a time, trim the artichokes as described on page 273. Cut each artichoke in half lengthwise and remove and discard any choke. Cut each half into two or more wedges and immerse in the lemon water. Trim the lettuce head and cut the leaves into narrow strips.

Chop the onion finely and brown it in a saucepan with the oil. Drain the artichokes and add them and all the remaining vegetables and 4 cups (1 liter) boiling water to the saucepan. Season with salt and pepper, cover, and cook over low heat until all the vegetables are perfectly cooked.

To serve, divide the bread slices among 4 bowls. Break an egg onto each slice and ladle the hot soup over the top. Sprinkle with the pecorino and serve.

Brodetto pasquale · Easter soup
Makes 8 servings

1 small white onion
1 whole clove
leaves from 1 small bunch flat-leaf parsley
1 pound (450 g) boneless beef, in one piece
1 pound (450 g) lamb breast, in one piece
1 carrot
1 small celery rib
salt
leaves from 1 small bunch marjoram
½ lemon
3 egg yolks
2 heaping tablespoons grated *parmigiano-reggiano*
freshly ground pepper
8 *crostini* (see page 273)

Peel the onion and stick it with the clove. Chop the parsley leaves. Put the meats in a pot (preferably earthenware), add about 3 quarts (3 liters) water, and bring to a boil over medium heat. Skim any foam and impurities from the surface and add the studded onion, carrot, celery, and parsley. Season with salt and cook over low heat for 1 hour. Lift out the lamb and set aside. Continue cooking the beef for 1 hour longer, always over low heat. When the beef is ready, remove it from the pot and set aside. Strain the broth into a saucepan. Set aside and keep warm.

Chop the marjoram leaves. Squeeze the juice from the lemon half into a food processor. Add the egg yolks and parmigiano and process until smooth. Return the broth to a boil and pour in the egg yolk mixture in a steady stream while stirring with a whisk to prevent lumps. Then add the marjoram and finally a grinding of pepper.

Ladle the *brodetto* into individual bowls, garnish with the *crostini,* and serve immediately. The boiled meats can be served separately as a tasty main dish.

La "cococciata" · Zucchini and tomato soup

Cococciata is a dialect term for *tegame di coccio*, an earthenware pot,
and by extension its contents.

Makes 4 servings

4 medium zucchini
2 large onions
4 tablespoons medium-fruity extra-virgin olive oil,
    preferably from Sabina
7 ounces (200 g) tomato purée
salt
1 heaping tablespoon minced flat-leaf parsley
2 eggs
2 heaping tablespoons grated pecorino, preferably
    pecorino romano
4 slices *casereccio* bread (see page 273)

Dice the zucchini. Slice the onions thinly and fry them in the oil until translucent. Add the zucchini and tomato purée and season with salt. Cover and finish cooking over a low flame until the zucchini is done.

Beat the eggs with a pinch of salt until blended. When the zucchini is ready, pour the eggs over the zucchini while stirring vigorously. Divide the bread slices among individual bowls, pour the soup over the bread, and sprinkle with the pecorino and the parsley. The soup is excellent hot or cold.

Boccette in brodo · Meatballs in broth

From the Roman Jewish tradition.

Makes 4 servings

1 soup bone
1 carrot
1 small white onion
1 small celery rib
1 small bunch flat-leaf parsley
salt
14 ounces (400 g) lean ground beef
1¾ ounces (50 g) beef marrow or butter

Put about 6 cups (1.5 liters) water in a pot. Add the soup bone, carrot, onion, celery, and parsley and bring to a boil. Salt lightly and cook the broth over medium heat for about 1 hour.

Meanwhile, form the ground beef into tiny meatballs and insert a little piece of marrow into the center of each ball. When the broth is ready, strain it, return it to the pot, and bring it back to a boil. Add the meatballs and cook over medium heat for about 15 minutes, or until cooked through. Ladle into individual bowls and serve immediately.

Fagioli con le cotiche · Beans and pork rinds
Makes 4 servings

3½ ounces (100 g) prosciutto rind
1 prosciutto bone with a little meat still attached
1 pound (450 g) dried cannellini beans, soaked and ready
   to cook
¼ white onion
1¾ ounces (50 g) prosciutto fat
1 garlic clove
2 small celery ribs
leaves from 1 small bunch flat-leaf parsley
5 ounces (150 g) canned tomatoes
salt
pepper
7 ounces (200 g) *cannolicchietti, maltagliati,* or other
   short soup pasta

Bring about 3 quarts (3 liters) lightly salted water to a boil. Drop in the rind and the bone, boil for 10 minutes, and drain. Trim the meat off the bone and cut into small pieces. Scrape the rind carefully to remove any hairs and then dice it. Put the beans, the bone, the pieces of meat, and the diced rind in a pan, pour in about 2 quarts (2 liters) water, and cook over low heat for about 1 hour, or until the beans are tender.

Meanwhile, chop together finely the onion, prosciutto fat, garlic, celery, and parsley leaves. Place everything in a saucepan and cook over medium heat for about 5 minutes. When the onion and the fat are translucent, add the tomatoes, season generously with salt and pepper, and continue cooking for 20 minutes longer.

When the beans are tender, discard the bone, add the tomato sauce, and bring back to a boil. Add the pasta and cook until al dente. Let rest for a few minutes before serving.

Farricello con le cotiche · Farro with pork rinds

A typical grain of northern Lazio, *farro* was used to make pasta and bread
until World War II because of the rarity and the high cost of wheat.
Considered almost a food of dire poverty, it had disappeared from
the market with the postwar prosperity. Today, it is once again
being used, often in the form of pasta.

Makes 6 servings

3½ ounces (100 g) prosciutto rind
leaves from 1 small bunch basil
leaves from 1 small bunch flat-leaf parsley
1 small white onion
1 garlic clove
1¾ ounces (50 g) prosciutto fat
leaves from 1 sprig marjoram
1 tablespoon intensely fruity extra-virgin olive oil
11 ounces (300 g) canned sauce tomatoes
salt
14 ounces (400 g) *farro spezzettato* (coarsely ground *farro*)
2 heaping tablespoons grated pecorino, preferably
     pecorino romano

Drop the rind into about 2 quarts (2 liters) boiling water, cover, boil for 10 minutes, and then drain. Scrape the rind carefully to remove any hairs and then cut
it into ⅜-inch (1-cm) squares. Drop the squares into boiling water (not salted).
Cover and simmer for about 30 minutes, or until tender. Do not drain.

Chop finely together the basil and parsley leaves and reserve. Chop together
the onion, garlic, prosciutto fat, and marjoram leaves and put into a pot with the
oil. Sauté over medium heat for about 5 minutes. When the onion and the fat are
translucent, add the basil, parsley, and tomatoes, then salt moderately. Let the
flavors blend over medium heat for 10 minutes. Add the rind squares with all
their water, season with salt, and then add the *farro* in a shower. Cover and finish
cooking the soup over low heat, stirring occasionally, for about 15 minutes.

Ladle into individual bowls, sprinkle with the pecorino, and serve.

Indivia rehaminà · Curly endive in broth
From the Roman Jewish tradition.
Makes 4 servings

4 cups (1 liter) meat broth
11 ounces (300 g) stale *casereccio* bread (see page 273)
1 head curly endive, about 11 ounces (300 g)
salt

Pour the broth into a pot. Slice the bread. Wash the endive carefully and chop the leaves.

Add the endive leaves to the broth and cover with the bread. Cover the pot, place over very low heat, and cook for about 1 hour. Season with salt, then serve hot.

*Minestra di ceci e "pennerelli" · Soup of chickpeas
and nervetti*
From the Roman Jewish tradition. *Pennerelli* is dialect for *nervetti*.
Makes 4 servings

11 ounces (300 g) beef *nervetti* (see page 274)
1 beef steak bone
1 small white onion
1 small celery rib
1 carrot
salt
5 ounces (150 g) tomato purée
1 pound (450 g) dried chickpeas, soaked and ready to cook

Clean the *nervetti* carefully, put them and the bone in a pot with 6 cups (1.5 liters) water, and bring to a boil. When the water comes to a boil, skim any scum and impurities from the surface and add the onion, celery, carrot, and some salt. Cook over low heat for about 1 hour.

Add the tomato purée and chickpeas and cook until the chickpeas are tender; the timing will depend on the age of the chickpeas. Check after 20 minutes and frequently thereafter. Discard the bone, taste and adjust the salt, and then ladle into bowls and serve.

Minestra di "cicerchiole" con i ceci · Soup of chickpeas
and homemade pasta
Makes 4 servings

1 pound (500 g) chickpeas, soaked and ready to cook
1 sprig rosemary
1 slice *lardo* or pancetta
1 garlic clove
1 ladleful tomato purée
salt
5 ounces (150 g) *cicerchiole* (*quadrucci,* a homemade *pastina;*
    see note on *minestra di quadrucci e piselli con il*
    "battuto," page 139)

Bring 2 quarts (2 liters) lightly salted water to a boil in a pot. Add the chickpeas and rosemary and cook over medium heat until the chickpeas are tender; the timing will depend on the age of the chickpeas. Check after 20 minutes and frequently thereafter. Drain the chickpeas, reserving the cooking water.

Chop together the *lardo* and garlic and sauté gently in a pan over low heat. Add the tomato purée, season with salt, and cook until the sauce is well reduced. Add the cooked chickpeas, the pasta, and 4 cups (1 liter) of the chickpea water and bring to a boil. When the pasta is al dente, transfer the soup to a tureen or ladle into individual bowls and serve.

Laganelle con i ceci · Whole-wheat noodles with chickpeas
Makes 4 servings

1⅓ pounds (600 g) chickpeas, soaked and ready to cook
1 white onion
1 celery rib
1 pound (450 g) fresh whole-wheat tagliatelle
6 tablespoons (90 ml) medium-fruity extra-virgin olive oil
pepper

Bring 6 cups (1.5 liters) salted water to a boil in a pot. Add the chickpeas, onion, and celery and cook over medium heat until the chickpeas are tender; the timing will depend on the age of the chickpeas. Check after 20 minutes and frequently thereafter.

Cut the pasta into irregular pieces, add to the pot containing the chickpeas, and cook until al dente. Remove the soup from the heat and let it cool somewhat. Dress with the oil and add a generous grinding of pepper, then serve.

Minestra di fagioli cannellini e bietola · Soup of cannellini beans and chard
Makes 4 servings

14 ounces (400 g) dried cannellini beans, soaked and
   ready to cook
14 ounces (400 g) chard
1 heaping tablespoon *battuto* (recipe on page 251)
2 tablespoons intensely fruity extra-virgin olive oil
5 ounces (150 g) tomato purée
salt
pepper
4 slices *casereccio* bread (see page 273), toasted

Bring about 6 cups (1.5 liters) lightly salted water to a boil in a pot. Add the beans and simmer over medium heat until tender; the timing will depend on the age of the beans. Check after 20 minutes and frequently thereafter. Remove from the heat and keep warm.

Trim and rinse the chard. Then, in another pot, cook the chard in just the rinsing water clinging to the leaves. Drain, chop, and transfer to the pot with the beans.

Put the *battuto* and oil in a pan (preferably earthenware) and sauté over low heat for 4 to 5 minutes, or until the *lardo* has completely melted. Add the tomato purée and cook over low heat for about 10 minutes. Add the beans and the chard with their cooking water, season with salt, and add a generous grinding of pepper. Continue cooking over medium heat for another 10 minutes.

Divide the bread slices among individual bowls and ladle the hot soup over the top. Serve immediately.

Minestra di fave fresche alla romana · Pasta and fresh fava beans
Makes 6 servings

1 heaping tablespoon *battuto* (recipe on page 251)
11 ounces (300 g) tomato purée

salt

pepper

6 cups (1.5 liters) vegetable broth

7 ounces (200 g) shelled fresh fava beans (not peeled)

5 ounces (150 g) *cannolicchietti, maltagliati,* or other short soup pasta

1 heaping tablespoon grated pecorino, preferably *pecorino romano*

Put the *battuto* in a pot and cook over low heat for 4 to 5 minutes. When the *lardo* has completely melted, add the tomato purée, season with salt and pepper, and cook the sauce over low heat for about 10 minutes, or until reduced. Meanwhile, put the broth in a pot and bring to a boil.

Add the favas and the boiling broth to the sauce and cook over low heat for 10 to 15 minutes. When the favas are tender, add the pasta and boil until al dente. Remove from the heat, add the pecorino, and stir vigorously. Let the soup rest for a few minutes before serving.

Minestra di magro con i fagioli cannellini e la bietola · *Meatless soup with white beans and chard*

Makes 4 servings

14 ounces (400 g) dried cannellini beans, soaked and ready to cook

14 ounces (400 g) chard

2 salt-packed anchovies, prepared as described on page 273

leaves from a few sprigs flat-leaf parsley

1 garlic clove

needles from 1 sprig rosemary

5 tablespoons intensely fruity extra-virgin olive oil

5 ounces (150 g) tomato purée

salt

pepper

4 slices *casereccio* bread (see page 273), toasted

Bring about 6 cups (1.5 liters) lightly salted water to a boil in a pot. Add the beans and simmer over medium heat until tender; the timing will depend on the age of the beans. Check after 20 minutes and frequently thereafter. Remove from the heat and keep warm.

Trim and rinse the chard. Put the chard in another pot, cover, and cook in just the rinsing water clinging to the leaves. Drain, chop, and transfer to the pot with the beans.

Chop the anchovies coarsely, and then mince them together with the parsley leaves, garlic, and the rosemary. Put everything in a pan with the oil and cook over low heat for 4 to 5 minutes, until the anchovies have completely dissolved. Add the tomato purée and let the flavors blend for about 20 minutes. Add the beans and the chard together with their cooking water, then season with salt and a grinding of pepper and cook the soup gently over low heat for about 6 minutes.

Divide the bread slices among individual bowls and ladle the hot soup over the top. Serve immediately.

Minestra di pasta e broccoli con le cotiche · Soup of pasta, broccolo, and pork rinds
Makes 4 servings

1¾ ounces (50 g) fresh pork rind
1 head *broccolo romanesco* (see page 273), about
    1⅓ pounds (600 g)
1¾ ounces (50 g) sliced prosciutto
1 small white onion
1 garlic clove
1 tablespoon intensely fruity extra-virgin
    olive oil
pepper
salt
5 ounces (150 g) spaghetti
2 ounces (60 g) grated pecorino, preferably
    pecorino romano

Drop the rind into about 2 quarts (2 liters) boiling water, cover, and simmer for 10 minutes, then drain. Scrape the rind carefully to remove any hairs, then dice and set aside. Discard the tough outer leaves and core of the *broccolo* and cut into florets. In the same pot, bring 2 quarts (2 liters) lightly salted water to a boil, add the florets, and simmer over medium heat until half cooked. Scoop out the florets with a slotted spoon and set aside; reserve the cooking water.

Cut the prosciutto into narrow strips. Chop together the onion and garlic and put in a pan (preferably earthenware) with the oil. Cook over medium heat for about 5 minutes. When the onion is almost translucent, add the prosciutto, the diced rind, and a little pepper and cook over low heat for a few minutes. Now add the *broccolo* florets and as much of their cooking water as needed to create a rather thick soup, then season with salt. Break the spaghetti into pieces, add to the pan, and boil until al dente.

Remove from the heat and serve, with the pecorino on the side.

Minestra di pasta e patate · Soup of pasta and potatoes

Shops used to sell remnants of pasta. In fact, the pasta was sold in bulk by weight, so there were always some broken bits left on the shelves. The shopkeeper would combine two or three shapes and the odd bits *(rimasugli)* and sell them for use in soups. Today factory-made *rimasugli* are sold.

Makes 4 servings

6 cups (1.5 liters) vegetable broth
4 or 5 small sauce tomatoes
1 heaping tablespoon *battuto* (recipe on page 251)
4 floury potatoes
salt
pepper
9 ounces (250 g) odd bits of fresh egg pasta
2 ounces (60 g) grated pecorino, preferably
   pecorino romano

Pour the broth into a pot and bring to a boil. Peel the tomatoes and chop the flesh. Put the *battuto* in a saucepan and cook over low heat for 4 to 5 minutes, or until the *lardo* has completely melted. Add the tomatoes and a few tablespoons of the boiling broth and continue cooking for 15 to 20 more minutes. Meanwhile, peel the potatoes and cut into small dice.

Add the potatoes to the tomato sauce, then add the remaining broth and season generously with pepper. Cook over low heat for another 15 to 20 minutes, or until the potatoes are tender. When almost done, add the pasta and cook until al dente.

Stir in the pecorino and serve immediately.

Minestra di quadrucci e piselli con il "battuto" · *Soup of pasta and fresh peas with battuto*

Quadrucci are small squares of fresh pasta, usually of egg dough, made by cutting fettuccine crosswise at intervals equal to the width of the noodle. Although any member of the large *pastina* family—small-format pastas for soup—will be good, the dish will lose its authenticity if anything other than *quadrucci* is used.

Makes 4 servings

1 heaping tablespoon *battuto* (recipe on page 251)
1 heaping tablespoon tomato paste
salt
11 ounces (300 g) shelled peas
pepper
7 ounces (200 g) fresh egg *quadrucci*
2 ounces (60 g) grated pecorino, preferably
   pecorino romano

Pour 6 cups (1.5 liters) water into a pot and bring to a boil. Put the *battuto* in a saucepan and cook over low heat for 4 to 5 minutes. Meanwhile, dilute the tomato paste in a ladleful of the boiling water. When the *lardo* is completely melted, add the diluted tomato paste and a little salt and cook this sauce over medium heat for about 20 minutes.

Add the peas and the remaining boiling water to the sauce, season with salt and pepper, and cook over low heat for 10 to 15 minutes. When the peas are tender, add the *quadrucci* and finish cooking the soup, about 5 minutes. It should be rather dense. Remove from the heat, stir in the pecorino, and serve immediately.

Minestra di quadrucci in brodo di pesce · *Small pasta in fish broth*
Makes 6 servings

1 small white onion
1 small leek
1 small celery rib
leaves from 1 sprig thyme
½ bay leaf
4 teaspoons (20 g) butter
14 ounces (400 g) soup fish (red mullet, squid, cuttlefish,
   scorpion fish, gurnard, conger eel, sole, or others) or cod

7 ounces (200 g) fish heads and bones
scant 1 cup (200 ml) dry white table wine
4 or 5 peppercorns
salt
5 ounces (150 g) fresh egg *quadrucci* (see note on *minestra di quadrucci e piselli con il "battuto,"* page 139)

Chop together (not too finely) the onion, leek, celery, and thyme leaves. Put in a large saucepan with the bay leaf and butter and sweat over low heat for about 15 minutes, or until the vegetables are completely wilted. Meanwhile, pour 4 cups (1 liter) water into a pot and bring to a boil.

Add the fish and fish heads and bones to the vegetables and sauté for 5 to 6 minutes, stirring. Add the wine and let it evaporate over medium heat until the odor of the alcohol has disappeared. Then add the boiling water, peppercorns, and a little salt. Cook the broth over medium heat for about 30 minutes.

Strain the broth and transfer to another pot. Bring to a boil, add the *quadrucci,* and cook for 3 to 4 minutes, or until al dente. Serve immediately.

Minestra di riso e cicoria con il battuto · Soup of rice and chicory with battuto
Makes 4 servings

1 pound (450 g) chicory
7 ounces (200 g) small sauce tomatoes
4 cups (1 liter) vegetable broth
1 heaping tablespoon *battuto* (recipe on page 251)
salt
pepper
7 ounces (200 g) *comune* or other rice for soup
2 ounces (60 g) grated pecorino, preferably *pecorino romano*

Trim and rinse the chicory. Drop it into 2 quarts (2 liters) lightly salted boiling water and cook for several minutes, or until tender. Drain, squeeze, and then chop the chicory, not too finely. Peel the tomatoes and chop the flesh. Pour the broth into a pot and bring to a boil.

Put the *battuto* in a pan (preferably earthenware) and cook over low heat for 4 to 5 minutes, or until the *lardo* is completely melted. Add the tomatoes and cook over low heat for about 15 minutes. Season with salt and pepper, add the chicory, and cook gently for 2 minutes, stirring. Now add the rice and the boiling broth and simmer the soup for about 15 minutes, or until the rice is tender.

The soup should be very dense. Ladle into individual bowls and serve immediately, with the pecorino on the side.

Minestra di riso e lenticchie · Rice and lentil soup
Makes 4 servings

> 9 ounces (250 g) lentils
> 4 cups (1 liter) meat or vegetable broth
> 1 small white onion
> 2½ ounces (70 g) sliced prosciutto
> 1 garlic clove
> 1 tablespoon intensely fruity extra-virgin olive oil
> 5 ounces (150 g) tomato purée
> salt
> pepper
> 7 ounces (200 g) *comune* or other rice for soup
> 2 ounces (60 g) grated pecorino, preferably
>   *pecorino romano*

Pour 2 quarts (2 liters) water into a pot and bring to a boil. Add the lentils and cook over medium heat for about 20 minutes, or until tender, then drain. Pour the broth into a pot and bring to a boil.

Chop together finely the onion, prosciutto, and garlic. Put the mixture into a pan with the oil and sauté over medium heat for 4 to 5 minutes. When the onion is almost translucent, add the tomato purée and continue cooking for about 15 minutes. Season with salt and pepper, add the rice and the boiling broth, and cook over low heat for 10 minutes. Just before the rice is done, stir in the lentils and heat through.

Serve immediately, with the pecorino on the side.

Minestra "spezzata" · "Broken" soup
From the Roman Jewish tradition.
Makes 6 servings

> 1 white onion
> 1 garlic clove

4 tablespoons medium-fruity extra-virgin olive oil
1 pound (450 g) canned tomatoes
1 pound (450 g) spaghetti
salt
leaves from 1 small bunch flat-leaf parsley

Chop the onion and crush the garlic clove. Put them both into a saucepan with the oil and sauté over medium heat for about 5 minutes. When the onion is almost translucent, add the tomatoes and simmer for about 20 minutes, mashing the tomatoes with a fork as needed to break them up.

Meanwhile, break the spaghetti into pieces. Pour 2 cups (500 ml) boiling water into the saucepan holding the sauce and bring to a boil. Season with salt, add the spaghetti, and cook until the spaghetti is al dente. The soup should end up rather brothy.

While the soup is finishing, chop the parsley leaves. Ladle the soup into individual bowls, sprinkle with the parsley, and serve hot.

Pasta "grattata" in brodo · "Grated" pasta in broth
Makes 6 servings

7 ounces (200 g) type 00 or all-purpose flour
1¾ ounces (50 g) semolina
3 eggs
salt
6 cups (1.5 liters) chicken or beef broth
2 ounces (60 g) grated pecorino, preferably
    pecorino romano

Sift the two flours together onto a wooden board, shape into a mound, and make a well in the center. Break the eggs into the well, add a pinch of salt, and begin to incorporate the egg into the flour with a fork. When the mixture is too stiff to use a fork any longer, begin forming the dough with your hands. Once it comes together in a fairly uniform ball, knead it energetically with your hands until you have a very firm dough. Cover with a dish towel and let rest for about 30 minutes. Then, using the large holes on a cheese grater, grate the dough onto a floured dish towel.

Pour the broth into a pot and bring to a boil. Add the grated pasta and cook over medium heat for 4 to 5 minutes, or until the pasta is al dente. Remove from the heat and serve immediately, with the pecorino on the side.

*Pasta e broccoli in brodo d'arzilla · Ray broth with pasta
and broccolo romanesco*
Makes 4 servings

1 head *broccolo romanesco* (see page 273), about 1 pound
   (500 g)
1 ray (skate; called *arzilla* in Rome), about 2¼ pounds (1 kg)
2 garlic cloves
1 small white onion
1 small bunch flat-leaf parsley
salt
1 salt-packed anchovy, prepared as described on page 273
2 tablespoons medium-fruity extra-virgin olive oil
scant ½ cup (100 ml) dry white table wine
small piece dried chile, ½ to ¾ inch (12 mm to 2 cm) long
7 ounces (200 g) canned tomatoes
7 ounces (200 g) spaghetti

Discard the tough outer leaves and core of the *broccolo* and cut into florets (you need about 11 ounces/300 g). Clean the fish and rinse well. Select a pan just large enough to hold the fish comfortably and put the onion, 1 garlic clove, and a few parsley stems (not leaves) in it. Pour in 6 cups (1.5 liters) water, add a pinch of salt, cover, and cook over low heat for 30 minutes. Add the fish and continue cooking for 20 minutes.

Remove the fish from the pan, let cool until it can be handled, then fillet it and set the flesh aside. Add the bones and odd pieces to the broth and continue to cook the broth over medium heat for 20 minutes longer. Strain the broth, then set aside and keep warm.

Chop together the leaves from all the parsley sprigs, the anchovy, and the remaining garlic clove. Put the mixture in a saucepan with the oil and sauté over low heat for a couple of minutes. Add the wine and let it reduce over medium heat until the odor of the alcohol has disappeared. Add the chile and tomatoes, season with salt, and continue cooking for about 20 minutes, mashing the tomatoes with a fork as needed to break them up.

Now add the *broccolo* florets to the sauce, pour in the broth, and let the flavors blend over medium heat for 5 minutes. Meanwhile, break the spaghetti into pieces. When the flavors have blended, add the spaghetti to the soup and simmer until al dente. Serve immediately.

The filleted fish can be served separately as a main course, but it is also excellent minced and put back into the broth before serving.

Pasta e ceci · *Pasta and chickpeas*
Makes 4 servings

2 sprigs rosemary
2 garlic cloves
1 pound (450 g) chickpeas, soaked and ready to cook
salt
pepper
4 oil-packed anchovy fillets
4 tablespoons intensely fruity extra-virgin olive oil
7 ounces (200 g) *cannolicchietti* or other short soup pasta

Tie tightly together 1 rosemary sprig and 1 garlic clove with kitchen twine. Put the chickpeas in a saucepan, pour in 2 quarts (2 liters) water, and add the rosemary-garlic bundle. Season with salt and a generous grinding of pepper and cook over low heat until tender; the timing will depend on the age of the chickpeas. Check after 20 minutes and frequently thereafter.

Drain the anchovies and chop very finely. Pour the oil into a separate pan, add the remaining garlic clove and the remaining rosemary sprig, and sauté over low heat for about 4 minutes, or until the garlic is golden brown. Discard the rosemary and garlic, add the anchovies, and mash them with a fork until they dissolve. Add everything to the chickpeas and let the flavors blend for a few minutes more. Add the pasta and cook until al dente (6 to 7 minutes for *cannolicchietti*). Serve immediately.

Riso in brodo con le rape · *Rice in broth with turnips*
From the Roman Jewish tradition.
Makes 4 servings

2 medium turnips
5 cups (1.2 liters) meat broth, preferably beef
11 ounces (300 g) *comune* or other rice for soup

Peel the turnips and slice very thinly. Put the slices in a bowl, cover with cold water, and soak for about 2 hours to eliminate the bitter taste.

Pour the broth into a pot and bring to a boil. Drain the turnips well and add them to the pot, then add the rice. Cook the soup over low heat for 7 to 8 minutes, or until the rice is just tender. Serve hot.

Stracciatella · Egg drop soup
Makes 6 servings

6 cups (1.5 liter) chicken or beef broth
leaves from 1 small bunch flat-leaf parsley
3 eggs
3 heaping tablespoons semolina
3 heaping tablespoons grated *parmigiano-reggiano*
nutmeg

Remove a cupful of cold broth and set aside. Pour the remaining broth into a pot and bring to a light boil. Chop the parsley leaves.

Break the eggs into a bowl, pour in the cold reserved broth, and add the semolina, parmigiano, parsley, and a grating of nutmeg. Mix everything with a whisk, then add the mixture to the broth (it should be at a gentle boil), pouring it in a steady stream while stirring with a whisk. Remove from the heat.

Pour the soup into a warmed tureen and serve immediately.

Zuppa di aragosta del Venerdì Santo · Lobster soup for Good Friday
Makes 4 servings

1 small spiny lobster
11 ounces (300 g) small shrimp
1 salt-packed anchovy, prepared as described on page 273
1 garlic clove
leaves from 1 small bunch flat-leaf parsley
2 tablespoons lightly fruity extra-virgin olive oil
small piece dried chile, to taste
7 ounces (200 g) tomato purée
4 cups (1 liter) fish broth
4 ounces (100 g) *crostini* (see page 273)

Boil the lobster in about 3 quarts (3 liters) lightly salted water for about 15 minutes. Drain the lobster and let cool. Remove the meat from the shell, discard the carapace, and then cut the meat into small pieces and reserve. Boil the shrimp in 3 quarts (3 liters) lightly salted water for about 10 minutes. Drain the shrimp and let cool, then peel them and reserve.

Chop together very finely the anchovy, garlic, and parsley leaves. Put in a saucepan with the oil, add the chile, and sauté over low heat for a couple of minutes. Add the tomato purée and continue cooking over medium heat for 15 minutes. Discard the chile.

Meanwhile, pour the broth into a pot and bring to a boil. When the tomato mixture is ready, add the broth to it and cook over medium heat for 5 minutes. Remove from the heat and add the lobster meat and shrimp.

Put the *crostini* in a warmed tureen and pour in the soup. Serve immediately.

Zuppa di luppoli · Hops soup
Makes 4 servings

11 ounces (300 g) hops
1¾ ounces (50 g) sliced prosciutto
1 garlic clove
2 tablespoons lightly fruity extra-virgin olive oil
salt
freshly ground pepper
2 eggs
4 slices *casereccio* bread (see page 273), toasted

Chop the hops coarsely. Chop together finely the prosciutto and garlic and put in a saucepan with the oil. Sauté over medium heat for about 4 minutes, or until the garlic is golden brown. Add the hops, salt, and a grinding of pepper and let the hops wilt over low heat for a couple of minutes, stirring. Add 4 cups (1 liter) hot water, salt lightly, and simmer the soup for 2 minutes.

Break the eggs into a bowl, add a pinch of salt, and beat lightly. Pour the eggs in a steady stream into the soup (it should be at a gentle boil) while stirring rapidly with a whisk. Divide the bread slices among individual bowls, ladle the soup over the top, and let rest for a few minutes before serving.

Zuppa di Natale dei Monti Cimini · Christmas soup
Makes 4 servings

11 ounces (300 g) dried chickpeas, soaked and ready to cook
11 ounces (300 g) dried chestnuts, soaked and ready to cook

1 garlic clove
needles from 1 sprig rosemary
small piece dried chile
4 tablespoons extra-virgin olive oil
4 slices stale good-quality bread
salt

Cook the chestnuts and the chickpeas together in lightly salted water. When they are tender, mash some of the chickpeas to make the soup creamy. Meanwhile, sauté the garlic, rosemary needles, and chile in the oil. Turn them into the pot with the chestnuts and the chickpeas. Let the flavors blend for a few minutes.

Put the bread in the bottom of a soup tureen and pour the soup over it. Let rest for 5 minutes before serving.

Zuppa di pesce e lattuga alla romana · *Fish and romaine lettuce soup*
Makes 6 servings

3¼ pounds (1.5 kg) soup fish (red mullet, squid, cuttlefish,
   scorpion fish, gurnard, conger eel, sole, or others)
1 pound (450 g) mussels
6 cups (1.5 liters) fish broth
2 hearts romaine lettuce
1 small leek
2 cups (500 ml) lightly fruity extra-virgin olive oil
1 bay leaf
leaves from 1 sprig thyme
salt
pepper
4 oil-packed anchovy fillets
2 cups (500 ml) dry white table wine, preferably from the
   Castelli Romani
2 garlic cloves
leaves from 1 small bunch flat-leaf parsley
6 slices *casereccio* bread (see page 273), toasted

Separate the firmer-fleshed cuttlefish and squid from the soft-fleshed fish (red mullet, scorpion fish, gurnard, conger eel, sole). Clean the cuttlefish and squid and cut into rings about ¾ inch (2 cm) wide. Clean and scrape the mussels and discard the beards. Rinse carefully and drain. Put the mussels in a pan, cover, and cook over a lively flame for a few minutes until they open. Remove the mussel meats from their shells, discarding any that failed to open, and set aside. Strain the pan broth and add it to the fish broth. Put the broth in a pot and reserve.

Cut the lettuce crosswise into strips about ¾ inch (2 cm) wide. Chop the leek finely. Put a scant ½ cup (100 ml) of the oil into a large pan (preferably earthenware), add the cuttlefish and squid, and fry over a lively flame for a few minutes. Add the lettuce, leek, bay leaf, and thyme leaves. Let the flavors blend over medium heat for about 5 minutes, then season with salt and pepper, cover, and continue cooking over low heat for about 10 minutes. Meanwhile, bring the broth to a boil.

Drain and chop the anchovy fillets and add them to the cuttlefish and squid. Add the wine and let it evaporate over medium heat for 5 minutes, or until the odor of the alcohol has disappeared. Now add the boiling broth and the rest of the fish. Continue cooking over medium heat for 10 minutes.

Crush the garlic cloves and put them in a saucepan with the remaining oil. Sauté over medium heat for 5 minutes, then discard the garlic and stir the oil into the soup. Continue cooking for 2 more minutes.

Chop the parsley leaves. Divide the bread slices among individual bowls and pour the soup over them. Sprinkle with the parsley and serve immediately.

Zuppa di telline · Clam soup
Makes 4 servings

about 2 pounds (1 kg) *telline* (see page 275)
1 salt-packed anchovy, prepared as described on page 273
1 garlic clove
leaves from 1 small bunch flat-leaf parsley
4 tablespoons medium-fruity extra-virgin olive oil
11 ounces (300 g) tomato purée
salt
pepper
4 slices *casereccio* bread (see page 273), toasted

Rinse the *telline* and put them in a large pan. Cover the pan and let them open over a lively flame. Extract the mollusks from their shells, discarding any that failed to open. Strain their broth, then set the mollusks and broth aside together.

Chop together finely the anchovy, garlic, and parsley leaves. Put everything in a saucepan with the oil and sauté over medium heat for about 4 minutes. When the anchovy has completely dissolved, add the tomato purée, cover, and cook the sauce over low heat for about 15 minutes. Meanwhile, bring 4 cups (1 liter) water to a boil.

Add the *telline,* their reserved broth, and a little salt and pepper to the sauce, then pour in the boiling water. Re-cover and cook the soup over low heat for 5 to 6 minutes.

Divide the bread slices among individual bowls and ladle the soup over them. Serve immediately.

SECONDI PIATTI · MAIN DISHES

Carne · Meat

"Pajata" di vitello in graticola · Grilled veal intestines
Makes 6 servings

about 2¼ pounds (1 kg) *pajata* (see page 274)
4 tablespoons intensely fruity extra-virgin olive oil
freshly ground pepper

Cut the *pajata* into lengths of about 6 inches (15 cm) each, bend each length into a ring, and tie the two ends together with kitchen twine.

Rub the rings generously with some of the oil and sprinkle with pepper. Put them on a grill, not too hot, and cook for 8 to 10 minutes, brushing often with oil. Serve piping hot.

Saltimbocca alla romana · Veal scallops with prosciutto and sage
Makes 4 servings

8 slices veal, about 2 ounces (60 g) each
8 slices prosciutto, both fat and lean
8 sage leaves
1¾ ounces (50 g) flour
4 tablespoons (60 g) butter
salt
pepper

scant ½ cup (100 ml) dry white table wine, preferably from
the Castelli Romani

Pound the veal slices gently with a meat tenderizer to flatten them a little and trim them all to a uniform size. Trim the prosciutto slices to the same size as the veal slices. Place first a sage leaf and then a prosciutto slice on each veal slice and secure them to the veal with a toothpick. Dredge in the flour.

Heat half the butter in a large skillet over a lively flame. Add the veal slices, arranging them close together. Sauté on both sides for 2 to 3 minutes total, or until the veal is cooked. Season in moderation with salt and pepper. Lift the veal from the pan, allowing any butter to drip back into the pan, and place on a platter; discard the toothpicks and keep warm. Add the wine to the pan juices and let it evaporate quickly over a lively flame. Remove from the heat, add the remaining butter, and allow it to melt, stirring.

Spoon the pan sauce over the veal and serve hot.

Abbacchio al forno con le patate · Oven-roasted milk-fed lamb with potatoes

In Rome and Lazio, *abbacchio* is milk-fed lamb that has never tasted grass.

Makes 6 servings

> 3 garlic cloves
> about 4½ pounds (2 kg) milk-fed lamb, from the leg or
>   shoulder or a combination of the two
> needles from 2 sprigs rosemary
> 2 tablespoons lard, or 4 tablespoons intensely fruity
>   extra-virgin olive oil
> freshly ground black pepper
> 1½ pounds (700 g) potatoes
> salt

Crush the garlic. Make small slits all over the meat and stick small pieces of the garlic together with a few rosemary needles into the slits. Rub the meat with 1 tablespoon of the lard or 2 tablespoons of the oil and a generous grinding of pepper. Put in a roasting pan.

Peel and dice the potatoes. Put them in the pan next to the meat. Salt everything and sprinkle with flakes of the remaining lard or drizzle with the remaining oil. Put in an oven preheated to 375°F (190°C) and roast for about 45 minutes, basting often with the pan juices. When the meat is tender, remove the pan from the oven. Serve hot.

Abbacchio brodettato · Milk-fed lamb in egg-lemon sauce
Makes 4 servings

1 white onion
2 ounces (60 g) sliced prosciutto
2 tablespoons lard, or 6 tablespoons (90 ml) intensely fruity
    extra-virgin olive oil
about 2¼ pounds (1 kg) milk-fed lamb from the leg or
    shoulder, in pieces (on the bone)
salt
pepper
nutmeg
½ cup (100 ml) dry white table wine
¾ ounce (20 g) flour
1 garlic clove
leaves from 1 small bunch flat-leaf parsley
½ lemon
2 egg yolks
1 heaping tablespoon grated pecorino (not too aged),
    preferably *pecorino romano*

Bring 2 cups (500 ml) water to a boil. Meanwhile, chop together finely the onion and prosciutto and put the mixture in a pan (preferably earthenware) together with the lard. Cook over medium heat for about 5 minutes. When the onion is almost translucent, add the lamb and sauté over medium heat for a few minutes. When a nice brown crust has formed on the meat, season it with salt and pepper and a grating of nutmeg. Add the wine and let it evaporate over medium heat until the odor of the alcohol has disappeared. Sprinkle on the flour and add a couple of ladlefuls of the boiling water. Cover and continue cooking over medium heat for about 30 minutes, or until the meat is tender, adding more of the water as needed to prevent the mixture from drying out.

Chop together the garlic clove and parsley leaves and put in a bowl. Squeeze the juice from the lemon half into the bowl, then add the egg yolks, and finally the pecorino. Stir until the sauce is smooth and well blended. Remove the pan from the heat. Pour in the egg mixture in a steady stream while stirring constantly for about a minute, just enough time for the sauce to warm up. Serve immediately.

Brasato di manzo ai funghi · *Braised beef with mushrooms*
Makes 6 servings

1 pound (450 g) fresh wild mushrooms such as *ovoli,* porcini,
    or chanterelles
1½ ounces (40 g) sliced *lardo*
2 garlic cloves
leaves from 1 small bunch marjoram
salt
freshly ground pepper
1½ pounds (700 g) eye round of beef, in a single piece
scant 1 cup (200 ml) medium-fruity extra-virgin olive oil
1 white onion
1 carrot
1 small celery rib
1 whole clove
1 bay leaf
nutmeg
7 ounces (200 g) canned tomatoes

Scrape the surface of the mushrooms gently with a small knife to remove any
clinging dirt, then wipe with a damp cloth. Cut them into very small pieces and
set aside. Chop together the *lardo,* 1 garlic clove, and the marjoram leaves. Put
in a bowl, add a pinch of salt, and season with a grinding of pepper. Rub the
meat with this mixture and then tie it with kitchen twine so it will keep its
shape. Put it in a saucepan with 6 tablespoons (90 ml) of the oil and brown uniformly over medium heat for a few minutes, or until it is a nice golden brown.
Lift it out of the pan and set aside in a warm place. Reserve the pan and its
contents.

Chop together finely the onion, carrot, celery, and the remaining garlic
clove. Put in the saucepan with the meat juices, add the clove, bay leaf, a grating
of nutmeg, and some salt, and sauté over low heat for 4 or 5 minutes. Then put
the meat back in the pan and add the tomatoes and as much water in a stream as
needed to cover the meat. Cook over medium heat for about 45 minutes, or
until the beef is tender and the tomatoes have broken down.

Meanwhile, put the mushrooms in a pan with the remaining oil and cook
for a couple of minutes. Season with salt and a grinding of pepper and cook
over a lively flame for 3 or 4 minutes, or until the mushrooms are tender. Set
aside.

When the meat is ready, lift it out of the sauce, transfer to a plate, and let rest, covered, for about 15 minutes. Transfer the pan juices to a food processor and process, then return them to the pan and add the mushrooms. Warm over low heat for a few minutes.

Snip the string, slice the meat, and arrange on a warmed platter. Pour the mushrooms and sauce over the slices and serve immediately.

Arrosto morto di gallinaccio · Turkey pot roast
Makes 4 servings

2 garlic cloves
1 turkey leg, about 1¾ pounds (800 g)
needles from 1 sprig rosemary
1 slice pancetta
leaves from 1 small bunch marjoram
leaves from 1 sprig thyme
salt
1 bay leaf
freshly ground pepper
2 tablespoons intensely fruity extra-virgin olive oil
scant 1 cup (200 ml) meat or vegetable broth

Sliver the garlic cloves. Make small slits all over the surface of the turkey leg and insert slivers of the garlic together with a few rosemary needles into the slits. Chop together finely the pancetta and the marjoram and thyme leaves. Put everything in a bowl, add a pinch of salt, the bay leaf, and a generous grinding of pepper. Spread this mixture evenly on the turkey and put the turkey in a pan just large enough to hold it.

Brush the leg with the oil and brown uniformly over medium heat until the meat takes on a nice color. Then cover and cook over low heat, adding the broth a few tablespoons at a time, for about 1 hour. Discard the bay leaf and serve immediately.

Animelle di vitello con i carciofi e i piselli · *Veal sweetbreads*
with artichokes and peas
Makes 4 servings

14 ounces (400 g) veal sweetbreads
4 large artichokes
juice of 1 lemon
14 ounces (400 g) peas
1 white onion
3 ounces (80 g) sliced prosciutto
1 tablespoon lard, or 3 tablespoons intensely fruity
   extra-virgin olive oil
salt
pepper
2 tablespoons dry Marsala
scant ½ cup (100 ml) vegetable broth

Soak the sweetbreads in several changes of cold water for about 1 hour, then drain. Drop the sweetbreads into a pot of lightly salted boiling water, lower the heat to medium, and leave for 5 minutes, then drain. Peel off the membrane and remove any fat from the surface and discard. Put the sweetbreads on a plate, top with a weight, and leave for about 2 hours. Cut them into small dice.

Fill a bowl with water and add half of the lemon juice. One at a time, trim the artichokes as described on page 273. Cut each artichoke in half lengthwise and remove and discard any choke. Cut each half into two wedges and immerse them in the lemon water. In a pot, bring about 3 quarts (3 liters) salted water to a boil. Add the remaining lemon juice and drop in the artichokes. Boil over medium heat for 7 to 8 minutes, or until the artichokes are tender, then drain.

Shell the peas. Bring 4 cups (1 liter) salted water to a boil, add the peas, and cook just until tender, then drain.

Chop the onion. Cut the prosciutto into strips. Put the onion and prosciutto in a saucepan with the lard and sauté over medium heat for about 5 minutes. When the onion is almost translucent, add the sweetbreads and cook gently over low heat for a few minutes. Season with salt and pepper, cover, and continue to cook over low heat for a few minutes more, or until the sweetbreads are tender, moistening every so often with the Marsala.

Transfer the sweetbreads to a warmed platter and keep warm. Add the artichokes and peas to the juices in the saucepan, then pour in the broth and finish cooking over a lively flame, stirring. Spoon the vegetables onto the platter next to the sweetbreads and serve.

Cinghiale in agrodolce · Sweet-and-sour wild boar
Makes 8 servings

3¼ pounds (1.5 kg) boneless boar meat
3 white onions
2 garlic cloves
2 carrots
2 whole cloves
leaves from 1 sprig thyme
1 bay leaf
1¼ cups (300 ml) dry white table wine
scant 1 cup (200 ml) white-wine vinegar
1 celery rib
1¾ ounces (50 g) *lardo*
3½ ounces (100 g) prosciutto
3½ tablespoons (50 g) lard, or 6 tablespoons (90 ml)
  medium-fruity extra-virgin olive oil
salt
pepper
1 ounce (30 g) raisins
1¾ ounces (50 g) unsweetened chocolate
2¼ ounces (70 g) sugar
2 heaping tablespoons mixed candied fruit
2 heaping tablespoons pine nuts

Put the boar meat in a large bowl. Slice 1 onion and cut 1 garlic clove and 1 carrot into small pieces. Put in a saucepan and add the cloves, thyme leaves, and bay leaf. Add a scant 1 cup (200 ml) of the wine and half of the vinegar and bring to a boil. Let cool completely, then pour over the meat. Cover and marinate in the refrigerator for 2 days, turning often.

Remove the meat from the marinade, dry it, and tie it with kitchen twine so it keeps its shape. Strain the marinade and set aside. Chop together the remaining 2 onions, 1 garlic clove, 1 carrot, and the celery. Dice the *lardo* and prosciutto very finely. Heat the lard in a saucepan 10 inches (25 cm) in diameter, just large enough to hold the meat comfortably but not too large. Add the meat and sauté over medium heat for a few minutes, or until nicely browned. Add the chopped onion mixture and then the *lardo* and prosciutto. Pour in the remaining wine and the strained marinade, then moisten with as much boiling water as needed just to cover the meat. Cover and finish cooking over low heat, about 2 hours. Season with salt and pepper only at the halfway point.

When the meat is ready, lift it out of the pan, transfer to a plate, and keep warm. Immerse the raisins in a small bowl of water to plump. Transfer the pan juices to a food processor and process, then return them to the pan. Grate the chocolate and add to the pan along with the remaining vinegar and the sugar. Let the flavors blend for a few minutes over low heat. Meanwhile, chop the candied fruit and drain the raisins. Add the candied fruit, raisins, and pine nuts to the sauce and cook over low heat for 5 to 6 minutes.

Snip the string, slice the meat, and arrange on a warmed platter. Pour the sauce over the slices and serve immediately.

Coda alla vaccinara · Stewed oxtail
Makes 8 servings

1 oxtail, 4½ pounds (2 kg), ready to cook
salt
1 leek
3¼ pounds (1.5 kg) celery
1 carrot
leaves from 1 sprig thyme
1 bay leaf
1 small white onion
leaves from 1 sprig marjoram
5 ounces (150 g) sliced prosciutto
2 tablespoons medium-fruity extra-virgin olive oil
scant 1 cup (200 ml) dry white table wine, preferably from
    the Castelli Romani
about 2¼ pounds (1 kg) tomato purée
pepper
¾ ounce (20 g) raisins
ground cinnamon
nutmeg
1 heaping tablespoon pine nuts

Rinse the oxtail in water and cut it into segments. Bring about 4 quarts (4 liters) lightly salted water to a boil and add the tail pieces. Remove the pot from the heat and leave the meat in the water for 10 minutes, then drain. Transfer the pieces to a pan, add cold water to cover, and bring to a boil. Add some salt, the leek, 1 celery rib, the carrot, the thyme leaves, and the bay leaf. Cover and continue cooking the tail over low heat for about 2 hours, then drain.

Chop together finely the onion, marjoram leaves, and prosciutto. Put the onion mixture in a pan (preferably earthenware) with the oil and sauté over medium heat for about 5 minutes. Add the tail pieces to the onion mixture, pour in the wine, let it evaporate over medium heat, stirring, until the odor of the alcohol has disappeared. Add the tomato purée, season with salt and pepper, and continue cooking over low heat for about 1 hour.

Immerse the raisins in a small bowl of water to plump. Pour 3 quarts (3 liters) water into a pot, add a pinch of salt, and bring to a boil. Add the remaining celery and boil for 4 to 5 minutes, or until it is tender. Drain and cut into segments.

As soon as the tail pieces are tender and the meat begins to fall off the bone, add the celery, a pinch of cinnamon, and a grating of nutmeg. Cook gently for a few minutes over low heat, then remove from the heat. Drain the raisins, add to the pan with the pine nuts, and stir.

Spoon into a warmed serving bowl and serve immediately.

Coniglio alla cacciatora · Rabbit with vinegar and herbs
Makes 4 servings

3 garlic cloves
1 cup dry white table wine
1 cup (240 ml) plus 1 tablespoon red- or white-wine vinegar
  or cider vinegar
2 sprigs rosemary
few sage leaves
1 rabbit, about 3¼ pounds (1.5 kg)
4 tablespoons extra-virgin olive oil
2 salt-packed anchovies, prepared as described
  on page 273
1 heaping tablespoon capers preserved in vinegar
small piece dried chile
1 tablespoon flour
salt
pepper

Crush 2 of the garlic cloves. Combine the 1 crushed garlic clove, the 1 cup (240 ml) wine, the vinegar, 1 sprig rosemary, and 2 small sage leaves in a nonreactive container. Cut the rabbit into pieces and add to the vinegar mixture. Marinate for 3 or 4 hours or, preferably, overnight in the refrigerator.

Put the oil in a skillet with the remaining crushed garlic clove and the chile and sauté over medium heat. When the garlic and chile are nearly browned, discard them. Remove the rabbit pieces from the marinade, dry them well, and then brown them in the flavored oil. Meanwhile, strain the marinade, and once the rabbit is browned, add the marinade to the pan, a little at a time, as the rabbit cooks. Cook the rabbit until tender.

Chop together the anchovies, capers, the remaining garlic clove, the needles from the remaining rosemary sprig, and the remaining sage leaves. Put the mixture in a small bowl and add the 1 tablespoon vinegar. Pour over the rabbit, sprinkle with the flour, and stir over a lively flame for a few minutes. Season with salt and pepper and serve.

Coniglio alla romana in padella · Pan-roasted rabbit
Makes 4 servings

1 rabbit, about 3¼ pounds (1.5 kg)
2½ ounces (70 g) prosciutto
4 tablespoons intensely fruity extra-virgin
   olive oil
1 garlic clove
leaves from 1 small bunch marjoram
scant 1 cup (200 ml) dry white table wine
7 ounces (200 g) tomato purée
salt
pepper

Cut the rabbit into pieces. Dice the prosciutto finely, put in a skillet with the oil, and add the rabbit pieces. Sauté for a few minutes over medium heat. Meanwhile, crush the garlic clove and chop the marjoram leaves. When the meat has a nice golden brown crust, add the garlic and marjoram. Pour in the wine and let it evaporate over medium heat until the odor of the alcohol has disappeared, then continue cooking over medium heat for 5 to 6 minutes.

Add the tomato purée, season with salt and pepper, and finish cooking over medium heat, about 30 minutes. At the end of cooking, the sauce should be quite reduced.

Coratella di abbacchio con i carciofi · Lamb organs with artichokes
Makes 4 servings

juice of 1 lemon
4 large artichokes
1⅓ pounds (600 g) *coratella* (heart, spleen, lung, and liver) of
    milk-fed lamb
3½ tablespoons (50 g) lard, or 6 tablespoons (90 ml)
    intensely fruity extra-virgin olive oil
salt
pepper
2 tablespoons dry Marsala or lemon juice

Fill a bowl with water and add about half of the lemon juice. One at a time, trim the artichokes, including their stems, as described on page 273. Cut each artichoke in half lengthwise and remove and discard any choke. Cut each half into two wedges and immerse them in the lemon water.

Rinse the *coratella* in a narrow stream of running water for 10 minutes. Drain and dry well, then cut the lung and heart into small pieces, keeping them separate. Slice the spleen and liver. Heat half the lard or 4 tablespoons of the oil in a pan (preferably earthenware) over medium heat. Add the lung pieces and cook for about 2 minutes, stirring constantly. Then add the heart and cook for another 5 to 6 minutes. Finally, add the liver and spleen and cook for 1 to 2 minutes. Remove from the heat and keep warm.

Drain the artichokes and pat dry. Heat the remaining lard or oil in a pan and add the artichoke wedges together with the remaining lemon juice (about 1 tablespoon). Season with salt and pepper and cook over medium heat for about 10 minutes. When the artichokes are tender, add them to the *coratella*. Next add the Marsala, put the pan back on the flame, stir, and let the liquid evaporate over medium heat until the odor of the alcohol has disappeared. Season with salt and pepper and serve.

Costarelle di maiale alla burina · Pork ribs with garlic and rosemary
Makes 4 servings

2 garlic cloves
needles from 1 sprig rosemary

freshly ground pepper
1¾ pounds (800 g) meaty pork ribs
4 tablespoons medium-fruity extra-virgin olive oil,
    preferably from Sabina
1½ cups (360 ml) dry white table wine
salt

In a mortar or a mini food processor, crush together the garlic, rosemary needles, and plenty of pepper. Rub the pork with 1 tablespoon of the oil and then with the garlic mixture and put in a shallow bowl. Drizzle with 1 cup (240 ml) of the wine and let rest for 1 hour.

Remove the ribs from the marinade, reserving the marinade, and pat them dry. In a skillet, brown the pork in the remaining oil over high heat. Then add the marinade, a little at a time, followed by the remaining ½ cup (120 ml) wine. Finish cooking over low heat until the pork is tender. Season with salt at the end of cooking.

Costolette di abbacchio "a scottadito" · Grilled baby lamb chops
Makes 4 servings

12 milk-fed lamb rib chops
2 tablespoons medium-fruity extra-virgin olive oil
freshly ground pepper
salt

Pound the chops lightly with a meat tenderizer to flatten them a little. Rub with the oil and sprinkle with pepper. Put them on a grill and cook on both sides for 3 or 4 minutes total. Sprinkle with salt and serve hot.

Cuore di vitello alla trasteverina · Marinated roast veal heart
Makes 6 servings

juice of 1 lemon
6 tablespoons (90 ml) intensely fruity extra-virgin olive oil
freshly ground pepper
1½ pounds (800 g) veal heart
piece of pork caul fat, large enough to wrap the heart pieces
salt

Put the lemon juice in a bowl and add the oil and a generous grinding of pepper. Trim the heart, then cut into pieces weighing about 1¾ ounces (50 g) each. Add to the marinade, stir to coat, and let marinate for 1 hour. Soak the caul fat in cold water to cover for 10 to 15 minutes, or until softened.

Remove the heart pieces from the marinade, reserving the marinade. Wrap each heart piece in a piece of caul fat, put in a baking pan, and salt lightly. Roast in an oven preheated to 350°F (180°C), basting often with the marinade, for about 30 minutes, or until tender.

Remove from the oven and transfer the pieces to a warmed platter. Pour the pan juices over the top and serve immediately.

Fegatelli di maiale all'alloro · *Pork liver with bay leaves*
Makes 4 servings

> 11 ounces (300 g) pork caul fat
> 1 pound (500 g) pork liver
> salt
> pepper
> 12 fresh bay leaves
> 2½ tablespoons (40 g) lard

Soak the caul fat in cold water to cover for 10 to 15 minutes, or until softened. Cut into squares about 6 inches (15 cm) on a side. You should have 12 squares. Remove the fibers and skin from the liver and cut it into small pieces weighing a scant 1½ ounces (40 g) each, or about the size of an average lemon cut in half lengthwise. You should have 12 pieces.

Line up the squares of caul fat on a work surface and sprinkle with salt and pepper. Put a bay leaf and a piece of liver in the center of each square. Roll up each square like a bundle (there is no need to tie them).

Heat the lard in a skillet over medium heat. Add the bundles and brown, turning them as needed, until cooked through and golden brown and crisp. Serve piping hot.

Fegatini di pollo con i carciofi · *Chicken livers with artichokes*
Makes 4 servings

> juice of 1 lemon
> 4 large artichokes

1⅓ pounds (600 g) chicken livers
1 small white onion
3 ounces (80 g) sliced prosciutto
1 tablespoon lard, or 3 tablespoons intensely fruity
   extra-virgin olive oil
salt
pepper
scant ½ cup (100 ml) dry white table wine

Fill a bowl with water and add the lemon juice. One at a time, trim the artichokes, including their stems, as described on page 273. Cut each artichoke in half lengthwise and remove and discard any choke. Cut each half into two wedges and immerse them in the lemon water. Trim away the green bile ducts from the livers and rinse the livers well. Soak the livers in cold water for about 15 minutes, then drain and cut into small pieces.

Chop the onion. Cut the prosciutto into strips. Heat the lard in a saucepan. Drain the artichokes well, add to the pan along with the onion, and season with salt and pepper. Sauté over medium heat for 5 minutes. Using a slotted spoon, transfer the artichokes to a platter and keep warm. Add the livers and prosciutto to the pan and cook over a lively flame for 4 to 5 minutes. Again using the slotted spoon, transfer the livers and prosciutto to the platter with the artichokes.

Pour the wine into the pan juices and let it evaporate over medium heat, stirring. When the odor of the alcohol has disappeared, remove the pan from the heat and pour the sauce over the artichokes and livers. Serve immediately.

––––––––––

Fegato di vitello fritto dorato · Fried calf's liver
Makes 4 servings

1 egg
8 slices calf's liver, about 2 ounces (60 g) each
1¾ ounces (50 g) flour
6 tablespoons (90 ml) medium-fruity extra-virgin olive oil
salt
1 lemon (optional)

Crack the egg into a bowl and beat with a fork. Dredge the liver slices in the flour, shaking off the excess, and then dip them briefly in the egg, coating evenly.

Heat the oil in a skillet. Fry the liver slices on both sides for not more than 1 or 2 minutes total. Drain, sprinkle with salt, and, if desired, squeeze the lemon over them. Serve immediately.

Fritto misto · *Mixed fry*

Artichokes are used in this recipe, but the vegetables can and should vary with the season. Eggplant and zucchini are good in summer, *ovoli* or other mushrooms in autumn. In winter, firm sweet custard cut into lozenge shapes can be added.

Makes 6 servings

14 ounces (400 g) lamb or veal brains
14 ounces (400 g) veal spinal cords, sweetbreads, or liver, or a combination
juice of 1 lemon
6 large artichokes
3 eggs
salt
1 pound (450 g) lard, or scant 1 cup (200 ml) medium-fruity extra-virgin olive oil
7 ounces (200 g) flour

Rinse the lamb brains. Dry them and cut into pieces. If using the spinal cords, parboil them, remove the skin, and cut them into small pieces. If using the sweetbreads and/or liver, trim, rinse, and dry.

Fill a bowl with water and add the lemon juice. One at a time, trim the artichokes, including their stems, as described on page 273. Cut each artichoke in half lengthwise and remove and discard any choke. Cut each half into two wedges and immerse them in the lemon water.

Break the eggs into a bowl, add a pinch of salt, and beat them lightly with a fork. Heat the lard in a skillet. Drain the artichoke wedges well and dip them first in the flour, shaking off the excess, and then in the beaten eggs. Working in small batches, drop them into the hot fat and fry until golden. Scoop out with a slotted spoon, drain on paper towels, and transfer to a warmed platter. Fry the pieces of lamb and veal the same way, drain them on paper towels, and put them next to the artichokes. Sprinkle with salt and serve immediately.

Involtini di carne e verza · *Stuffed Savoy cabbage*
Makes 6 servings

12 large leaves Savoy cabbage
2½ ounces (70 g) stale bread, soaked in meat broth
leaves from 2 bunches flat-leaf parsley

14 ounces (400 g) mixed ground meats (veal, lamb, pork)
1 egg
1 heaping tablespoon grated *parmigiano-reggiano*
1 heaping tablespoon grated pecorino, preferably
   pecorino romano
salt
pepper
1 small white onion
1½ ounces (40 g) prosciutto fat, or 6 tablespoons (90 ml)
   medium-fruity extra-virgin olive oil
1 small celery rib
1 small carrot
½ garlic clove
1 pound (450 g) tomato purée

Bring 4 cups (1 liter) water to a boil and drop in the cabbage leaves. Drain them after a few minutes and spread them out on a dish towel to cool. Remove the hard central rib. Chop the leaves from 1 bunch parsley.

Squeeze the bread and put it in a bowl. Add the ground meats, egg, parmigiano, pecorino, chopped parsley, pinch of salt, and a grinding of pepper. Mix for a long time to blend all the ingredients thoroughly. Divide the mixture into 12 equal portions. Spread 1 portion on each cabbage leaf. Roll up each leaf into a roulade and secure with toothpicks so the filling doesn't escape during cooking.

Chop together the onion, prosciutto fat (if using), celery, carrot, garlic, and the remaining parsley leaves and put the mixture in a pan (preferably earthenware). If you have not used the prosciutto fat, add the oil to the pan. Sauté over medium heat for about 5 minutes. When the onion and the fat begin to become translucent, add the tomato purée. Cook for 10 minutes, then add the *involtini*, arranging them close together, and season with salt and pepper. Cover and continue to cook over medium heat for 20 more minutes. Transfer the *involtini* to a warmed platter, discard the toothpicks, and serve.

Involtini di manzo · *Beef rolls*
Makes 6 servings

2 small celery ribs
2 small carrots
12 thin slices boneless beef
12 slices prosciutto

3½ ounces (100 g) flour
¼ yellow onion
1 garlic clove
1 ounce (30 g) prosciutto fat
1 tablespoon intensely fruity extra-virgin olive oil
1 whole clove
1 bay leaf
1⅓ pounds (600 g) sauce tomatoes
scant 1 cup (200 ml) dry white table wine
salt
pepper
nutmeg

Cut 1 celery rib and 1 carrot into small strips. Pound the meat slices lightly with a meat tenderizer to flatten them a little. Lay a prosciutto slice on each beef slice, then divide the carrot and celery strips evenly among the prosciutto slices, scattering them on top. Roll up each slice into a roulade and secure with toothpicks so the filling doesn't escape during cooking. Dredge the rolls in the flour, shaking off the excess, and set aside.

Chop together finely the onion, the remaining celery and carrot, the garlic clove, and the prosciutto fat. Put in a pan, preferably earthenware, with the oil, then add the clove and the bay leaf. Sauté over medium heat for about 5 minutes. When the onion and the fat begin to become translucent, add the meat rolls and brown gently on all sides. Meanwhile, peel the tomatoes, cut them into strips, and reserve. Remove and discard the bay leaf and clove, pour in the wine, and let it evaporate over medium heat. When the odor of the alcohol has disappeared, add the tomatoes and season with salt, pepper, and a grating of nutmeg.

Cover and continue cooking over low heat for 25 to 30 minutes, or until the meat is tender. Using a slotted spoon, transfer the *involtini* to a warmed platter and keep warm. Pour the pan juices into a food processor and process. Discard the toothpicks from the *involtini,* pour the sauce over the stop, and serve.

Lenticchie in umido con le salsicce · Lentils and sausages
Makes 4 servings

1 pound (450 g) lentils, rinsed and ready to cook (most
    lentils need no soaking)
1 onion
1 celery rib

1 carrot
leaves from 1 small bunch marjoram
2 tablespoons extra-virgin olive oil
9 fresh pork sausages
1 cup dry white table wine
11 ounces (300 g) tomato purée
salt
pepper

Cook the lentils in lightly salted water until tender, then drain.

Meanwhile, chop together the onion, celery, carrot, and marjoram leaves. Put in a pan (preferably earthenware) with the oil and sauté over low heat for 5 to 6 minutes, or until tender. Skin 1 sausage, crumble the meat, add to the pan, and cook until the sausage fat has completely melted. Add the wine and let it evaporate over medium heat until all the alcohol odor has disappeared. Then add the remaining sausages and brown them on all sides. Add the tomato purée and continue cooking for 10 minutes.

Season with a grinding of pepper and taste for salt. Finally, add the lentils to the pan and cook gently over low heat for a few minutes to let the flavors blend.

Lesso rifatto con le cipolle · Leftover boiled beef with onions
Makes 5 servings

1½ pounds (700 g) boneless boiled beef
1 pound (450 g) white onions
7 ounces (200 g) lard, or 6 tablespoons (90 ml) intensely
    fruity extra-virgin olive oil
scant ½ cup (100 ml) dry white table wine, preferably from
    the Castelli Romani
4 tablespoons meat or vegetable broth
salt
pepper

Slice the meat. Slice the onions very thinly, put them in a pan with the lard, and sauté over medium heat for about 5 minutes, or until the onions begin to become translucent.

Add the meat slices, then add the wine and let it evaporate over medium heat until the odor of the alcohol has disappeared. Moisten with the broth, season moderately with salt and pepper, and let the flavors blend over low heat for 5 to 6 minutes. Transfer to a warmed platter and serve piping hot.

Lesso rifatto in umido con le patate · Leftover boiled beef with potatoes
Makes 5 servings

1½ pounds (700 g) boneless boiled beef
1 pound (450 g) boiling potatoes
leaves from 1 small bunch basil
leaves from 1 small bunch marjoram
14 ounces (400 g) yellow onions
3½ ounces (100 g) lard, or 3 to 4 tablespoons intensely fruity
   extra-virgin olive oil
14 ounces (400 g) tomato purée
salt
pepper

Slice the meat. Peel the potatoes and cut them into wedges. Bring about 2 quarts (2 liters) salted water to a boil and drop in the potatoes. Drain them when they are half done and set aside. Chop together finely the basil and marjoram leaves.

Thinly sliced the onions, put them in a pan with the lard, and sauté over medium heat for 5 minutes. When they begin to become translucent, add the tomato purée and the chopped basil and marjoram and season with salt and pepper. Cook over medium heat for 20 minutes. Add the potatoes and let the flavors blend for a few minutes, then add the meat slices and cook gently for 3 to 4 minutes to heat through and finish cooking the potatoes. Remove from the heat and serve immediately.

Lingua di bue in agrodolce · Sweet-and-sour beef tongue
Makes 8 to 10 servings

1 beef tongue, about 3¼ pounds (1.5 kg)
8 pitted prunes
½ ounce (15 g) raisins
½ white onion
½ carrot
leaves from 1 small bunch marjoram
leaves from 1 small bunch flat-leaf parsley
1 ounce (25 g) unsweetened chocolate

3½ tablespoons (50 g) lard, or 6 tablespoons (90 ml)
   medium-fruity extra-virgin olive oil
1 bay leaf
¾ ounce (20 g) sugar
scant ½ cup (100 ml) white-wine vinegar diluted with scant
   ½ cup (100 ml) water
salt
2 heaping tablespoons mixed candied orange and citron
   rinds
5 ounces (150 g) pitted sour cherries
1 heaping tablespoon pine nuts

Bring 2 quarts (2 liters) lightly salted water to a boil. Add the tongue and boil for 30 to 40 minutes, or until tender. Drain the tongue, let it cool until it can be handled, and then skin and trim it. Put the tongue back in the pot to keep it warm in its broth.

Immerse the prunes and raisins in separate small bowls of water to plump. Chop together finely the onion, carrot, and marjoram and parsley leaves. Grate the chocolate. Put the onion mixture in a saucepan with the lard and sauté over medium heat for 5 minutes. When the onion is almost translucent, add the bay leaf, sugar, and chocolate and mix well. Add the diluted vinegar and a pinch of salt and bring to a boil.

Meanwhile, slice the tongue and chop the candied rinds, not too small. Add the tongue slices to the sauce and let the flavors blend over very low heat for a couple of minutes. Drain the prunes and raisins and add to the pan along with the candied rinds, cherries, and pine nuts. Continue cooking over low heat for 2 more minutes. Serve immediately.

Lombello allo spiedo · Spit-roasted pork fillet
Makes 6 servings

12 slices *casereccio* bread (see page 273)
12 slices prosciutto
6 slices pork fillet, each about 4 ounces (120 g) and ¾ inch
   (2 cm) thick
2 tablespoons (30 g) lard, or 5 tablespoons medium-fruity
   extra-virgin olive oil
salt
pepper

Trim the bread and prosciutto to the same size as the pork slices. Thread onto a spit a bread slice, a prosciutto slice, and a pork slice. Repeat in this order until all the ingredients are used up.

Rub all the ingredients generously with the lard, then put the spit in a rotisserie-equipped oven preheated to 400°F (200°C) or over an open fire. The meat will be ready in about 20 minutes. Season with salt and pepper when about half done. Serve piping hot.

Piccatine al limone · Veal scallops with lemon
Makes 4 servings

1 pound (450 g) veal fillet, thinly sliced
pepper
1¾ ounces (50 g) flour
4½ tablespoons (70 g) butter
salt
1 lemon
leaves from 1 small bunch flat-leaf parsley
1½ ounces (40 g) sliced prosciutto

Trim the veal slices to make uniform rounds. Sprinkle them with pepper and then dip them quickly in the flour, shaking off the excess. Melt half the butter in a skillet over medium heat until it foams. Add the meat slices and cook, turning once, for about 3 minutes total. Using a slotted spoon, remove the slices from the pan and place them, overlapping, on a warmed platter. Sprinkle with salt and cover to keep them warm. Reserve the pan juices in the pan.

Squeeze the juice from the lemon and finely chop the parsley leaves. Cut the prosciutto in strips and add it to the reserved pan juices. Add the remaining butter and sauté over medium heat for about 4 minutes. When the prosciutto has colored, add the chopped parsley and 3 tablespoons lemon juice. Cook the sauce over a lively flame for not more than 1 minute.

Spoon the sauce over the meat slices and serve immediately.

Pollo al rosmarino · Pan-roasted chicken with tomatoes,
rosemary, and garlic
Makes 4 servings

1 medium-size whole chicken
2 garlic cloves
1 chicken bouillon cube
7 ounces (200 g) canned tomatoes
4 tablespoons extra-virgin olive oil
needles from 2 sprigs rosemary
small piece dried chile
scant 1 cup (200 ml) dry white table wine
salt

Cut the chicken into large pieces. Crush 1 garlic clove flat. Crumble the bouillon cube. Dice the tomatoes.

Heat the oil and crushed garlic in a skillet and brown the chicken, turning as needed, until it takes on a nice color on all sides. Discard the garlic and add the bouillon cube, the rosemary needles from 1 sprig, and the chile. Mix well, add the wine, and let it evaporate over medium heat. When the odor of alcohol has disappeared, add the tomatoes, taste for salt, and continue cooking until the chicken is tender and the sauce is well reduced.

Finely chop together the remaining garlic clove and the remaining rosemary needles. Add to the chicken and cook over low heat for a few minutes to blend the flavors. Serve immediately.

Pollo alla moda di Scandriglia · Pan-roasted chicken
in vinegar sauce
Makes 4 servings

1 whole chicken, about 3¼ pounds (1.5 kg)
scant ½ cup (100 ml) medium-fruity extra-virgin olive oil,
   preferably from Sabina
salt
pepper
4 oil-packed anchovy fillets
2 garlic cloves
1½ ounces (40 g) capers preserved in vinegar

needles from 1 sprig rosemary
scant ½ cup (100 ml) white- or red-wine vinegar or cider
vinegar, not too strong

Cut the chicken into smallish pieces. Heat the oil in a skillet and brown the chicken pieces, turning them frequently. Sprinkle lightly with salt and pepper.

While the chicken is cooking, drain the anchovies. In a wooden mortar, mash together thoroughly the anchovies, garlic, capers, rosemary needles, and a few tablespoons of the vinegar. Add the remaining vinegar and mix well.

When the chicken is almost done, pour in the vinegar mixture. Finish cooking, stirring often and letting the liquid evaporate completely. Serve immediately.

Pollo alla romana con i peperoni · *Chicken with bell peppers*
Even simple chicken with tomatoes, without the peppers,
is typical of *cucina romana.*
Makes 4 servings

1 whole chicken, about 3¼ pounds (1.5 kg)
11 ounces (300 g) sauce tomatoes, preferably San Marzano
2 garlic cloves
leaves from 1 small bunch marjoram
1¾ ounces (50 g) sliced prosciutto
6 tablespoons (90 ml) intensely fruity extra-virgin olive oil,
    or 1½ ounces (40 g) lard
salt
pepper
scant ½ cup (100 ml) dry white table wine
2 large yellow or red bell peppers

Cut the chicken into large pieces. Peel the tomatoes and cut them into ¾-inch (2-cm) dice. Crush the garlic cloves. Chop the marjoram leaves. Cut the prosciutto into strips.

Put the prosciutto in a skillet with 2 tablespoons of the oil or 1 tablespoon of the lard. Sauté over medium heat for about 4 minutes. When the prosciutto has colored, add the chicken and brown evenly over medium heat for 5 minutes. Stir in 1 garlic clove, the marjoram, and the tomatoes. Season with salt and pepper and continue cooking over a lively flame for about 20 minutes, moistening with the wine a little at a time.

Meanwhile, cut the peppers in half, remove the seeds and membranes, and cut lengthwise into strips. Put the strips in a skillet with the remaining oil (or lard) and the remaining garlic clove. Cook over medium heat for 5 to 6 minutes, or until the peppers are tender. When both the chicken and peppers are cooked, put them both in a warm serving dish and mix well. Serve immediately.

Pollo coi capperi · Chicken with capers
Makes 4 servings

1 whole chicken, about 3¼ pounds (1.5 kg)
2 tablespoons extra-virgin olive oil
scant 1 cup (200 ml) dry white table wine
2 oil-packed anchovy fillets
1¾ ounces (50 g) salt-packed capers, rinsed thoroughly to
  remove the salt
leaves from 1 small bunch parsley
2 garlic cloves
pepper
1½ ounces (40 g) pine nuts

Cut the chicken into serving pieces. Heat the oil in a skillet over a lively flame and brown the chicken pieces, turning frequently. Add the wine and let it evaporate over medium heat until the alcohol odor has disappeared.

Meanwhile, drain the anchovies and put in a food processor. Add the capers, parsley leaves, garlic, and some pepper and process until smooth. Pour over the chicken. Cover and continue to cook, adding a few tablespoons hot water if needed to keep the dish moist. Finally, add the pine nuts, heat for a few minutes, stirring, and serve.

Pollo ripieno alla papalina · Stuffed chicken
Makes 6 servings

1 whole chicken, about 3¼ pounds (1.5 kg), including
  the giblets
2 fresh pork sausages, skinned and crumbled
¾ ounce (20 g) dried porcini mushrooms
scant 1 ounce (25 g) black truffle
3 tablespoons lightly fruity extra-virgin olive oil
scant 1 cup (200 ml) meat broth

1¾ ounces (50 g) crustless bread
1 egg
10 vacuum-packed peeled chestnuts (or roast and peel
fresh chestnuts)
salt
pepper
nutmeg

Trim the giblets, eliminating the green bile ducts from the liver. Rinse them for a good, long time, then cut them into small pieces. Skin the sausages and crumble the sausage meat. Soak the dried porcini for 20 minutes in at least two changes of warm water. Drain, rinse, and squeeze well, then chop, not too finely. Grate the truffle.

Put the liver and the sausages in a small pan with 2 tablespoons of the oil and a few tablespoons of the broth and sweat over low heat for about 6 minutes. Using a slotted spoon, remove the livers and sausages from the pan and set aside. Add the remaining broth and the bread to the pan juices and let the bread absorb all the liquid. Transfer the contents of the pan to a food processor, add the livers and sausages, egg, chestnuts, and mushrooms, season with salt and pepper, and process until the mixture is smooth. Transfer the mixture to a bowl, add a grating of nutmeg and the grated truffle, and stir well.

Fill the chicken cavity with the stuffing and sew the opening closed with coarse thread. Put the bird in a roasting pan, then brush the bird with the remaining 1 tablespoon oil and season lightly with salt and pepper. Put the pan in an oven preheated to 400°F (200°C) and roast, brushing every so often with the pan juices, for about 1 hour, or until the juices run clear when a thigh is pierced.

Remove from the oven and let cool somewhat, then carve the chicken and serve. This chicken is also excellent served at room temperature.

Polmoncino di vitello in intingolo · Veal lung in sauce
Makes 4 servings

1 pound (450 g) veal lung
1 ounce (30 g) dried porcini mushrooms
2 ounces (60 g) sliced prosciutto
4 teaspoons (20 g) lard, or 4 tablespoons intensely fruity
extra-virgin olive oil
1 tablespoon chopped white onion
1 ounce (30 g) flour

scant 1 cup (200 ml) dry white table wine
salt
pepper
scant 1 cup (200 ml) meat broth (if needed)

Clean the veal lung, then drop it into 3 quarts (3 liters) lightly salted boiling water and simmer for about 30 minutes. Drain, pat dry, and remove and discard the white membrane covering it. Cut into small ⅜-inch (1-cm) dice. Soak the dried porcini for 20 minutes in at least two changes of warm water. Drain, rinse, and squeeze well, then chop very finely.

Chop the prosciutto very finely and put it in a saucepan with the lard. Add the onion and mushrooms and sauté over medium heat for about 4 minutes. When the onion is golden brown, add the diced lung. Let it color over medium heat, then sprinkle on the flour and stir to mix. Add the wine and evaporate over medium heat. When the odor of the alcohol has disappeared, season with salt and pepper, cover, and finish cooking over low heat, adding the broth, a little at a time, when the pan begins to dry. Serve hot.

Polpette di lesso alla casalinga · *Meatballs of boiled beef*
Makes 5 servings

1¾ ounces (50 g) crustless bread
scant ½ cup (100 ml) heavy cream or milk
leaves from 1 small bunch flat-leaf parsley
2 garlic cloves
1 pound (450 g) boiled boneless beef
2 heaping tablespoons mixed grated cheese, equal amounts
    pecorino, preferably *pecorino romano,* and
    parmigiano-reggiano
3 eggs
salt
pepper
3½ ounces (100 g) flour
7 ounces (200 g) dried bread crumbs
scant 1 cup (200 ml) medium-fruity extra-virgin olive oil
1½ cups (350 ml) ready-made tomato sauce with basil

Soak the bread in the cream, then squeeze it well, discarding the excess cream. Chop together finely the parsley leaves and garlic. Trim the meat, removing any fat and membranes, then chop it. Put it in a bowl and add the parsley and garlic mixture, the bread, the cheese, and 1 egg. Season with salt and pepper and mix until well blended.

Break the remaining 2 eggs into another bowl and beat gently with a little salt. Form the meat mixture into small patties. Dredge them first in the flour, shaking off the excess, then dip them in the eggs, and then finally in the bread crumbs. Heat the oil in a skillet over medium heat. Working in batches, fry the patties on both sides for a few minutes total, or until nicely colored and just cooked through. Drain on paper towels; set aside and keep warm.

Heat the tomato sauce in a saucepan. Add the meat patties to the sauce and let the flavors blend over low heat for a couple of minutes. Serve piping hot.

Polpettone di pollo · Chicken meat loaf
From the Roman Jewish tradition.
Makes 6 servings

3½ ounces (100 g) stale crustless bread
scant 1 cup (200 ml) meat or vegetable broth
14 ounces (400 g) ground chicken breast
2 eggs
salt
pepper
ground cinnamon
1 carrot
1 artichoke stem
4 tablespoons intensely fruity extra-virgin olive oil
6 tablespoons (90 ml) dry white table wine

Soak the bread in the broth, then squeeze it well, discarding the excess broth. Transfer the bread to a bowl, add the chicken, season with salt, pepper, and a pinch of cinnamon, and mix thoroughly. With oiled hands, form the meat mixture into a meat loaf. Cut off the tough bottom and peel off the stringy outer layers of the artichoke stem, exposing the tender core. Chop together finely the carrot and the artichoke stem.

Put the meat loaf and the oil in a shallow saucepan just large enough to hold it. Brown over medium heat, turning often with the help of two large spoons, until a nice crust has formed on the surface of the meat. Add the carrot and the artichoke stem, then pour in the wine and let it evaporate over medium heat. When the smell of the alcohol has completely disappeared, pour in just enough boiling water to cover the meat loaf. Season with salt and pepper and cook over low heat for about 1 hour, or until the liquid is substantially reduced.

Let the meat loaf cool, then cut into slices. Ladle the sauce over the slices and serve.

Rognone di manzo in umido · Stewed beef kidney
Makes 4 servings

2 beef kidneys, about 1½ pounds (700 g) total
scant 1 cup (200 ml) white wine vinegar
leaves from 1 small bunch flat-leaf parsley
1 large white onion
2 tablespoons (30 g) lard, or 4 tablespoons intensely fruity
  extra-virgin olive oil
14 ounces (400 g) canned tomatoes
salt
pepper
scant ½ cup (100 ml) dry white table wine

Soak the kidneys in the vinegar and enough water to cover for 10 minutes. Drain and slice the kidneys. Put the slices in a skillet and sauté over a lively flame for about 2 minutes, or until the liquid that they throw off evaporates. When the pan is perfectly dry, set aside and keep warm.

Chop the parsley leaves. Chop the onion and put it in a pan with the lard. Cook over medium heat for 5 minutes. When it is almost translucent, add the tomatoes and cook over medium heat for about 20 minutes, mashing the tomatoes with a fork as needed to break them up. Add the kidney slices, season with salt and pepper, and then pour in the wine and evaporate over medium heat, stirring. When the odor of the alcohol has disappeared, remove from the heat, sprinkle with the parsley, and serve.

Rollè di vitello in casseruola · Rolled veal pot roast
Makes 8 servings

about 2 pounds (1 kg) veal breast, in a single piece
1 garlic clove
leaves from 1 small bunch flat-leaf parsley

2 ounces (60 g) grated pecorino, preferably *pecorino romano*
2 eggs
pepper
1 sprig rosemary
4 tablespoons intensely fruity extra-virgin olive oil
scant ½ cup (100 ml) meat broth

Pound the veal breast lightly with a meat tenderizer to flatten a little. Chop together the garlic clove and parsley leaves and put in a bowl. Add the pecorino and eggs and mix thoroughly, then season with pepper. Spread the mixture on the veal breast and roll the breast up tightly. Lay the rosemary sprig lengthwise on the roll and tie securely with kitchen string.

Put the roll with the oil in a pan, ideally oval and just large enough to hold the meat. Sauté over a lively flame, turning with the help of two large spoons, until a golden brown crust has formed on the surface of the roll. Put in an oven preheated to 350°F (180°C), cover, and continue cooking for about 1 hour, adding a little of the broth from time to time. Instead of the oven, the meat can also be cooked on the stove top over medium heat.

Let rest for about 20 minutes, then slice and serve.

Salsicce con indivia, patate, "gobbi" e broccoli · Sausages with curly endive, potatoes, cardoons, and broccolo romanesco
Makes 4 servings

1 head cardoons, about 7 ounces (200 g)
1 tablespoon medium-fruity extra-virgin olive oil
  (for blanching the cardoons)
14 ounces (400 g) boiling potatoes
1 head *broccolo romanesco* (see page 273), about 14 ounces
  (400 g)
1 head curly endive, about 12 ounces (350 g)
2 tablespoons (30 g) lard, or 4 tablespoons medium-fruity
  extra-virgin olive oil
4 fresh pork sausages

Trim the cardoons, discarding all the leaves and tougher, stringier outer ribs that surround the heart. Bring 2 quarts (2 liters) lightly salted water to a boil and add 1 tablespoon of the oil. Drop in the cardoons, lower the heat to medium, and simmer for 10 minutes, or until the cardoons are almost white. Drain and cut into ¾-inch (2-cm) lengths.

In the same pot, bring another 2 quarts (2 liters) lightly salted water to a boil, add the cardoon pieces, and simmer for about 1 hour, or until tender. Drain and set aside.

Peel the potatoes and cut them into about ¾-inch (2-cm) dice. Discard the tough outer leaves and core of the *broccolo* and cut into florets. Trim the endive, drop it into a large pot of boiling salted water, and cook until tender, 3 to 4 minutes. Lift it out with a sieve, squeeze it, and then chop it, not too finely. Set aside. Keep the water at a boil and now drop in the potatoes. When they are just tender, lift them out and drop in the *broccolo* florets. When they are tender, drain and set aside. (You can now discard the water.)

Melt the lard in a large skillet. Add the sausages and brown them over a lively flame for a couple of minutes. Now add all the vegetables and cook gently over low heat for 6 to 7 minutes, stirring constantly. Serve piping hot.

---

*Salsicce e broccoli affogati · Sausages and broccolo romanesco
in white wine*
Makes 4 servings

> 1 head *broccolo romanesco* (see page 273), about
>   2 pounds (1 kg)
> 2 garlic cloves
> 8 fresh pork sausages
> 3 tablespoons intensely fruity extra-virgin olive oil
> ⅜-inch (1-cm) piece dried chile
> salt
> ½ cup (100 ml) dry white table wine

Discard the tough outer leaves and core of the *broccolo* and cut into florets. Crush the garlic cloves. Put the sausages in a skillet with 3 tablespoons water. Cover and cook the sausages over medium heat for a few minutes. When the sausages are nicely browned, remove them from the pan and keep warm. Reserve the pan and its contents.

Place the *broccolo* florets in the reserved skillet, add the oil, and then the garlic and chile. Season moderately with salt, cover, and sweat the florets over very low heat for 10 minutes, stirring often. When they are tender, add the sausages. Then add the wine, a little at a time, and let it evaporate completely. Cook for 2 more minutes to allow the flavors to blend, then remove from the heat. Serve immediately.

*Salsicce e fagioli alla trasteverina · Sausages and beans
in tomato sauce*
Makes 4 servings

> 1 pound (450 g) shelled fresh cannellini beans
> 8 fresh pork sausages
> 1 small white onion
> 1 small celery rib
> 1 garlic clove
> 3 tablespoons intensely fruity extra-virgin olive oil
> 1 pound (450 g) tomato purée
> salt
> pepper

Boil the beans in about 2 quarts (2 liters) lightly salted water. When tender, drain and set aside. Put the sausages in a skillet and add 3 tablespoons water. Sauté over medium heat for a few minutes, or until a golden brown crust forms on the surface of the sausages. Remove the sausages from the pan and keep warm. Reserve the pan and its contents.

Chop together finely the onion, celery, and garlic. Put in the reserved skillet, add the oil, and sauté over medium heat for about 5 minutes. When the onion is almost translucent, add the tomato purée and season with salt and pepper. Continue cooking over medium heat for 20 minutes. Add the beans and sausages to this sauce and let the flavors blend over low heat for 3 minutes. Serve hot.

Scaloppine con la lattuga · Veal scaloppine with romaine lettuce
From the Roman Jewish tradition.
Makes 4 servings

> 1 head romaine lettuce, about 9 ounces (250 g)
> 8 slices veal, about 2 ounces (60 g) each
> 2½ ounces (70 g) flour
> 5 tablespoons medium-fruity extra-virgin olive oil
> 1½ ounces (40 g) beef marrow
> salt
> pepper

Discard the outer leaves of the lettuce; separate the remaining leaves, rinse, and dry well. Pound the veal slices lightly with a meat tenderizer to flatten them a little. Dredge them in the flour, shaking off the excess.

Pour 4 tablespoons of the oil into a skillet over medium heat. Add the veal slices and cook on both sides for a few minutes. When a golden brown crust has formed on the surface, remove the slices with tongs or a slotted spoon. Grease a baking pan with the remaining 1 tablespoon oil and put half the meat slices in a single layer on the bottom, arranging them close together. Cover with a layer of lettuce, then with the remaining 4 meat slices, followed by another layer of lettuce. Crumble the marrow over the surface and season with salt and pepper.

Bake in an oven preheated to 400°F (200°C) for about 20 minutes. Serve hot.

Spalla di castrato con i fagioli cannellini · Lamb shoulder with cannellini beans
Makes 6 servings

3½ ounces (100 g) prosciutto rind
1 slice *lardo*
1 small carrot
1 small celery rib
1 small bunch flat-leaf parsley
1 small white onion
1 whole clove
3¼ pounds (1.5 kg) shoulder of *castrato* (see page 273)
salt
pepper
4 tablespoons medium-fruity extra-virgin olive oil
3¼ cups (750 ml) dry red table wine
3¼ cups (750 ml) meat or vegetable broth
12 ounces (350 g) dried cannellini beans, soaked and ready
    to cook

Drop the rind into about 2 quarts (2 liters) boiling water, cover, boil for 10 minutes, and then drain. Scrape the rind carefully to remove any hairs. Cut the *lardo* into narrow strips. Tie together the carrot, celery, and parsley with kitchen string. Peel the onion and stick with the clove.

Bone the lamb and reserve the bones. Pound the lamb lightly with a meat tenderizer to flatten. Make small slits all over the meat and stick the *lardo* strips into the slits. Sprinkle the lamb on both sides with salt and pepper. Roll it up and tie tightly with kitchen string. Put the roll in a large saucepan with the oil and brown over medium heat for a few minutes. When a nice golden brown crust has formed on the surface of the roll, add the pork rind, the carrot bundle, the onion, and the reserved bones. Pour in the wine and broth and continue cooking the meat over medium heat for about 1 hour.

When the lamb is quite tender, remove it from the liquid, draining it well, and put on a warmed platter. Remove the prosciutto rind and place on a cutting board. Strain the pan juices, then scoop off the fat from the surface. Pour the juices back in the saucepan and keep warm.

Meanwhile, put the beans in a pot with about 2 quarts (2 liters) salted water and bring to a boil. Lower the heat and simmer for about 20 minutes, or until tender; the timing will depend on the age of the beans. Check after 20 minutes and frequently thereafter.

Add the beans to the pan juices. Cut the prosciutto rind into strips and add to the beans. Cook gently over low heat for a few minutes. Slice the lamb, garnish with the beans and prosciutto rind, and moisten with the pan juices. Serve hot.

Spalla di montone con le olive · *Mutton with olives*
From the Roman Jewish tradition.
Makes 6 servings

1 shoulder of mutton, about 3¼ pounds (1.5 kg)
salt
pepper
1 tablespoon ground cinnamon
1 whole clove
3 white onions
2 carrots
7 ounces (200 g) green olives
4 tablespoons intensely fruity extra-virgin olive oil
scant ½ cup (100 ml) meat or vegetable broth

Bone the mutton, then pound lightly with a meat tenderizer to flatten. Sprinkle with salt and pepper and the cinnamon and put the clove on the center. Roll up the mutton and tie it tightly with kitchen string.

Thickly slice the onions and slice the carrots. Pit half the olives and chop coarsely. Pit the remaining olives and leave whole.

Put the roll in a large saucepan with the oil and brown over medium heat for a few minutes, turning often with two large spoons. When a nice golden brown crust has formed on the surface, add the onions and carrots and continue cooking over low heat for about 30 minutes, adding the broth a few tablespoons at a time. Now add all the olives and continue cooking until the meat is tender, about 1 hour. Serve hot.

***

Spezzatino di abbacchio e funghi alla cacciatora · *Lamb stew with mushrooms*
Makes 4 servings

11 ounces (300 g) fresh wild mushrooms such as *ovoli,*
    porcini, or chanterelles
1 sprig sage
1 sprig rosemary
about 2¼ pounds (1 kg) milk-fed lamb (leg, ribs, and kidney)
10 tablespoons (150 ml) intensely fruity extra-virgin olive oil
salt
2 garlic cloves
¾-inch (2-cm) piece dried chile
11 ounces (300 g) tomato purée

Scrape the surface of the mushrooms gently with a small knife to remove any clinging dirt, then wipe with a damp cloth and slice. Tie the sage and rosemary together with kitchen string.

Cut the lamb into large pieces. Put the lamb and 6 tablespoons (90 ml) of the oil in a pan over medium heat and sauté for 4 to 5 minutes, or until a nice golden brown crust forms. Sprinkle the lamb with salt, then remove it from the pan; set aside and keep warm. Reserve the pan juices in the pan. Put the mushrooms in a skillet with the remaining 4 tablespoons (60 ml) oil, sprinkle with salt, and sauté over medium heat for 4 to 5 minutes, or until tender. Remove from the heat and set aside.

Crush the garlic cloves, put them in the reserved lamb pan, and add the chile and herb bundle. Brown the garlic over medium heat for about 4 minutes. Add the tomato purée and a little salt and continue cooking for about 20 minutes. Now add the lamb pieces and finish cooking over medium heat, stirring carefully, for about 20 minutes. A few minutes before the lamb is ready, add the mushrooms to heat through. Discard the herb bundle and the chile and serve hot.

Spezzatino di castrato con le patate · Lamb stew with potatoes
Makes 4 servings

> about 2 pounds (1 kg) boneless *castrato* or lamb
> 1 pound (450 g) boiling potatoes
> 1 white onion
> 4 tablespoons intensely fruity extra-virgin olive oil
> 1 cup (200 ml) dry red table wine
> 2 quarts (1 kg) tomato purée
> 1 sprig rosemary
> 2 sage leaves
> ground cinnamon
> salt
> pepper

Cut the lamb into large pieces. Peel the potatoes, cut them into wedges, and set aside in bowl of cold water. Chop the onion.

Put the onion in a pan (preferably earthenware) with the oil and sauté over medium heat for 3 to 4 minutes, or until almost translucent. Add the lamb pieces and brown over medium heat, turning frequently. Add the wine and let it evaporate. When the odor of the alcohol has disappeared, add the tomato purée, the rosemary, the sage leaves, and a pinch of cinnamon and season with salt and pepper. Cook over medium heat for about 15 minutes.

Drain and dry the potatoes. Add them to the meat and finish cooking over low heat, stirring often, for about 30 minutes. Serve hot.

Spezzatino di vitello con l'erbetta · Veal stew with parsley
From the Roman Jewish tradition.
Makes 4 servings

> 1½ pounds (700 g) veal stew meat
> 2 garlic cloves
> 4 tablespoons intensely fruity extra-virgin olive oil
> salt
> pepper
> leaves from 1 bunch flat-leaf parsley

Cut the meat into large pieces. Crush the garlic cloves and put them in a saucepan with the meat and the oil. Sauté over a lively flame for a few minutes.

When the meat is lightly browned, discard the garlic, season the meat with salt and pepper, and lower the flame to the minimum. Cover and continue cooking for about 20 minutes, adding a few tablespoons boiling water if needed to moisten.

Chop the parsley leaves finely and add half to the stew, which by now should be half done. Continue cooking over low heat for 20 minutes longer. When the meat is tender, remove it from the stove and sprinkle with salt and with the rest of the parsley.

Let cool a bit before serving. This dish is also excellent served at room temperature.

Spezzatino con i peperoni · Veal stew with sweet peppers
Makes 4 servings

1½ pounds (700 g) veal stew meat
2 fleshy yellow sweet peppers
1 green onion
5 or 6 ripe San Marzano tomatoes
4 tablespoons medium-fruity extra-virgin olive oil,
    preferably from Sabina
scant ½ cup (100 ml) dry white table wine
salt
pepper
1 heaping tablespoon minced flat-leaf parsley

Cut the meat into small cubes. Cut the sweet peppers in half, remove and discard the seeds and membranes, and cut into lengthwise strips. Thinly slice the green onion. Peel and dice the tomatoes.

Brown the meat in the oil over medium heat in a large saucepan, stirring often. Add the wine and let it evaporate. When the odor of the alcohol has disappeared, add the sweet peppers, onion, and tomatoes to the meat, mix well, and season with salt and pepper. Cover and continue cooking over a very low flame, adding a few tablespoons boiling water if the pan begins to dry. When the meat is tender, let the stew rest for 20 minutes, then sprinkle with the parsley and serve.

Trippa alla romana · *Tripe with tomato sauce and pecorino*
Makes 6 servings

leaves from 1 small bunch Roman mint (see page 274)
3½ ounces (100 g) mixed grated cheese, equal amounts
    pecorino romano and *parmigiano-reggiano*
about 2 pounds (1 kg) veal tripe, cleaned and ready to cook
2 cups (500 ml) *sugo d'umido* (recipe on page 253) or
    ready-made tomato sauce

Chop the mint leaves very finely and put in a bowl. Add the grated cheese and mix well.

Cut the tripe into strips. Put the *sugo* in a pan, add the tripe, cover, and cook over low heat for about 30 minutes, or until tender. Sprinkle with the cheese mixture and serve immediately.

Uccelletti scappati · *Beef birds*
These skewers are excellent cooked on a grill over a moderate fire.
Makes 6 servings

3 slices *casereccio* bread (see page 273)
1¾ ounces (50 g) slab pancetta, or 1½ ounces (40 g) *lardo*
12 slices beef, each about 3 ounces (80 g), about 3¼ inches
    (9 cm) long, and ¾ inch (2 cm) wide
12 slices prosciutto, both fat and lean
24 sage leaves
1 tablespoon lard, or 2 tablespoons medium-fruity
    extra-virgin olive oil
salt
pepper

Cut the bread and pancetta into cubes. Pound the beef slices lightly with a meat tenderizer to flatten a little. Trim the prosciutto slices to the same size as the meat slices. Lay a slice of prosciutto on each meat slice and top with a sage leaf. Roll up each meat slice and secure closed with a toothpick.

Thread the meat rolls onto wooden skewers, alternating them with the bread and pancetta cubes and the remaining sage leaves. Brush the skewers with the lard, then sprinkle with salt and pepper. Bake in an oven preheated to 400°F (200°C) for about 20 minutes. Serve piping hot.

Pesce · Fish

Anguilla alla moda di papa Martino · *Grilled eel skewers*
Makes 4 servings

1 large eel, about 1¾ pounds (800 g)
7 ounces (200 g) coarse salt
2 cups (500 ml) Vernaccia or other sweet
  white wine
1 garlic clove
1 small bunch flat-leaf parsley
6 bay leaves
peppercorns
salt
2 tablespoons white wine vinegar

Rub the eel with the coarse salt to eliminate any sliminess on the skin. (This step will make it easier to grip the eel.) Make a circular cut at the base of the head and then cut down to the tail and slip off the skin. Discard the head. Rinse the eel well and cut it crosswise into segments about 2 inches (5 cm) long. Pour the wine into a large nonreactive container. Crush the garlic and add to the wine with a few parsley sprigs, 1 bay leaf, and 5 or 6 peppercorns. Put the eel segments in this mixture and marinate in the refrigerator for about 12 hours.

Remove the eel segments from the marinade, reserving the marinade. Cut the remaining bay leaves in half. Thread the eel segments onto wooden skewers, alternating them with the bay leaf halves. Grill over charcoal, turning often and basting with the marinade. When done, sprinkle with salt. Arrange the skewers on a platter and sprinkle with the vinegar. Let cool a bit before serving.

The skewers can also be cooked under a broiler or roasted in an oven preheated to 350°F (180°C).

Anguilla in guazzetto · *Eel with raisins and pine nuts*
Makes 4 servings

1 large eel, about 1¾ pounds (800 g)
7 ounces (200 g) coarse salt
3 white onions
1¾ ounces (50 g) raisins
1 ladleful vegetable broth
3 tablespoons medium-fruity extra-virgin olive oil
2 heaping tablespoons pine nuts
salt
pepper

Rub the eel with the coarse salt to eliminate any sliminess on the skin. (This step makes it easier to grip the eel.) Make a circular cut at the base of the head and then cut down to the tail and slip off the skin. Discard the head. Rinse the eel well and cut crosswise into segments about 1¼ inches (3 cm) long. Chop the onions. Immerse the raisins in a bowl of water to plump. Bring the broth to a boil in a small saucepan and keep hot.

Put the onions in a pan with the oil and sweat them over low heat for 5 to 6 minutes. When they are almost translucent, add the eel pieces and sauté over low heat for about 5 minutes, turning gently often. Add the broth and let it evaporate, then drain the raisins and add to the pan along with the pine nuts. Cover and finish cooking over low heat for about 15 minutes. Season with salt and pepper and serve immediately.

Baccalà al forno alla monticiana · *Baked salt cod and tomatoes*
Makes 6 servings

about 2 pounds (900 g) salt cod, soaked to remove the
   salt and ready to cook
1 pound (450 g) sauce tomatoes
leaves from 1 small bunch flat-leaf parsley
leaves from 1 small bunch basil
1 garlic clove
pepper
6 tablespoons (90 ml) intensely fruity extra-virgin
   olive oil

Scrape the skin off the cod and discard. Bone the fish carefully and cut it into pieces each weighing about 1¾ ounces (50 g). Rinse and pat dry. Peel the tomatoes and cut them into strips. Chop together the parsley and basil leaves and the garlic, put in a bowl, and season generously with pepper.

Put the fish in a pan in a single layer, add water just to cover, and bring to a boil. Lower the heat to medium and cook for about 3 minutes. Remove the cod from the water and discard the water.

Grease a baking pan with 2 tablespoons of the oil. Arrange the cod in a single layer in the pan. Cover with the tomato strips and the herbs, then drizzle with the remaining oil. Sprinkle with pepper, put into an oven preheated to 375°F (190°C), and cook for about 30 minutes. Let rest for a few minutes before serving.

Baccalà con i peperoni · Salt cod with bell peppers
Makes 5 servings

4 yellow bell peppers
1¾ pounds (800 g) salt cod, soaked to remove the salt and
  ready to cook
7 ounces (200 g) flour
14 ounces (400 g) white onions
scant 1 cup (200 ml) intensely fruity extra-virgin olive oil
14 ounces (400 g) canned tomatoes
salt
pepper

Hold the peppers over a gas flame until blistered on all sides (or blister under the broiler). Transfer them to a closed container, such as a paper bag or a pot with a lid, and leave for about 30 minutes. Then, peel, halve lengthwise, remove the seeds and membranes, and cut lengthwise into strips. Scrape the skin off the fish and discard. Bone the fish carefully, then rinse and dry and cut into serving pieces. Dredge in the flour, shaking off the excess, and set aside.

Thinly slice the onions and put in a saucepan with 3 tablespoons of the oil. Sauté over medium heat for about 5 minutes. When the onions are almost translucent, add the tomatoes and season with salt and pepper. Cook over low heat, breaking up the tomatoes with a fork as needed, for about 20 minutes. Add the pepper strips and cook for 10 minutes longer, still over low heat.

Heat the remaining oil in a skillet. Fry the cod on both sides until golden brown. Remove with a slotted spoon and add to the saucepan with the tomato sauce and peppers. Cook gently over medium heat for a few minutes. Serve hot.

Baccalà in agrodolce alla romana · *Sweet-and-sour salt cod*
Makes 6 servings

about 2¼ pounds (1 kg) salt cod, soaked to remove the salt
   and ready to cook
2 cups (500 ml) intensely fruity extra-virgin olive oil
11 ounces (300 g) flour
8 pitted prunes
1 ounce (30 g) raisins
2 rennet or Granny Smith apples
½ pesticide-free lemon
1 small white onion
2 garlic cloves
leaves from 1 small bunch flat-leaf parsley
scant ½ cup (100 ml) dry white table wine
2 tablespoons white wine vinegar
1 teaspoon (10 g) sugar
1 pound (450 g) tomato purée
1 tablespoon pine nuts
salt
pepper
¾-inch (2-cm) piece dried chile

Scrape the skin off the fish and discard. Bone the fish carefully and cut it in
half lengthwise and then into pieces about 2 inches (5 cm) wide. Rinse and dry.
Dredge the cod in the flour, shaking off the excess. Heat the oil in a skillet over
medium heat. Fry the cod on both sides until golden brown. Transfer with a
slotted spoon to paper towels to drain and keep warm. Reserve the pan with
the oil.

Immerse the prunes and raisins in separate bowls of water to plump. Peel
and slice the apples. Grate 1 tablespoon rind (colored part only) from the lemon.
Chop together finely the onion, garlic cloves, and parsley leaves. Put the mixture
in the reserved skillet and cook over medium heat for 5 minutes. When the onions are almost translucent, add the wine, vinegar, and sugar and let the liquids
evaporate over a lively flame for 5 minutes, stirring constantly. Now drain the
prunes and raisins and add them to the pan along with the tomato purée, apple
slices, pine nuts, and grated rind. Season with salt and pepper and continue cooking over medium heat for about 15 minutes.

Add the fried cod to the skillet with the sauce, then add the chile, cover, and
cook gently over medium heat, stirring gently, for about 15 minutes. If the sauce

has reduced too much, add a few tablespoons hot water. Discard the chile and serve hot.

Baccalà in guazzetto · Salt cod with raisins and pine nuts
Makes 5 servings

1¾ pounds (800 g) salt cod, soaked to remove the salt and
  ready to cook
4 white onions
6 tablespoons (90 ml) intensely fruity extra-virgin olive oil
2 heaping tablespoons pine nuts
1¾ ounces (50 g) raisins
14 ounces (400 g) tomato purée

Scrape the skin off the fish and discard. Bone the fish carefully and cut it into 2-inch (5-cm) pieces. Rinse and dry. Thinly slice the onions. Put the oil in a pan that will later hold all the fish pieces in a single layer. Add the onions and sweat them over medium heat for 6 to 7 minutes.

Put the fish in the pan with the onions and cook over low heat for about 6 minutes, turning gently. Add the pine nuts, raisins, and tomato purée. Cover and continue cooking over low heat for about 20 minutes. Serve immediately.

Calamari ripieni alla romana · Stuffed squid
Makes 4 servings

1¾ pounds (800 g) medium-size squid
3 garlic cloves
leaves from 1 small bunch flat-leaf parsley
3½ ounces (100 g) crustless bread
6 tablespoons (90 ml) medium-fruity extra-virgin olive oil
salt
freshly ground pepper
1 large white onion
9 ounces (250 g) tomato purée
scant ½ cup (100 ml) fish or vegetable broth

Clean the squid. Detach the heads from the body tubes. Discard the cartilaginous bone and guts in the tubes. Rinse the tubes and set aside. Discard the beak. Rinse the tentacles and chop very finely.

Chop 2 of the garlic cloves and the parsley leaves and put in a bowl. Crumble the bread finely into the bowl and add the chopped tentacles. Mix well, add 4 tablespoons of the oil, and mix well again. Season with salt and a generous grinding of pepper. Fill the squid with this mixture and sew the openings closed with coarse thread.

Chop the onion and put it in a large pan with the remaining oil. Cook over medium heat for about 5 minutes. When the onion is almost translucent, add the squid, lining them up in a single layer in the pan. Pour in the tomato purée and broth, cover, and cook over low heat for about 30 minutes, or until the sauce is quite thick. Transfer the squid to a warmed platter, snip and remove the thread, and spoon the sauce over the top. Serve hot.

Cefalo in gratella · Roasted gray mullet
This recipe also works well with grouper, gilt-head bream,
sea bass, or similar fish.
Makes 4 servings

1 lemon
1 gray mullet, about 2 pounds (1 kg), cleaned
    and ready to cook
salt
pepper
2 tablespoons intensely fruity extra-virgin
    olive oil

Cut the lemon in half. Squeeze the juice from half the lemon and reserve the juice. Cut the other half into wedges and set aside.

Rinse and dry the fish, then sprinkle with the lemon juice, salt, and pepper. Put a rack on a wide baking pan to collect the juices as the fish cooks and put the pan in an oven. Preheat the oven to 375°F (190°C). Brush the fish with the oil, place it on the hot rack, and roast for about 15 minutes, turning gently after 7 to 8 minutes and brushing with the liquid that has fallen into the pan. Remove from the oven, put the fish on a warmed oval plate, top with a second warmed oval plate, and set aside to rest for about 10 minutes on the door of the warm oven. Remove the top plate, garnish the fish with the lemon wedges, and serve.

Ciriole alla fiumarola · Small eels with anchovies and capers

Throughout Lazio and in the city of Rome, the small eel is also called *ciriola* or *fiumarola*. The large eel is known, incorrectly, as *capitone*.

Makes 4 servings

1½ pounds (700 g) small eels
1½ ounces (40 g) salt-packed anchovies, prepared as
　described on page 273
1¾ ounces (50 g) salt-packed capers, rinsed thoroughly to
　remove the salt
2 garlic cloves
2 tablespoons intensely fruity extra-virgin olive oil
salt
pepper
scant 1 cup (200 ml) dry white table wine
leaves from 1 small bunch flat-leaf parsley

Remove and discard the head of each eel. Rinse the eels carefully and dry them. Cut them into lengths of about 2 inches (5 cm).

Chop together finely the anchovies, capers, and garlic cloves. Put in a saucepan with the oil and sauté over medium heat for about 4 minutes. When the garlic begins to color, add the eel pieces and sprinkle with salt and pepper. Sauté over low heat for 2 to 3 minutes. Moisten with the wine, a little at a time, and finish cooking, about 15 minutes. Meanwhile chop the parsley leaves.

Remove from the heat, sprinkle with the parsley, and serve immediately.

Ciriole con i piselli · Small eels with peas
Makes 4 servings

1½ pounds (700 g) small eels
leaves from 1 small bunch marjoram
2 small white onions
1 pound (450 g) peas
2 tablespoons intensely fruity extra-virgin olive oil
9 ounces (250 g) canned tomatoes
scant ½ cup (100 ml) vegetable broth
salt

pepper

4 tablespoons dry white table wine

Remove and discard the head of each eel. Rinse the eels carefully and dry them. Cut them into lengths of about 2 inches (5 cm). Chop the marjoram leaves and the onions. Shell the peas.

Put the onions and oil in a saucepan over medium heat and cook for about 5 minutes. When the onions are almost translucent, add the peas, tomatoes, marjoram, and broth. Season with salt and pepper and cook over low heat for about 10 minutes, breaking up the tomatoes with a fork as needed. Add the eel pieces and finish cooking over low heat, stirring gently and basting with the wine, a tablespoon at a time, for about 10 minutes. Serve hot.

Filetti di trota in salsa ai tartufi · Trout fillets in truffle sauce
Makes 4 servings

1 trout, about 2 pounds (1 kg), cleaned and ready to cook

scant ½ cup (100 ml) milk

1 lemon

1 small black truffle

1 garlic clove

scant ½ cup (100 ml) medium-fruity extra-virgin olive oil, preferably from Sabina

1 tablespoon white-wine vinegar

salt

pepper

Poach the trout in lightly salted water to cover, mixed with the milk and flavored with a slice cut from the lemon. Let the fish cool in its broth, then fillet the fish and carefully remove the skin from each fillet. Put the fillets on a platter.

Grate the truffle. Crush the garlic clove. Put the oil in a small skillet, add the garlic and truffle, and cook over medium heat until the garlic just begins to color. Add the vinegar and let it evaporate for a minute or two. Discard the garlic and add the juice of the lemon, a pinch of salt, and a grinding of pepper. Cook the sauce over low heat for a few minutes, then pour it over the cooled fillets. Serve immediately.

Frittata di ranocchie · *Frog frittata*
Makes 4 servings

1 pound (450 g) small frogs
7 ounces (200 g) flour
2 cups (500 ml) lightly fruity extra-virgin olive oil
1 or 2 lemons
5 eggs
salt
pepper

Rinse, decapitate, and skin the frogs. Make an incision in the belly with a pointed knife and eviscerate them. Rinse carefully and dry.

Dredge the frogs in the flour, shaking off the excess. Heat the oil in a skillet over medium heat. Fry the frogs on both sides for 1 to 2 minutes on each side. Using a slotted spoon, transfer the frogs to a plate. Discard the oil in the pan, then return the frogs to the pan.

Halve and squeeze the lemons, measure out 3 tablespoons of the juice, and set aside. Break the eggs into a bowl and beat lightly with salt and pepper. Pour the eggs into the skillet with the frogs and add the lemon juice. Cook over medium heat, stirring, until the eggs begin to set. Lower the flame, cover, and cook the frittata for 3 to 4 minutes total, using a plate to turn the frittata (see page 274) when the first side is browned. Serve warm or at room temperature.

Gratin di pesce alla casalinga · *Fish gratin*
Makes 4 servings

3 eggs
1 pound (450 g) leftover cooked fish fillets
7 ounces (200 g) leftover mashed potatoes
6 tablespoons (80 g) butter
1 tablespoon dried bread crumbs

Separate the eggs. Beat the whites with a fork until stiff peaks form. Break up the fish, removing any errant bones. Mix the fish with the mashed potatoes and put the mixture in a saucepan. Add 3 tablespoons (40 g) of the butter and heat over low heat, stirring constantly, until hot. Remove from the heat and add the egg yolks, one at a time, beating well after each addition. Finally, fold in the beaten whites, using a rotary movement from the top to the bottom of the pan.

Grease an ovenproof dish with 1½ teaspoons (10 g) of the butter and pour in the fish mixture. Dust the surface with the bread crumbs and dot with the remaining butter. Bake in an oven preheated to 400°F (200°C) for about 20 minutes, or until the top is golden brown. Let the gratin rest for a few minutes before serving.

Luccio brodettato alla romana · Pike in egg-lemon sauce
This recipe is also good made with other freshwater fish of about the same size.
Makes 4 servings

1 pike, about 1¾ pounds (800 g)
1 carrot
1 celery rib
1 bay leaf
2 cups (500 ml) dry white table wine, preferably from
   the Castelli Romani
salt
pepper
2 tablespoons (30 g) butter
¾ ounce (20 g) flour
juice of ½ lemon
2 egg yolks
leaves from 1 small bunch flat-leaf parsley

With a knife, make an incision along the belly of the fish and remove and discard the guts. Discard the dorsal and ventral fins. Rinse and dry.

Cut the carrot and celery into large pieces. Put the fish in a fish poacher and add the carrot, celery, and bay leaf. Pour in the wine and enough water just to cover the fish. Season with salt and pepper and bring just to a boil. Reduce the heat to low and cook for 20 minutes. Leave the fish in its broth and keep warm.

Melt the butter in a saucepan. When it foams, add the flour and toast it over low heat for 1 minute, stirring constantly. Add a few ladlefuls of the fish broth and cook for 10 minutes longer over low heat. Remove from the heat, add the lemon juice, season with salt and pepper, and add the egg yolks, one at a time, beating steadily with a whisk. Chop the parsley leaves.

Transfer the fish to a warmed platter and gently remove the skin. Nap the fish with the sauce and sprinkle with the parsley. Serve immediately.

Merluzzo al gratin · *Cod gratin*
Makes 4 servings

2 cod, about 1 pound (450 g) each
1 garlic clove
leaves from 1 small bunch flat-leaf parsley
3 salt-packed anchovies, prepared as described on page 273
6 tablespoons (90 ml) medium-fruity extra-virgin olive oil
freshly ground pepper
1 tablespoon dried bread crumbs

Remove the head and tail from each fish. Make an incision along the belly of each fish and remove and discard the guts, then remove and discard the backbone, leaving the fillets attached. Rinse and dry.

Chop together finely the garlic clove and parsley leaves. Put the anchovies in a mortar and add 2 tablespoons of the oil and a generous grinding of pepper. Crush with a pestle until the anchovies are almost reduced to a paste. Add the garlic and parsley and mix well.

Grease a baking pan with 1 tablespoon of the oil. Lay the fillets, close together and skin side down, on the bottom. Spread the fillets with the anchovy sauce, sprinkle with the bread crumbs, and drizzle with the remaining 3 tablespoons oil. Put in an oven preheated to 400°F (200°C) for about 15 minutes, or until just cooked through. Let rest for a few minutes before serving.

Ombrina al forno · *Oven-roasted ombrine*
Sea bass (*spigola*) or gilt-head bream (*orata*) may be used instead of *ombrina,* a Mediterranean fish prized for its delicate flesh.
Makes 4 servings

4 *ombrina* steaks, about 5 ounces (150 g) each
1 pound (450 g) boiling potatoes
1 garlic clove
2 oil-packed anchovy fillets
leaves from 1 small bunch flat-leaf parsley
3 small white onions
6 tablespoons (90 ml) intensely fruity extra-virgin olive oil
salt
pepper

Rinse and dry the fish. Bring about 2 quarts (2 liters) water to a boil and drop in the potatoes. Drain them when they are half done, then peel and slice. Drain the anchovies, then chop together finely together with the garlic clove and parsley leaves. Thinly slice the onions.

Grease a baking pan with 1 tablespoon of the oil. Divide the potatoes in half and lay half of the slices in a single layer in the baking pan. Sprinkle with the onions and half the chopped anchovy mixture. Drizzle with 2 tablespoons of the oil and lay the fish slices on top, close together. Season with salt and pepper and arrange the remaining potato slices on top in a single layer. Spread the remaining anchovy mixture over the potatoes and drizzle with the remaining oil.

Bake in an oven preheated to 400°F (200°C) for about 20 minutes, or until lightly browned on top. Let rest for a few minutes before serving.

Palombo alla romana con i piselli · Dogfish with peas

The *palombo*, known as dogfish or smooth hound in English, is a small Mediterranean shark (at most about three feet/one meter long, usually shorter).

Makes 4 servings

4 dogfish steaks, about 5 ounces (150 g) each
1 small white onion
leaves from 1 small bunch flat-leaf parsley
2 pounds (1 kg) peas
1 tablespoon tomato paste
4 tablespoons medium-fruity extra-virgin olive oil
salt
pepper

Rinse and dry the fish. Chop together finely the onion and parsley leaves. Shell the peas. Dilute the tomato paste in 1 ladleful hot water.

Sweat the onion and parsley in the oil in a pan over low heat for a few minutes. Add the peas, the diluted tomato paste, and as much boiling water as needed just to cover the peas. Season with salt and pepper and continue cooking over medium heat for about 8 minutes, or until the peas are tender.

Add the fish steaks and cook over low heat for 2 to 3 minutes, turning them gently. The pan juices should have thickened quite a bit. Serve immediately.

Pesce cappone imprigionato · Red gurnard in a pastry crust

Imprigionato means "imprisoned." The *pesce cappone,* known by numerous names in Italy, has a reddish skin, large, bony head, and protruberant eyes. Its white flesh is delicate and delicious.

Makes 8 servings

1⅓ pounds (600 g) Manila clams

1 red gurnard, about 2½ pounds (1.2 kg)

24 small shrimp

1 garlic clove

2 tablespoons medium-fruity extra-virgin olive oil

9 ounces (250 g) fresh button mushrooms

1 small white onion

leaves from 1 small bunch flat-leaf parsley

4 teaspoons (20 g) butter

salt

pepper

4 cups (960 ml) béchamel sauce

1 egg yolk

1⅓ pounds (600 g) *pâte brisée* (see note on *panzerotti di maiale,* page 103)

Soak the clams for a few hours in lightly salted water to purge them. With a long, sharp knife, make an incision along the backbone of the fish. Open the fish and remove the first fillet. Discard the backbone and remove the second fillet, discarding the guts as you go. Peel the fillets and rinse gently. Dry them, then cut each fillet into several pieces. Rinse and peel the shrimp. Crush the garlic clove.

Drain and rinse the clams carefully. Crush the garlic clove and put it in a pan with the oil. Add the clams, cover, and cook over a lively flame for about 5 minutes, or just until the clams open. Lift the clams out of the pan and remove them from their shells, discarding any that failed to open. Strain the pan broth. Set broth and clams aside.

Using a small knife, gently scrape the surface of the mushrooms to eliminate any clinging dirt. Wipe with a damp cloth and thinly slice.

Chop together finely the onion and parsley leaves. Put in a saucepan with the butter and sauté over medium heat for about 5 minutes. When the onion is almost translucent, add the mushrooms, season with salt and pepper, and cook over a lively flame for about 10 minutes.

Put the béchamel in a bowl, add the clam broth, fish pieces, shrimp, clams, and the cooked mushrooms with their pan juices. Mix well and adjust the salt.

Beat the egg yolk in a bowl. Roll out the *pâte brisée* into a rectangle about 14 by 8 inches (35 by 20 cm) and spread the fish mixture along the long axis a bit below the center. Fold the pastry over and press the edges to seal closed, as though making a large *raviolo*. Transfer the pastry package to a baking pan and brush the surface with the beaten yolk. Bake in an oven preheated to 400°F (200°C) for about 20 minutes, or until golden brown. Let rest for a few minutes before serving.

Tortino di sarde e carciofi · *Baked sardines and artichokes*
From the Roman Jewish tradition.
Makes 6 servings

1¾ pounds (800 g) fresh sardines
juice of 1 lemon
6 artichokes
leaves from 1 small bunch flat-leaf parsley
6 tablespoons (90 ml) intensely fruity extra-virgin olive oil
salt
pepper
1 tablespoon dried bread crumbs

Remove and discard the heads of the sardines. Make an incision along the belly of each fish, gut the fish, and then open it up like a book and remove the backbone. Rinse the fish well and close them up again.

Fill a bowl with water and add the lemon juice. One at a time, trim the artichokes, including their stems, as described on page 273. Cut each artichoke in half lengthwise and remove and discard any choke. Thinly slice the artichoke halves and the stems lengthwise and immerse them in the lemon water. Chop the parsley leaves finely.

Grease an ovenproof dish with 2 tablespoons of the oil. Arrange half the artichokes in a layer on the bottom of the dish. Arrange half the sardines in a single layer on top. Sprinkle with half the parsley, season with salt and pepper, and drizzle with 2 tablespoons of the oil. Layer the remaining artichokes on top and finish with a layer of sardines. Sprinkle with the remaining parsley and the bread crumbs and season with salt and pepper. Drizzle with the remaining 2 tablespoons oil.

Bake in an oven preheated to 350°F (180°C) for about 30 minutes, or until the surface is lightly browned. Serve hot.

Sarde ripiene e fritte · Fried stuffed sardines
Makes 6 servings

24 fresh sardines
7 ounces (200 g) spinach
4 teaspoons (20 g) butter
salt
2 eggs
2 ounces (60 g) flour
1¼ cups (300 ml) intensely fruity extra-virgin olive oil

Remove and discard the heads of the sardines. Make an incision along the belly of each fish, gut the fish, and then open it up like a book and remove the backbone. Trim and rinse the spinach. Put it in a pot, cover, and cook over medium heat in just the rinsing water clinging to the leaves. Drain the spinach, squeeze well, and chop.

Melt the butter in a saucepan over medium heat. When it foams, add the spinach and cook gently for about 3 minutes. Season with salt and remove from the heat. Lay the sardines flat, skin side down. Spread an equal amount of the spinach on each sardine, then roll up each sardine and secure closed with a toothpick.

Break the eggs into a bowl and beat gently with a little salt. Dredge the sardine rolls first in the flour, shaking off the excess, then in the beaten egg. Heat the oil in a skillet over medium heat. Fry the sardine rolls on both sides for about 5 minutes total, or until golden brown. Drain them on paper towels and serve hot.

Seppie con i carciofi · Cuttlefish with artichokes
Makes 4 servings

1½ pounds (700 g) small cuttlefish
4 artichokes
1 lemon
scant 1 cup (200 ml) fish broth
1 small white onion
1 garlic clove
4 tablespoons intensely fruity extra-virgin olive oil
salt
pepper
leaves from 1 small bunch flat-leaf parsley

Wash and dry the cuttlefish and cut them into rings. (If the cuttlefish are not very small, you will need to remove the beak from each one.)

Fill a bowl with water. Halve the lemon and squeeze the juice from half the lemon into the water. One at a time, trim the artichokes, including their stems, as described on page 273. Cut each artichoke in half lengthwise and remove and discard any choke. Cut each half into two wedges and immerse them in the lemon water. Squeeze the other half of the lemon and reserve the juice.

Bring the broth to a boil in a small pan. Chop together finely the onion and garlic clove and put in a saucepan with the oil. Sauté over medium heat for about 5 minutes. When the onion is almost translucent, drain the artichokes well and add them to the pan. Cook over low heat for 5 to 6 minutes, or until the artichokes are tender, adding a few tablespoons of the boiling broth, a little at a time.

Add the cuttlefish and cook gently over low heat for a couple of minutes, stirring. Add the rest of the boiling broth, season with salt and pepper, and continue cooking over low heat for about 10 minutes. Meanwhile, chop the parsley leaves.

Remove the cuttlefish from the heat and sprinkle with the reserved lemon juice and the chopped parsley. Mix well and serve immediately.

Spigola alla romana · Sea bass with mushrooms
Makes 4 servings

2 sea bass, about 1 pound (450 g) each
pepper
7 ounces (200vg) fresh button mushrooms
1 tablespoon flour
leaves from 1 small bunch flat-leaf parsley
3 small white onions
1 garlic clove
2 oil-packed anchovy fillets
4 tablespoons medium-fruity extra-virgin olive oil
4 teaspoons (20 g) butter
4 tablespoons dry white table wine, preferably from the
    Castelli Romani
salt

With a long, sharp knife, make an incision along the backbone of the fish. Open the fish and remove the first fillet. Discard the backbone and remove the second fillet, discarding the guts as you go. Rinse and dry the fillets. Sprinkle the fillets with pepper and set aside.

Using a small knife, gently scrape the surface of the mushrooms to eliminate any clinging dirt. Wipe with a damp cloth and thinly slice. Toss the mushroom slices with the flour. Chop the parsley leaves.

Chop together finely the onions and garlic clove. Drain the anchovies and chop finely. Put the onions and garlic in a saucepan with the oil and butter and sauté over medium heat for about 5 minutes. When the onions are almost translucent, add the anchovies and cook, crushing them with a fork, until dissolved. Add the fish fillets and then the wine and season moderately with salt. Cook over medium heat, turning once, for just a few minutes on each side. Remove the fillets from the pan, being careful not to break them, and place on a warmed platter. Keep warm. Reserve the pan juices in the pan.

Put the mushrooms in the fish pan, season with salt and pepper, and cook over a lively flame for 5 or 6 minutes. Remove from the heat, sprinkle with the parsley, and pour the mushroom sauce over the fillets. Serve immediately.

Storione in fricandò · Stewed sturgeon
Makes 4 servings

1 piece sturgeon, about 1¾ pounds (800 g) and 8 inches
   (20 cm) long
1¾ ounces (50 g) *lardo*
salt
pepper
1¾ ounces (50 g) flour
1 pesticide-free lemon
scant ½ cup (100 ml) meat broth
2 tablespoons lightly fruity extra-virgin olive oil
4 teaspoons (20 g) butter
scant ½ cup (100 ml) dry white table wine, preferably from
   the Castelli Romani

Rinse and dry the fish. Cut the *lardo* into strips and then into small dice. Sprinkle with salt and pepper. Make small slits all over the fish and stick the *lardo* pieces into the slits. Tie the fish with kitchen string as if it were a meat roast, then dredge in the flour, shaking off the excess. Grate half of the lemon rind (colored part only), then halve the lemon and squeeze the juice from both halves.

Bring the broth to a boil in a small saucepan. Heat the oil and butter in a pot just large enough to hold the fish. Brown the fish over medium heat for 1 to 2 minutes, turning gently with the help of two spoons to brown all sides. Add the wine and let it evaporate over a lively flame. When the odor of the alcohol has disappeared, add the grated rind. Continue cooking over low heat for 20 minutes, adding the broth a little at a time.

When the fish is cooked, transfer it to a warmed platter and pour the lemon juice over the top. Let rest for 10 minutes, then slice. Serve the slices drenched in the sauce.

Stufato di alici e indivia · Stew of anchovies and curly endive
From the Roman Jewish tradition.
Makes 6 servings

about 2 pounds (1 kg) fresh anchovies
1 head curly endive, about 2 pounds (1 kg)
1 garlic clove
6 tablespoons (90 ml) intensely fruity extra-virgin
  olive oil
salt
pepper

Remove the heads and the guts from the anchovies. Rinse very well and blot dry.

Separate the endive leaves. Crush the garlic clove. Bring 4 cups (1 liter) lightly salted water to a boil, drop in the endive leaves, and leave for a few seconds. Drain the leaves, squeeze well, and put them in a skillet with the garlic and 4 tablespoons of the oil. Cook gently over medium heat for a few minutes, then remove from the heat.

Grease a baking pan with the remaining 2 tablespoons oil and line the bottom with half the endive leaves. Lay the anchovies on top, close together, then sprinkle with salt and pepper. Top with the remaining endive leaves. Bake in an oven preheated to 350°F (180°C) for about 20 minutes. Serve hot.

Triglie con i pinoli e l'uvetta · Red mullet with pine nuts and raisins
From the Roman Jewish tradition.
Makes 4 servings

8 red mullets
1 ounce (30 g) raisins
4 tablespoons medium-fruity extra-virgin olive oil

scant ½ cup (100 ml) white-wine vinegar
1 tablespoon pine nuts
salt

With a knife, make an incision along the belly of each fish and remove and discard the guts. Discard the fins and scale the fish, then rinse and dry. Immerse the raisins in a small bowl of water to plump.

Grease a wide pan just large enough to hold the fish with 1 tablespoon of the oil. Put the fish close together in the pan and moisten with the vinegar. Drain the raisins and sprinkle them and the pine nuts over the top. Season with salt.

Cover and cook over a lively flame for 6 to 7 minutes, shaking the pan gently. Turn the fish to cook both sides. When the fish are done, transfer them to a warmed platter. Return the pan with the pan juices to the stove top and reduce over medium heat for a couple of minutes. Pour the contents of the pan over the fish and serve immediately.

Triglie di scoglio alla romana · Red mullet with tomato sauce
Makes 4 servings

4 red mullets, about 7 ounces (200 g) each
salt
pepper
juice of ½ lemon
2 garlic cloves
leaves from 1 small bunch flat-leaf parsley
leaves from 2 sprigs oregano
1 pound (450 g) sauce tomatoes
4 tablespoons medium-fruity extra-virgin olive oil
1 tablespoon dried bread crumbs

With a knife, make an incision along the belly of each fish and remove and discard the guts. Discard the fins and scale the fish, then rinse and dry. Season lightly with salt and pepper inside and out, then sprinkle with 1 tablespoon lemon juice.

Chop together finely the garlic cloves and the parsley and oregano leaves. Peel the tomatoes and cut into strips. Grease a baking pan just large enough to hold the fish with 1 tablespoon of the oil. Put the fish close together in the pan. Sprinkle first with the chopped herb mixture and then with the bread crumbs. Sprinkle the tomatoes over the top, season moderately with salt, and then drizzle with the remaining oil.

Bake in an oven preheated to 400°F (200°C) for about 15 minutes, or until the surface is lightly browned. Let rest for a few minutes before serving.

VERDURE E LEGUMI · VEGETABLES AND LEGUMES

"Frittata" di patate e cipolle alla romana · Eggless potato and onion "frittata"

This is actually a *tortino,* a sort of flan, but in Rome it is always called a frittata. A tasty variant is the addition of a tablespoon of pork cracklings (or finely diced prosciutto) to the onions as you sauté them.

Makes 4 servings

4 pounds (800 g) floury potatoes
14 ounces (400 g) white onions
1¾ ounces (50 g) lard, or 6 tablespoons (90 ml) medium-fruity extra-virgin olive oil
salt
pepper

Bring about 3 quarts (3 liters) lightly salted water to a boil and drop in the potatoes. When the potatoes are tender, drain, peel, and slice them.

Slice the onions thinly. Put them in a large skillet with the lard and sauté over medium heat for about 5 minutes. When they are almost translucent, add the potatoes and mash with a wooden spoon into a paste. Season with salt and pepper and sauté over medium heat for 5 minutes, or until browned on the first side. Use a plate to turn the frittata (see page 274) and cook until nicely colored on the second side. Serve warm or room temperature.

Bietole al pomodoro · Chard with tomatoes
Makes 4 servings

1¾ pounds (800 g) chard
9 ounces (250 g) sauce tomatoes, preferably San Marzano
5 oil-packed anchovy fillets
2 garlic cloves
3 tablespoons intensely fruity extra-virgin olive oil
pepper

Discard the toughest ribs and rinse the chard. Put in a pot, cover, and cook in just the rinsing water clinging to the leaves until wilted. Drain the chard, squeeze well, and chop, not too finely. Peel the tomatoes and cut them into small pieces.

Drain the anchovy fillets. Crush the garlic cloves and put them in a pan with the oil and the anchovy fillets. Sauté over medium heat for about 2 minutes, or until the anchovies have dissolved. Add the tomatoes and cook the sauce over medium heat for about 15 minutes. Discard the garlic, add the chard, sprinkle with pepper, and let the flavors blend over low heat for a few minutes. Serve piping hot.

Puntarelle in salsa di alici · Puntarelle with anchovy dressing

In Rome, the stalks of the Catalonian chicory (*la catalogna*) are known as *puntarelle,* and this recipe is a peculiarly Roman way of treating it. The plant consists of an elongated head with pointed leaves surrounding a center formed of hollow stalks, which are the basis of this dish, but only after painstaking trimming. *Puntarelle* are increasingly available outside Italy, but if you can't find them, the dressing is delicious on curly endive, romaine, radicchio, or any other salad that can defend itself against the strong flavors.

Makes 4 servings

2 heads Catalonian chicory
8 oil-packed anchovy fillets
1 garlic clove
2 tablespoons white-wine vinegar
4 tablespoons intensely fruity extra-virgin olive oil
freshly ground pepper

Remove the outer leaves of the chicory and reserve for another use. Cut off the shoots about 4 inches (10 cm) above the base. With a small sharp knife, cut the shoots lengthwise into narrow strips. As you work, drop the strips into a bowl of cold water and set the bowl aside until the strips have curled.

Drain the anchovy fillets, cut each fillet into a few pieces, and put them in a mortar. Add the garlic clove and vinegar and begin to work the mixture energetically with a pestle. When the ingredients are completely mashed into a paste, pour in the oil and mix to make a very fluid sauce. Drain the *puntarelle* well and put in a salad bowl. Dress first with the sauce and then with a generous grinding of pepper. Toss, then let rest for 10 to 15 minutes before serving.

Broccoletti "strascinati" · *Sautéed broccoli rabe*

If the broccoli rabe is young and tender, it can be cooked
directly in the skillet without parboiling. *Strascinati* means
"dragged," as the vegetable through the flavored oil.

Makes 4 servings

3¼ pounds (1.5 kg) broccoli rabe
2 garlic cloves
½- or ¾-inch (1- to 2-cm) piece dried chile
4 tablespoons intensely fruity extra-virgin olive oil
salt

Remove the stems, strings, and the toughest leaves from the broccoli rabe. Bring
3 quarts (3 liters) salted water to a boil, drop in the broccoli rabe, and parboil for
2 minutes. Drain well and chop, not too finely. Crush the garlic cloves.

Put the garlic cloves and chile in a large skillet with the oil. Cook over medium heat for about 4 minutes, or until almost browned. Discard the garlic
and chile and add the broccoli rabe. Cook gently over medium heat for a few
minutes, stirring constantly. At the end of cooking, sprinkle with salt and
serve hot.

Broccoli al prosciutto · *Broccoli with prosciutto*

This recipe works well with cauliflower, too.

Makes 4 servings

1 head *broccolo romanesco* (see page 273), about
    2¼ pounds (1 kg)
4 ounces (100 g) sliced prosciutto
3½ tablespoons (50 g) lard, or 2 tablespoons intensely fruity
    extra-virgin olive oil
salt
pepper

Discard the tough outer leaves and core of the *broccolo* and cut into florets.
Bring 2 quarts (2 liters) salted water to a boil and drop in the florets. Cook until
al dente, then drain. Cut the prosciutto into strips.

Heat the lard in a skillet over medium heat. Add the *broccolo* florets and cook gently for a few minutes. Add the prosciutto strips, season with salt and pepper, and finish cooking for 6 to 7 minutes, stirring. Serve hot.

Broccoli stufati · Broccolo romanesco in red wine
Makes 4 servings

1 head *broccolo romanesco* (see page 273), about 3 pounds (1.3 kg)
1 garlic clove
scant 1 cup (200 ml) intensely fruity extra-virgin olive oil
scant 1 cup (200 ml) dry red table wine
salt
pepper

Discard the tough outer leaves from the *broccolo*. Cut off the base and dice the core. Cut the head into florets. Crush the garlic clove. Put all the *broccolo* florets and core pieces and the garlic in a pan with the oil. Sauté over medium heat for about 3 minutes, then add the wine and season with salt and pepper.

Cover and cook over low heat for 10 to 15 minutes, or until the *broccolo* is tender. Serve hot.

Cappelle di porcini arrosto · Roast porcini caps
Makes 4 servings

8 large fresh porcini mushrooms
4 tablespoons intensely fruity extra-virgin olive oil
leaves from 1 small bunch flat-leaf parsley
1 garlic clove
salt
pepper

Remove the stems from the mushrooms. Scrape the surface of the caps gently with a small knife to remove any clinging dirt, then wipe with a damp cloth. Grease a baking pan with 1 tablespoon of the oil and put the mushroom caps, close together and head down, in the pan.

Chop together finely the parsley and garlic clove and put them in a small bowl. Add 2 tablespoons of the oil and a pinch each of salt and pepper. Mix well, then pour over the mushrooms. Drizzle the remaining 1 tablespoon oil over the caps.

Bake in an oven preheated to 350°F (180°C) for about 20 minutes. Serve hot.

Carciofi alla giudia · Deep-fried whole artichokes
From the Roman Jewish tradition.
Makes 4 servings

juice of 1 lemon
4 large artichokes
about 1⅔ cups (400 ml) lightly fruity olive oil for
    deep-frying
salt
pepper

Fill a bowl with water and add the lemon juice. One at a time, trim the artichokes as described on page 273, but remove the stems, and immerse them in the lemon water. When all the artichokes are trimmed, drain and let dry. One at a time, put the artichokes head down on a flat surface and press them gently while giving them a little twist with the flat of the hand so the remaining leaves open like a flower.

Heat the oil in a saucepan to 300°F (150°C), then lower the heat slightly. Put the artichokes, head down, in the hot oil, press down with a fork, and cook until they are just golden brown. Turn the artichokes over and continue to fry, still pressing with the fork, until the heart is tender. Drain on paper towels. Sprinkle with salt and pepper just before serving.

Carciofi alla romana · Braised whole artichokes
Makes 4 servings

juice of 1 lemon
8 artichokes
2 garlic cloves
leaves from 1 small bunch flat-leaf parsley
leaves from 1 small bunch *mentuccia* (see page 274)

1¼ cups (300 ml) intensely fruity extra-virgin olive oil
salt
pepper

Fill a bowl with water and add the lemon juice. One at a time, trim the artichokes, including about 2¾ inches (7 cm) of their stems, as described on page 273, and immerse in the lemon water. When all the artichokes and stems are trimmed, remove the stems from the lemon water and chop together with the garlic cloves and the parsley and *mentuccia* leaves. Put everything in a bowl, add 1 tablespoon of the oil, and season with salt and pepper. Mix thoroughly. Fill the cavity in the center of the each artichoke with an equal amount of this mixture, and sprinkle the outside of the artichokes with salt.

Put the artichokes, head down and close together, in a deep pan (preferably earthenware) just large enough to hold them. Pour the remaining oil over the artichokes and then add a scant 1 cup (200 ml) water to the pan. Put a cloth or a piece of thick paper (like a grocery bag) between the pan and its lid. Bring to a boil and then reduce the heat to low. After about 20 minutes, check to see if the artichokes are tender. They should be quite tender and the water completely evaporated.

Let rest for 10 minutes before serving to allow the artichokes to absorb the cooking liquid. These artichokes are also excellent served at room temperature.

Carciofi con i piselli · Artichokes with peas
Makes 4 servings

juice of 1 lemon
4 artichokes
1 small white onion
2 ounces (60 g) sliced prosciutto
2 ounces (60 g) lard, or 4 tablespoons intensely fruity
   extra-virgin olive oil
salt
pepper
11 ounces (300 g) shelled peas

Fill a bowl with water and add the lemon juice. One at a time, trim the artichokes, including their stems, as described on page 273. Cut each artichoke in half lengthwise and remove and discard any choke. Cut each half into two wedges. Slice the stems. Put all the artichoke pieces in the lemon water.

Chop together finely the onion and prosciutto. Put in a pan with the lard and sauté over medium heat for about 4 minutes. When the onion is almost translucent, drain the artichoke wedges and stem slices well and add them to the onion. Season with salt and pepper and cook over medium heat until half done. Add the peas and continue cooking over low heat for about 15 minutes, stirring. Serve hot.

Carciofi con il guanciale · Artichokes with guanciale
Makes 4 servings

juice of 1 lemon
8 small artichokes
3½ ounces (100 g) *guanciale* or pancetta
2 tablespoons (30 g) lard, or 5 tablespoons intensely fruity
  extra-virgin olive oil
6 tablespoons (90 ml) dry white table wine, preferably from
  the Castelli Romani
salt
freshly ground pepper

Fill a bowl with water and add the lemon juice. One at a time, trim the artichokes, including about 2 inches (5 cm) of their stems, as described on page 273. Cut each artichoke in half lengthwise and remove and discard any choke. Cut each half into two wedges. Put all the artichoke pieces in the lemon water.

Dice the *guanciale* and put in a pan (preferably earthenware) with the lard. Cook over medium heat for 4 to 5 minutes. When the fat has almost completely melted, drain the artichokes well and add them to the pan. Cook gently for a few minutes, stirring. Moisten with the wine, season with salt and a grinding of pepper, and finish cooking over low heat, about 10 minutes. Serve hot.

Carciofi fritti alla romana · Deep-fried artichoke wedges
Makes 4 servings

2 eggs
1¾ ounces (50 g) flour
2 cups (500 ml) lightly fruity extra-virgin olive oil
salt

pepper
juice of 1 lemon
4 large artichokes

Break the eggs into a bowl. Add the flour, 2 tablespoons of the oil, and a pinch each of salt and pepper. Whisk until the batter is smooth. Let rest for about 1 hour.

Fill a bowl with water and add the lemon juice. One at a time, trim the artichokes, including their stems, as described on page 273. Cut each artichoke in half lengthwise and remove and discard any choke. Cut each half into six wedges. Put all the artichoke wedges in the lemon water.

Heat the oil in a deep skillet to 300°F (150°C), then lower the heat slightly. Meanwhile, drain the artichokes well, then dip them in the batter and allow the excess to drip off. Drop the pieces into the hot oil, a few at a time; they will cook in just a few minutes. Scoop them out with a slotted spoon and drain on paper towels. Just before serving, no sooner, sprinkle them with salt. Serve piping hot.

Carciofi in fricassea alla romana · Artichokes in cream
Makes 4 servings

1½ lemons
12 small artichokes
leaves from 1 small bunch flat-leaf parsley
leaves from 1 small bunch marjoram or basil
5 eggs
6 tablespoons (90 ml) heavy cream
salt
pepper
3½ tablespoons (50 g) butter

Fill a bowl with water and squeeze in the juice of 1 lemon. One at a time, trim the artichokes, including their stems, as described on page 273. Cut each artichoke in half lengthwise and remove and discard any choke. Cut each half into two wedges and immerse in the lemon water.

Bring 4 cups (1 liter) lightly salted water to a boil. Drain the artichokes, add them to the boiling water, and boil for about 10 minutes. Meanwhile, chop together finely the parsley and marjoram leaves and put in a small bowl. Break the eggs into a bowl. Squeeze in the juice from the remaining lemon half and add the cream and a pinch each of salt and pepper. Beat lightly and set aside.

Melt the butter in a large skillet. When the butter foams, drain the artichokes well, add them to the pan, and cook gently over low heat for a few minutes. Add the egg mixture and stir with a fork until the eggs are lightly set but still creamy, 1 to 2 minutes. Serve hot.

Cavolfiore fritto in pastella · Batter-fried cauliflower
Makes 4 servings

2 tablespoons dry white table wine
½ ounce (14 g) fresh cake yeast
1 whole egg plus 1 yolk
7 ounces (200 g) flour
2½ cups (600 ml) lightly fruity extra-virgin olive oil
salt
pepper
1 cauliflower, about 2 pounds (1 kg)

Put the wine in a bowl and crumble in the yeast. Mix gently, then cover the bowl and let the yeast sit for 6 to 7 minutes, or until it begins to foam. Pour the yeast mixture into a food processor, add the whole egg and the egg yolk, the flour, 2 tablespoons of the oil, and a pinch each of salt and pepper. Process until a smooth batter forms. Let rest for about 2 hours.

Meanwhile, trim the cauliflower and cut into florets. Bring 2 quarts (2 liters) lightly salted water to a boil. Drop in the cauliflower florets and boil until al dente, then drain.

When the batter has rested for enough time, heat the oil in a deep skillet to 300°F (150°C), then lower the heat slightly. Dip the florets in the batter and allow the excess to drip off. Drop the florets into the hot oil, a few at a time; they will cook in 3 to 4 minutes. Scoop them out with a slotted spoon and drain on paper towels. Serve hot.

Cavolfiore in tegame con le alici · Cauliflower with anchovies
Makes 4 servings

1 cauliflower, about 2 pounds (1 kg)
5 tablespoons white-wine vinegar
4 oil-packed anchovy fillets, drained

2 garlic cloves
4 tablespoons intensely fruity extra-virgin olive oil
salt
freshly ground pepper

Trim the cauliflower and cut it into florets. Rinse the florets in water acidulated with the vinegar. Bring 2 quarts (2 liters) lightly salted water to a boil. Drop in the cauliflower florets and boil until al dente, then drain. Meanwhile, drain the anchovies, then chop finely with the garlic cloves.

Heat the oil in a skillet over medium heat and cook the anchovies and garlic for 4 to 5 minutes, or until the anchovies have completely dissolved. Drain the cauliflower and add to the pan. Cook gently over low heat for a few minutes, stirring gently. Season with salt and pepper and serve hot.

Ceci al rosmarino · Chickpeas with rosemary
Makes 4 servings

1⅓ pounds (600 g) dried chickpeas, soaked and ready to
  cook
½ white onion
3 tablespoons intensely fruity extra-virgin olive oil
needles from 1 sprig rosemary
freshly ground pepper

Bring 2 quarts (2 liters) salted water to a boil. Add the chickpeas and cook over very low heat until tender; the timing will depend on the age of the chickpeas. Check after 20 minutes and frequently thereafter.

Meanwhile, thinly slice the onion. Put it in a saucepan with the oil and the rosemary needles and cook over medium heat for about 5 minutes. When the onion is almost translucent, drain the chickpeas and add to the onion. Season with a generous grinding of pepper and let flavors blend over low heat for 5 or 6 minutes, stirring. Serve hot.

Cianfotta · Mixed summer vegetables
Makes 4 servings

1 pound (500 g) sweet peppers
1 large eggplant

1 large, ripe tomato
14 ounces (400 g) potatoes (any kind)
3 large onions
1 garlic clove
4 tablespoons extra-virgin olive oil
3½ ounces (100 g) Gaeta or similar black olives
salt
pepper
leaves from 1 small bunch basil
leaves from 1 small bunch parsley
pinch of dried oregano

Halve the peppers, remove the seeds and membranes, and cut lengthwise into strips. Dice the eggplant and tomato. Peel and dice the potatoes. Chop the onions. Crush the garlic clove.

Sauté the onions and garlic in a large pan with the oil. Add all the prepared vegetables and the olives, season with salt and pepper, cover, and cook over medium heat for about 40 minutes, stirring often.

Meanwhile, chop together the basil and parsley leaves and add them to the pan when the vegetables are done. Add the oregano, then stir and let any remaining liquid evaporate over a lively flame. Serve hot or cold.

Cicoria "strascinata" · Sautéed chicory
Makes 4 servings

3¼ pounds (1.5 kg) wild chicory
2 garlic cloves
½- or ¾-inch (1- to 2-cm) piece dried chile
2½ tablespoons (40 g) lard, or 5 tablespoons intensely fruity
   extra-virgin olive oil

Trim the chicory carefully, without separating the leaves at the base. Bring about 3 quarts (3 liters) salted water to a boil. Add the chicory and boil until al dente.

Meanwhile, crush the garlic cloves and crumble the chile. Put them in a skillet with the lard and sauté over medium heat for about 5 minutes. When the garlic is almost golden, drain the chicory but leave it still dripping wet and add it to the pan. Cook gently, stirring constantly, until the water evaporates completely. Serve hot.

Cipolle al forno · Baked white onions
Makes 4 servings

> 4 large white onions, preferably flat, of uniform size with
>   their skin
> 6 tablespoons (90 ml) intensely fruity extra-virgin olive oil
> 2 tablespoons white-wine vinegar
> salt
> pepper

Wipe the onions with a damp cloth but do not peel. Put them in a baking pan in which they fit snugly. Cook in an oven preheated to 350°F (180°C) for about 30 minutes, or more if they are large.

Let the onions cool, peel them, and cut them into wedges. Toss with the oil, vinegar, salt, and pepper and serve.

Cipolline alla romana in agrodolce · Sweet-and-sour onions
Makes 4 servings

> 1⅓ pounds (600 g) *cipolline* (very small, flat onions)
> 1 ounce (30 g) prosciutto fat
> 1 garlic clove
> 4 teaspoons (20 g) lard, or 4 tablespoons intensely fruity
>   extra-virgin olive oil
> 2 ounces (60 g) sugar
> salt
> scant ½ cup (100 ml) white-wine vinegar

Soak the onions in water to cover for about 1 hour.

Drain the onions. Chop together finely the prosciutto fat, garlic clove, and 2 of the onions. Put the mixture in a pan (preferably earthenware) with the lard and cook over medium heat for about 5 minutes. Add the remaining whole onions, the sugar, and a pinch of salt. Pour in the vinegar and then just enough water to cover (about a scant ½ cup/100 ml) the onions. Cook over medium heat for about 30 minutes, or until the liquid is completely evaporated. The onions should be tender and covered with a light coating of glistening sauce.

Fagioli cannellini con il tonno · Cannellini beans with tuna
Makes 4 servings

1⅓ pounds (600 g) dried cannellini beans, soaked and ready
   to cook
2 garlic cloves
1 bay leaf
leaves from 1 small bunch flat-leaf parsley
5 ounces (150 g) oil-packed tuna
3 tablespoons intensely fruity extra-virgin olive oil
1 tablespoon white-wine vinegar
salt
freshly ground pepper

Put the beans in a pot. Crush 1 garlic clove and add to the pot along with the bay leaf. Add 2 quarts (2 liters) lightly salted water, bring to a boil, lower the heat, and simmer, covered, until tender; the timing will depend on the age of the beans. Check after 20 minutes and frequently thereafter. Drain the beans and discard the garlic and bay leaf. Let cool.

Chop together finely the remaining garlic clove and the parsley leaves. Drain the tuna, put it in a large bowl, and break it up with a fork. Add the beans, garlic, and parsley. Dress with the oil, vinegar, a pinch of salt, and a generous grinding of pepper. Mix well before serving.

Fagioli con la lattuga · Beans with romaine lettuce
From the Roman Jewish tradition.
Makes 6 servings

about 2 pounds (1 kg) romaine lettuce
leaves from 1 small bunch flat-leaf parsley
1 garlic clove
2 cups (500 ml) vegetable or meat broth
3 tablespoons intensely fruity extra-virgin olive oil
salt
pepper
1 pound (450 g) dried borlotti (cranberry) beans, soaked and
   ready to cook
7 ounces (200 g) tomato purée

Discard the outer leaves from the romaine heads and cut the remainder into strips. Chop the parsley leaves. Crush the garlic clove. Heat the broth in a pot.

Put the garlic in a saucepan with the oil. Cook over medium heat for about 5 minutes, or until the garlic has colored slightly, then discard the garlic. Add the lettuce, parsley, and a pinch each of salt and pepper and sweat over low heat for about 5 minutes. Now add the beans, the hot broth, and the tomato purée. Cook over low heat until the beans are tender; the timing will depend on the age of the beans. Check after 20 minutes and frequently thereafter. Serve hot.

Fagioli freschi al pomodoro · *Fresh beans in tomato sauce*
Makes 4 servings

2½ pounds (1.2 kg) fresh borlotti (cranberry) or other fresh
    shelling beans, shelled
salt
1½ ounces (40 g) prosciutto fat
1 small white onion
1 small celery rib
leaves from 1 small bunch flat-leaf parsley
4 teaspoons (20 g) lard, or 4 tablespoons intensely fruity
    extra-virgin olive oil
14 ounces (400 g) tomato purée
salt
pepper

Put the beans in a pot, cover generously with cold water, bring to a boil, and lower the heat. When the beans are about half done, season with salt and continue cooking until tender.

Meanwhile, chop together finely the prosciutto fat, onion, celery, and parsley leaves. Put in a pan together with the lard and sauté over medium heat for about 5 minutes, or until the onion and the fat are almost translucent. Add the tomato purée, season with salt and pepper, and cook over low heat for about 15 minutes.

Drain the beans (but reserve the water), add to the tomato mixture, and cook gently for a few minutes over low heat. If the sauce reduces too much, add a few tablespoons of the bean water. Serve hot.

Fagiolini "a corallo" in umido · _Green beans with tomatoes_

Nobody can agree on why these large, flat green beans are named for coral, but they are a fixture of the Roman summer. Elsewhere they are often labeled romano or Italian beans.

Makes 4 servings

1¾ pounds (800 g) flat green beans

14 ounces (400 g) canned tomatoes

1 small white onion

2 tablespoons (30 g) lard, or 5 tablespoons intensely fruity
    extra-virgin olive oil

salt

pepper

leaves from 1 small bunch flat-leaf parsley

Cut off the ends of the beans and pull off any strings. Cut the tomatoes into pieces. Thinly slice the onion.

Put the onion in a saucepan with the lard and sauté over medium heat for about 5 minutes. When the onion is almost translucent, add the tomatoes and cook over medium heat for 15 minutes. Add the beans, season with salt and pepper, cover, and continue cooking over medium heat for about 15 minutes. Add a few tablespoons of boiling water if the sauce reduces too much.

Chop the parsley leaves and sprinkle them over the beans just before serving.

Fagiolini verdi in padella · _Pan-cooked green beans_

Makes 4 servings

1⅓ pounds (600 g) green beans

leaves from 1 small bunch flat-leaf parsley

1 small white onion

4 teaspoons (20 g) lard, or 4 tablespoons intensely fruity
    extra-virgin olive oil

9 ounces (250 g) tomato purée

salt

pepper

Cut off the ends of the beans and pull off any strings. Bring about 2 quarts (2 liters) lightly salted water to a boil, drop in the beans, and boil until tender, then drain well. Chop the parsley leaves finely. Slice the onion.

Put the onion in a saucepan with the lard and sauté over medium heat for about 5 minutes. When the onion is almost translucent, add the tomato purée and parsley and season with salt and pepper. Cook over medium heat for about 15 minutes. Add the beans to the sauce and continue cooking for a few minutes to allow the flavors to blend. Serve hot.

Fave con il pecorino · Raw fava beans with pecorino cheese

The first sweet, tender fava beans of spring are always eaten raw.

Freshly picked young fava beans in their pods
Young pecorino cheese, preferably pecorino romano

Set out the fava beans, still in their pods. Break the pecorino into chunks with an almond-shaped cheese knife and place alongside the beans. Each person shells his or her own beans. There is no need to skin the individual beans.

Fave fresche con il guanciale · Fresh fava beans with guanciale

Makes 4 servings

1 small white onion, finely chopped
4 ounces (120 g) *guanciale,* or, only if necessary, slab pancetta, finely diced
1 ounce (30 g) lard, or 3 tablespoons intensely fruity extra-virgin olive oil
1⅓ pounds (600 g) shelled fresh fava beans
salt
pepper

Finely chop the onion and finely dice the *guanciale.* Put them in a pan with the lard and sauté over medium heat for about 5 minutes. When the onion is almost translucent, add the favas and a little salt (the quantity depends on how salty the *guanciale* is) and pepper. Cook over low heat for about 10 minutes, or until the favas are tender, moistening every so often with a few tablespoons of hot water. Serve immediately.

Finocchi al tegame · Sautéed fennel
Makes 4 servings

2 large fennel bulbs
salt
2 garlic cloves
6 tablespoons (90 ml) medium-fruity extra-virgin
 olive oil
pepper

Cut off the stalks and leaves from the fennel bulbs, then remove the outer layer from each bulb. Put the bulbs in a pot, cover generously with water, add a big pinch of salt, and bring to a boil. When the fennel is half done, drain and cut into rather large wedges.

Crush the garlic cloves and put them in a skillet with the oil. Sauté over medium heat for about 5 minutes, or until the garlic begins to color. Add the fennel wedges, season lightly with salt, grind in some pepper, and continue cooking, always over medium heat and turning as needed to color evenly, for about 10 minutes, or until golden brown. Serve hot.

Frittata coi funghi di bosco · Frittata of wild mushrooms
The traditional version of this recipe includes some combination of porcini, *piopparelli, ovoli, russule, gallinelle, manine, spugnole,* and other wild mushrooms, still found in the region's woods.
Makes 4 servings

1 pound (500 g) fresh wild mushrooms
2 garlic cloves
5 eggs
1 heaping tablespoon minced flat-leaf parsley
salt
pepper
2 tablespoons medium-fruity extra-virgin olive oil,
 preferably from Sabina

Scrape the surface of the mushrooms gently with a small knife to remove any clinging dirt, then wipe with a damp cloth. Slice the mushrooms. Crush the garlic cloves.

Break the eggs into a bowl, add the parsley, a pinch of salt, and abundant pepper, and beat with a fork just until blended.

Put the mushrooms and garlic in a skillet with the oil and sauté over medium heat until the garlic is golden brown and the mushrooms are cooked. Discard the garlic. Pour the eggs over the mushrooms and stir for a moment until the eggs begin to set. Then cook the frittata for 3 to 4 minutes, or until browned on the first side. Use a plate to turn the frittata (see page 274) and cook until nicely colored on the second side. Serve warm or at room temperature.

Frittata di carciofi · Frittata of artichokes
Makes 4 servings

juice of 1 lemon
2 large artichokes
leaves from 1 small bunch flat-leaf parsley
6 eggs
4 teaspoons (20 g) lard, or 3 tablespoons intensely fruity
   extra-virgin olive oil
salt
pepper

Fill a bowl with water and add the lemon juice. One at a time, trim the artichokes, including their stems, as described on page 273. Cut each artichoke in half lengthwise and remove and discard any choke. Slice the artichokes lengthwise and immerse in the lemon water. Chop the parsley leaves.

Break the eggs into a bowl, add the parsley and a pinch of salt, and beat just until blended.

Drain the artichokes well. Heat the lard in a skillet over medium heat, add the artichokes, season with salt and pepper, and cook for 5 to 6 minutes. Add a few tablespoons water and continue cooking the artichokes for 2 minutes longer, stirring constantly. Remove from the heat and let cool somewhat. Add the artichokes to the bowl with the beaten eggs and then pour the mixture back into the skillet. Cook the frittata over medium heat for 3 or 4 minutes, or until browned on the first side. Use a plate to turn the frittata (see page 274) and cook until nicely colored on the second side. Serve warm or at room temperature.

Frittata di cipolle e ruchetta · Frittata of onions and arugula
Makes 4 servings

> 1 pound (500 g) green onions
> 6 tablespoons (90 ml) medium-fruity extra-virgin olive oil,
>   preferably from Sabina
> 1 small bunch arugula
> salt
> pepper
> 4 eggs

Cut off and discard the green tops of the onions and thinly slice the white portions. Soak the onions in water to cover for 1 hour.

Drain the onions well. Put them in a skillet with the oil and cook slowly, without browning, until translucent. Add the arugula, season with salt and pepper, and let wilt for a few minutes, stirring.

Break the eggs into a bowl, season lightly with salt and pepper, and beat just until blended. When the arugula is wilted, pour in the eggs and stir just until the eggs begin to set. Level the surface with the back of a spoon, cover the skillet, and cook the frittata over low heat until browned on the first side. Use a plate to turn the frittata (see page 274), re-cover, and cook over low heat until nicely colored on the second side. This frittata is excellent warm or at room temperature.

Frittata di patate e guanciale · Frittata with potatoes and guanciale
Makes 4 servings

> 2 large boiling potatoes
> 7 ounces (200 g) *guanciale*
> 6 eggs
> 1 heaping tablespoon minced flat-leaf parsley
> salt
> pepper
> 1 teaspoon lard

Peel the potatoes and slice them razor thin. Cut the *guanciale* into strips. Break the eggs into a bowl, add the parsley, season with salt and pepper, and beat just until blended.

Put the potatoes and *guanciale* in a skillet with the lard and brown over medium heat. Pour off and reserve the fat from the potatoes and *guanciale*, leaving them in the pan. Pour the eggs on top along with 1 to 2 tablespoons of the reserved fat. Cook the frittata over low heat on the first side until a crisp crust forms. Use a plate to turn the frittata (see page 274) and cook until browned and crisp on the second side. Serve warm or at room temperature.

Frittata di zucchine · Zucchini frittata
Makes 4 servings

3 medium zucchini
4 tablespoons intensely fruity extra-virgin olive oil
leaves from 1 small bunch flat-leaf parsley
3 Roman mint leaves (see page 274)
6 eggs
salt
pepper

Cut off and discard the ends from the zucchini and slice thinly. Put the slices in a skillet with the oil and a few tablespoons water and cook over low heat until golden brown.

Meanwhile, chop the parsley and mint leaves. Break the eggs into a bowl, add the herbs, season with salt and pepper, and beat just until blended. When the zucchini are ready, pour the eggs over the top and cook for 4 to 5 minutes, or until the first side is nicely browned. Use a plate to turn the frittata (see page 274) and cook until nicely browned on the second side. Serve warm or at room temperature.

Frittelle di borragine · Borage fritters
Makes about 12 fritters

7 ounces (200 g) flour
2 teaspoon baking powder
2 eggs
2 heaping tablespoons grated *parmigiano-reggiano*
salt
pepper
leaves from 1 bunch borage
olive oil for deep-frying

Sift together the flour and baking powder. Break the eggs into a blender, add a scant 1 cup (200 ml) water, the cheese, a pinch each of salt and pepper, and the flour mixture and process until the batter is smooth. Pour into a bowl, cover, and let rest for 2 hours.

Cut the borage leaves into little strips, add to the batter, and mix well. Pour the oil to a depth of about 1 inch (2.5 cm) into a deep skillet and heat over medium-high heat until a little of the batter dropped into the oil sizzles and turns lightly golden on contact. Working in batches, drop the borage mixture by the spoonful into the hot oil and fry for a few minutes, or until golden. Scoop the fritters out of the oil with a slotted spoon and drain on paper towels. Serve piping hot.

Frittura di ovoli · Batter-fried wild mushrooms

Ovoli are hard to find even in Italy. If necessary,
you can use other kinds of wild mushrooms.

Makes 4 servings

about 2½ pounds (1.2 kg) fresh *ovoli* mushrooms, caps closed
   and quite firm
2 cups (500 ml) lightly fruity extra-virgin olive oil
2 eggs
salt
about 7 ounces (200 g) flour

Scrape the surface of the mushrooms gently with a small knife to remove any clinging dirt, then wipe with a damp cloth. Cut into wedges.

Heat the oil in a skillet. Meanwhile, break the eggs into a bowl, add a pinch of salt, and beat just until blended. When the oil is hot, dredge the mushrooms in the flour, shaking off the excess, dip them in the eggs, and drop them into the skillet. Fry the mushrooms, a few at a time, over medium heat until they are golden brown. Scoop the mushrooms out of the oil with a slotted spoon and drain on paper towels. Serve piping hot.

Insalata di asparagi di campo · Wild asparagus salad

Makes 4 servings

about 2 pounds (1 kg) wild asparagus
salt
½ lemon

4 tablespoons lightly fruity extra-virgin olive oil
pepper

Cut off and discard the tough lower part of each asparagus stalk so that all the spears are more or less the same length. Gather the spears into a bunch and tie with kitchen twine. Stand them vertically, tips up, in a tall, narrow pot. Add water to reach halfway up the sides of the bunch. Add a pinch of salt, cover, and cook over low heat for 8 to 10 minutes, or until just tender. Transfer to a serving plate and snip the string.

Squeeze the juice from the lemon half into a small bowl. Add the oil and a pinch each of salt and pepper and mix well. Pour this dressing over the asparagus and serve.

Insalata di cipolle con le alici · Onion and anchovy salad
Makes 4 servings

11 ounces (300 g) green onions
6 salt-packed anchovies, prepared as described on page 273
2 tablespoons white-wine vinegar
4 tablespoons intensely fruity extra-virgin olive oil
salt
pepper

Cut off and discard the green tops of the onions and thinly slice the white portions. Soak the onions in water to cover for 1 hour. Cut the anchovies into very narrow strips.

Drain the onions well, put them in a salad bowl, and add the anchovies.

Put the vinegar in a small bowl. Add the oil and a pinch each of salt and pepper and mix well. Pour this dressing over the onions and anchovies and serve.

Insalata di finocchi e sedano · Fennel and celery salad
Makes 4 servings

1 large fennel bulb
1 large white celery heart
4 tablespoons intensely fruity extra-virgin olive oil
salt
freshly ground pepper

Cut off the stalks and leaves from the fennel bulb, then remove the outer layer from the bulb. Discard the tough outer ribs from the celery heart. Cut the fennel and celery into very narrow strips.

Put the fennel and celery strips in a bowl, drizzle with the oil, season with the salt and pepper, and toss to mix.

Insalata di pomodori al basilico · Tomato and basil salad
Makes 4 servings

> 2 large, slightly green salad tomatoes
> 1 garlic clove
> leaves from 1 small bunch basil
> 4 tablespoons intensely fruity extra-virgin olive oil
> salt
> pepper

Halve the tomatoes. Discard the seeds and juices. Cut each tomato into several wedges.

Rub the garlic clove vigorously on the bottom and sides of a salad bowl, then add the tomatoes. Chop the basil leaves and put them in a small bowl. Add the oil and a pinch each of salt and pepper. Pour this dressing over the tomatoes and toss to mix. Let the salad rest for 15 minutes, mixing often, then serve.

Lattughe farcite · Stuffed romaine lettuce
From the Roman Jewish tradition.
Makes 4 servings

> 4 small heads romaine lettuce
> 1¾ ounces (50 g) oil-packed anchovy fillets
> 1 tablespoon salt-packed capers, rinsed thoroughly to remove
>   the salt
> 3½ ounces (100 g) pitted black olives
> 4 tablespoons medium-fruity extra-virgin olive oil
> salt

Discard the tougher outer lettuce leaves and any damaged leaves from each romaine head. Leave the others attached to the core. Rinse and drain the heads well.

Drain the anchovies, then chop together the anchovies, capers, and olives. Put the mixture in a bowl and add 2 tablespoons of the oil. Mix very well.

Open the lettuce leaves gently and sprinkle the inside of each head with a heaping spoonful of the anchovy mixture. Close the heads and place them in a single layer in a pan, arranging them very close together. Dress with the remaining oil and a pinch of salt. Cover the pan and cook over very low heat for about 15 minutes, or until the lettuce leaves are completely wilted. If the pan begins to dry out, add a tablespoon of water. Serve warm.

Melanzane a funghetto · Sautéed eggplant

The name, *a funghetto,* or "mushroom style," came about because eggplant cooked this way has a mushroomlike taste.

Makes 4 servings

> 2 long, firm large eggplants
> 2 garlic cloves
> scant 1 cup (200 ml) intensely fruity extra-virgin olive oil
> salt
> pepper

Trim away the green tip from each eggplant. Finely dice the eggplants and put them in a nonstick skillet without adding fat. Stir over medium heat until wilted.

Meanwhile, crush the garlic cloves and put them in a pan with the oil. Sauté over medium heat for about 3 minutes. When the garlic begins to color, add the eggplants, season with salt and pepper, and sauté for a few minutes, or until tender. Serve immediately.

Melanzane arrostite all'aglio · Garlic-roasted eggplants

Makes 4 servings

> 2 garlic cloves
> 2 long, firm large eggplants
> salt
> pepper
> 2 tablespoons intensely fruity extra-virgin olive oil

Finely chop the garlic. Trim away the green tip from each eggplant, then halve the eggplants lengthwise. Remove and discard any seeds and make deep incisions in a grid pattern in the cut side of each half. Sprinkle the incisions with the chopped garlic, then season generously with salt and pepper. Put the eggplants, cut side up and very close together, in a baking pan. Drizzle the oil over the eggplants.

Bake in an oven preheated to 350°F (180°C) for about 20 minutes, or until the eggplants are tender and a nice golden brown crust has formed on the surface. Let rest for a few minutes before serving. These eggplants are also excellent served at room temperature.

Melanzane ripiene · Stuffed eggplants
Makes 4 servings

4 long, firm small eggplants
7 ounces (200 g) *provatura* (see page 275) or mozzarella
4 tablespoons intensely fruity extra-virgin olive oil
salt
pepper
2 tablespoons ready-made tomato sauce

Discard the green tip of the eggplants and halve lengthwise. Remove the pulp with a tablespoon, leaving a shell about ⅜ inch (1 cm) thick. Chop the eggplant pulp and the *provatura* very finely and put in a small bowl. Add 2 tablespoons of the oil and a pinch each of salt and pepper and mix well. Divide this mixture evenly among the eggplant halves.

Select a baking pan in which the eggplants will fit snugly and grease it with 1 tablespoon of the oil. Arrange the stuffed eggplants in the pan. Spoon the tomato sauce evenly over the top and drizzle with the remaining oil. Bake in an oven preheated to 375°F (190°C) for about 30 minutes. Let rest for a few minutes before serving.

Peperonata · Bell peppers with onions and tomatoes
Makes 4 servings

about 2 pounds (1 kg) red or yellow bell peppers
2 white onions
2 garlic cloves
scant 1 cup (200 ml) intensely fruity extra-virgin olive oil

salt

1 pound (450 g) sauce tomatoes, preferably San Marzano

Halve the peppers lengthwise, remove the seeds and membranes, and cut lengthwise into wide strips. Chop the onions coarsely with the garlic cloves. Put them in a skillet with the oil and sauté over medium heat for about 5 minutes. When the onions are almost translucent, add the peppers, season with salt, and cook over a lively flame, stirring, for about 10 minutes.

Meanwhile, peel and dice the tomatoes. Add them to the peppers, season with a little more salt, and finish cooking over medium heat for about 15 minutes. Serve immediately.

Peperoni con il guanciale · Bell peppers with guanciale
Makes 4 servings

6 large green bell peppers

1 small white onion

2 tablespoons (30 g) lard, or 4 tablespoons intensely fruity
  extra-virgin olive oil

salt

pepper

2½ ounces (70 g) *guanciale* or slab pancetta

Halve the peppers lengthwise, remove the seeds and membranes, and cut each half lengthwise into several pieces, not too wide. Thinly slice the onion.

Put the onion in a pan with the lard and sauté over medium heat for 5 minutes. When it is almost translucent, add the peppers and season with salt and pepper. Cook over medium heat for 7 to 8 minutes. Meanwhile, cut the *guanciale* into very narrow strips. When the peppers are almost cooked, add the *guanciale* and cook over low heat for a few minutes until its fat melts. Serve immediately.

Peperoni imbottiti · Stuffed bell peppers
Makes 4 servings

6 large yellow bell peppers

¾ ounce (20 g) raisins

8 oil-packed anchovy fillets

1½ ounces (40 g) capers preserved in vinegar

7 ounces (200 g) pitted black olives

leaves from 1 small bunch basil

leaves from 1 small bunch flat-leaf parsley

3½ ounces (100 g) crustless bread, soaked in milk

2 heaping tablespoons pine nuts

salt

pepper

6 tablespoons (90 ml) intensely fruity extra-virgin olive oil

1¼ cups (300 ml) ready-made tomato sauce

Hold the peppers over a gas flame until blistered on all sides (or blister under a broiler). Transfer them to a closed container, such as a paper bag or a pot with a lid, and leave for about 30 minutes. Then peel, cut off the tops carefully and reserve, and remove the seeds. Immerse the raisins in a small bowl of water to plump.

Drain the anchovies. Chop together the anchovies, capers, olives, basil leaves, and parsley leaves. Put the mixture in a small bowl. Squeeze the bread, crumble into pieces, and add to the bowl. Drain the raisins and add to the bowl along with the pine nuts. Add just a little salt and pepper, then add 4 tablespoons of the oil. Mix well.

Fill the peppers with the mixture and put the tops on like lids. Place close together in a baking pan just large enough to hold them. Pour the tomato sauce over the peppers, then drizzle them with the remaining oil. Bake in an oven preheated to 350°F (180°C) for about 20 minutes, until the filling is piping hot. The peppers are also excellent served at room temperature.

Piselli al prosciutto · Peas with prosciutto

If you don't have the typical Roman small peas and have to use larger ones, add a pinch of sugar along with the peas.

Makes 4 servings

3 romaine lettuce leaves

about 2 pounds (1 kg) peas in their pods

1 small white onion

3½ ounces (100 g) sliced prosciutto

4 teaspoons (20 g) lard, or 3 tablespoons medium-fruity
  extra-virgin olive oil

scant 1 cup (200 ml) vegetable broth
salt

Cut the lettuce leaves into narrow strips. Shell the peas. Chop together finely the onion and prosciutto.

Put the onion and prosciutto mixture in a saucepan with the lard and sauté over medium heat for about 4 minutes, or until golden brown. Add the lettuce and let it wilt for a couple of minutes, stirring constantly.

Now add the peas and the broth, season with salt, and continue cooking over medium heat for about 10 minutes. At the end, the broth should be almost completely evaporated and the peas tender. Serve immediately.

Pomodori ripieni alla trasteverina · Stuffed tomatoes
Makes 6 servings

6 firm tomatoes, all about the same size and not too ripe
1¾ ounces (50 g) dried porcini mushrooms
1 white onion
2½ ounces (70 g) crustless bread
milk
leaves from 1 small bunch flat-leaf parsley
1 celery rib
6 tablespoons (90 ml) intensely fruity extra-virgin olive oil
salt
pepper
1 egg
2 heaping tablespoons grated *parmigiano-reggiano*

Cut off and discard the top of each tomato. Scoop out the pulp (with a melon baller or a tablespoon), leaving a shell about ⅜ inch (1 cm) thick. Sprinkle the inside of each hollowed-out tomato with salt, then put the tomatoes, cut side down, on an inclined plane to drain. Remove and discard the seeds from the pulp, then chop the pulp and put it in a small bowl.

Soak the dried porcini for 20 minutes in at least two changes of warm water. Drain, rinse, and squeeze well, then chop finely. Soak the bread in a little milk but do not squeeze out. Chop together finely the onion, parsley leaves, and celery and put in a pan with 3 tablespoons of the oil. Cook over medium heat for about 5 minutes. When the onion is almost translucent, add the mushrooms and bread, season with salt and pepper, and cook over low heat until all the liquid has evaporated. Remove the pan from the heat.

Break the egg into a small bowl, add the cheese, and beat lightly. Add the egg mixture to the mixture in the pan, season with salt and pepper, and mix well. Fill the tomatoes with the mixture.

Select a baking pan in which the tomatoes will fit snugly and grease the bottom of the pan with 1 tablespoon of the oil. Arrange the tomatoes in the pan. Drizzle the remaining oil over the tomatoes. Bake in an oven preheated to 400°F (200°C) for about 20 minutes, or until the surface of the tomatoes is lightly browned. Let rest for a few minutes before serving.

Pomodori ripieni di riso · *Rice-stuffed tomatoes*
Makes 6 servings

12 tomatoes, all about the same size and not too ripe
salt
2 garlic cloves
leaves from 1 small bunch Roman mint (see page 274)
leaves from 1 small bunch flat-leaf parsley
5 ounces (150 g) Vialone Nano, Arborio, or other rice for
     risotto
6 tablespoons (90 ml) lightly fruity extra-virgin olive oil
pepper

Cut off and reserve the top of each tomato. Scoop out the pulp (with a melon baller or a tablespoon), leaving a shell about ⅛ inch (1 cm) thick. Sprinkle the inside of each hollowed-out tomato with salt, then put the tomatoes, cut side down, on an inclined plane to drain. Remove and discard the seeds from the pulp, then chop the pulp and put it in a small bowl.

Chop together finely the garlic cloves and mint and parsley leaves. Add to the tomato pulp along with the rice and 3 tablespoons of the oil. Mix well, then season with salt and pepper. Fill the tomatoes with the rice mixture and cover with the reserved tops.

Select a baking pan in which the tomatoes will fit snugly and grease the bottom of the pan with 1 tablespoon of the oil. Arrange the tomatoes in the pan. Drizzle the remaining oil over the tomatoes. Bake in an oven preheated to 375°F (190°C) for 30 minutes. Serve the tomatoes slightly warm. They are also excellent served at room temperature.

Porcini al coccio · *Porcini mushrooms with tomatoes*
Makes 4 servings

about 2¼ pounds (1 kg) fresh porcini mushrooms
4 oil-packed anchovy fillets
leaves from 1 small bunch *mentuccia* (see page 274)
11 ounces (300 g) very ripe sauce tomatoes, preferably San
   Marzano
2 garlic cloves
4 tablespoons intensely fruity extra-virgin olive oil
salt
pepper

Scrape the surface of the mushrooms with a small knife to remove any clinging dirt, then wipe with a damp cloth and slice them. Drain the anchovies and chop into tiny pieces. Chop the *mentuccia* leaves. Cut up the tomatoes without peeling them.

Crush the garlic cloves and put them in a pan (preferably earthenware) with the oil. Add the anchovies and cook gently for about 5 minutes. When the anchovy pieces have almost dissolved, add the porcini and sauté over a lively flame for a few minutes. Add the tomatoes and *mentuccia* and season with salt and pepper. Cover the pan and cook over medium heat for about 6 minutes, or until the porcini are tender. Discard the garlic and serve.

Porcini trifolati al burro d'alice · *Porcini mushrooms
with anchovy butter*
Makes 4 servings

about 2¼ pounds (1 kg) fresh porcini mushrooms
2 garlic cloves
3 oil-packed anchovy fillets
leaves from 1 small bunch flat-leaf parsley
½ lemon
4 tablespoons lightly fruity extra-virgin olive oil
salt
pepper
4½ tablespoons (70 g) butter

Scrape the surface of the mushrooms with a small knife to remove any clinging dirt, then wipe with a damp cloth and slice them. Chop the garlic cloves. Drain the anchovies, then chop together with the parsley leaves. Squeeze the juice from the lemon half and measure 1 tablespoon.

Heat the oil in a skillet and sauté the garlic over medium heat for about 5 minutes. Add the porcini and sauté over a lively flame for 5 to 6 minutes. When the mushrooms are tender, season with salt and pepper, then remove with a slotted spoon and keep warm. Reserve the pan and its contents.

Add the butter to the mushroom pan and melt over low heat. Add the anchovies and parsley and stir for a few minutes over medium heat until the anchovies have completely dissolved. Remove from the heat and add the lemon juice. Stir and pour over the porcini. Serve piping hot.

Sedani in umido alla romana · *Stewed celery*
Makes 4 servings

2 large heads celery
1 white onion
3½ ounces (100 g) sliced prosciutto
leaves from 1 small bunch flat-leaf parsley
3 tablespoons medium-fruity extra-virgin olive oil
14 ounces (400 g) tomato purée
salt
pepper

Trim the celery, discarding the leaves and the toughest strings from the ribs. Cut the rest into pieces about 2 inches (5 cm) long. Bring a pot filled with lightly salted water to a boil, add the celery, boil for 2 minutes, and drain.

Chop together finely the onion, prosciutto, and parsley leaves. Put the mixture in a saucepan with the oil and sauté over medium heat for about 5 minutes. Add the tomato purée, season with salt and pepper, and continue cooking for about 20 minutes, always over medium heat.

When the sauce is ready, add the celery pieces, cover, and cook over low heat for about 10 minutes. At the end, the celery should be tender and flavorful. Serve hot.

Spinaci in padella alla trasteverina · Spinach with raisins and pine nuts
Makes 4 servings

1¾ ounces (50 g) raisins
2 pounds (1 kg) spinach
4 teaspoons (20 g) lard or butter
1 heaping tablespoon pine nuts
salt
pepper

Immerse the raisins in a small bowl of water to plump. Trim and rinse the spinach. Put it in a pot, cover, and cook over medium heat in just the rinsing water clinging to the leaves. Drain the spinach and squeeze well.

Heat the lard in a skillet, add the spinach, stir to coat it with the fat, and cook for a couple of minutes. Drain the raisins and add to the pan along with the pine nuts, then season with salt and pepper. Continue to cook the spinach gently over low heat for 2 more minutes. Serve hot.

Verdure miste all'agro · Mixed vegetables in green sauce
Makes 4 servings

2 medium boiling potatoes
1 beet
3 artichokes
3½ ounces (100 g) green beans
3½ ounces (100 g) asparagus tips
3½ ounces (100 g) cauliflower florets
6 tablespoons (90 ml) *salsa verde* (recipe on page 252)

Peel the potatoes and beet. Trim the artichokes as described on page 273. Then remove all the leaves and the stem from each artichoke and keep only the heart. Cut off the ends of the beans and pull off any strings. Cut the green beans into lengths of about 1¼ inches (3 cm), the artichoke hearts into small wedges, and the potatoes and beet into dice. Leave the asparagus tips and cauliflower florets whole.

Cook the vegetables separately in salted water until tender. Drain and let cool.

Dress the vegetables separately with the *salsa verde,* then transfer them, keeping them separate, to a platter and serve.

Zucchine al forno alla moda di Sezze · Baked zucchini
Makes 4 servings

about 2 pounds (1 kg) zucchini
salt
1 tablespoon flour
leaves from 1 small bunch parsley
2 garlic cloves
2 heaping tablespoons grated *parmigiano-reggiano* cheese
pepper
4 tablespoons extra-virgin olive oil

Cut off and discard the ends from the zucchini and slice thinly. Salt the slices lightly and leave them in a colander to lose their water for a few hours. Dry the zucchini slices, flour lightly, and put in a bowl. Chop together the parsley leaves and garlic cloves and add to the zucchini along with the parmigiano and a grinding of pepper. Toss gently to mix.

Put the zucchini mixture in a baking pan, drizzle with the oil, and bake in an oven preheated to 400°F (200°C) for about 20 minutes, or until tender and golden. Serve hot or at room temperature.

Zucchine al tegame · Zucchini with tomatoes
Makes 4 servings

4 medium zucchini
1 white onion
3 tablespoons intensely fruity extra-virgin olive oil
9 ounces (250 g) canned tomatoes
salt
pepper
leaves from 1 small bunch flat-leaf parsley

Cut off and discard the ends from the zucchini. Quarter each zucchini lengthwise, and cut crosswise into lengths of about 1½ inches (4 cm). Chop the onion.

Put the onion in a pan with the oil and cook over medium heat for about 5 minutes. When it is almost translucent, add the tomatoes and cook over medium heat for about 15 minutes, mashing them with a fork as needed to break them up. Add the zucchini, season with salt and pepper, and continue cooking over low heat for 10 to 15 minutes more.

Meanwhile, chop the parsley leaves. When the zucchini are ready, remove the pan from the heat, sprinkle with the parsley, and serve immediately.

Zucchine marinate · Marinated zucchini
Makes 4 servings

2 cups (500 ml) white-wine vinegar
¾-inch (2-cm) piece dried chile, or 1 teaspoon red pepper
    flakes
salt
8 large zucchini
2 cups (500 ml) lightly fruity extra-virgin olive oil

Pour the vinegar into a small nonreactive pan, crumble in the chile, and add a pinch of salt. Simmer this marinade for about 10 minutes. Let cool.

Meanwhile, cut off and discard the ends from the zucchini and cut into slices ¼ inch (6 mm) thick. Heat the oil in a skillet over medium heat. Fry the zucchini slices, a few at a time, for a couple of minutes, or until golden. Remove with a slotted spoon to paper towels to drain.

When all the zucchini slices are fried, put them in a bowl and pour the marinade over them. There should be just enough to cover them. Let rest for at least 1 day in a cool place, stirring occasionally, before serving.

Zucchine ripiene · Meat-filled zucchini
Makes 4 servings

1½ ounces (40 g) crustless bread
7 ounces (200 g) ground beef
2 eggs
2 heaping tablespoons grated *parmigiano-reggiano*
4 tablespoons intensely fruity extra-virgin olive oil
nutmeg

salt

pepper

4 medium-large zucchini

2 Roman mint leaves (see page 274)

5 ounces (150 g) tomato purée

Crumble the bread into a bowl. Add the beef, eggs, parmigiano, 1 tablespoon of the oil, a grating of nutmeg, and a pinch each of salt and pepper. Blend all the ingredients very well until you have a smooth mixture.

Cut off and discard the ends from the zucchini, then cut them in half crosswise. Using a zucchini corer or a small, sharp knife, carefully remove the pulp from each half, leaving a sturdy shell. Fill the zucchini halves with the stuffing and put them close together in a pan just large enough to hold them. Chop the mint.

Pour the remaining oil over the zucchini and cook over medium heat for a few minutes, turning them with two forks to color lightly on all sides. Add the tomato purée, mint, and a little salt and pepper. Cook over low heat for about 10 minutes. The filling should be cooked through and the zucchini tender. Serve immediately. The zucchini are also good served at room temperature.

SFIZI · SAVORIES

Olive nere condite · Black olives with citrus rind
Makes 4 servings

7 ounces (200 g) dry-cured black olives

rind of ½ pesticide-free orange (colored part only)

rind of ½ pesticide-free lemon (colored part only)

small piece dried chile, or 1 teaspoon red pepper flakes

2 tablespoons lemon juice

3 tablespoons medium-fruity extra-virgin olive oil, preferably from Sabina

leaves from 1 small bunch marjoram

salt

Soften the olives in lukewarm water, drain and dry them, and put them in a serving bowl. Cut the orange and lemon rind into very narrow strips and add to the bowl. Crumble in the chile and add the lemon juice, oil, marjoram, and a pinch of salt. Stir to combine, then let the flavors blend for a couple of hours before serving. Serve the olives with aperitifs.

Alici salate · Salted anchovies

In popular cooking, salt-packed anchovies have become mainly a condiment, as can be seen from the recipes in this book, but they are also delicious on bread, with or without butter. This is the quantity needed for the annual consumption of an average family in the Lazio region.

11 pounds (5 kg) fresh anchovies
6½ pounds (3 kg) coarse salt
20 to 30 bay leaves

Remove the heads and the guts from the anchovies. Rinse them very well and blot dry.

Put a layer of coarse salt in a wide-mouthed glass or porcelain jar and arrange a layer of anchovies, close together, on top. Cover with another layer of salt and then another layer of anchovies. Continue this way, creating alternating layers of salt and anchovies and adding a bay leaf every so often, until all the ingredients are used up, finishing with a layer of salt. Top the final salt layer with a glass, wooden, or other nonmetallic disk a little smaller than the mouth of the jar, and place a cylindrical weight of 2 to 5 pounds (1 to 2.3 kg) on top of the disk.

Let the jar rest like that in a cool, level spot for 1 to 2 months. During this time, brine will form; the anchovies should always be immersed in the brine. If the brine begins to overflow, remove the excess, leaving only a thin layer covering the anchovies. After 1 to 2 months, remove the anchovies from the jar as needed and prepare as described on page 273.

Bruschetta classica · Classic garlic toast
Makes 4 servings

8 slices *casereccio* bread (see page 273)
1 garlic clove
6 tablespoons (90 ml) intensely fruity extra-virgin olive oil
such as just-pressed *olio di frantoio*
salt

Toast the bread slices on both sides on a grill. Remove them and rub vigorously with the garlic clove. Dress the slices generously with the oil and salt lightly. Serve hot.

Bruschetta con il pomodoro · Tomato bruschetta
Makes 4 servings

7 ounces (200 g) cherry tomatoes
leaves from 1 small bunch basil
8 slices *casereccio* bread (see page 273)
1 garlic clove
3 tablespoons intensely fruity extra virgin olive oil such as
  just-pressed *olio di frantoio*
salt

Dice the tomatoes finely and set aside. Mince the basil leaves.

Toast the bread slices on both sides on a grill. Remove them and rub vigorously with the garlic clove. Dress the slices generously with the oil and salt lightly. Spoon on the tomatoes and sprinkle with the basil. Serve hot.

Capitone marinato · Marinated eel
Makes 4 servings

1 large eel, about 2 pounds (1 kg)
7 ounces (200 g) coarse salt
extra-virgin olive oil for frying
2 cups red wine vinegar
1 garlic clove
1 bay leaf
5 peppercorns
salt

Rub the eel with the coarse salt to eliminate any sliminess on the skin. (This step makes it easier to grip the eel.) Cut off the head of the eel and discard, then cut the eel into 2-inch (5-cm) lengths without skinning it. Heat the oil in a skillet over medium heat and fry the eel pieces until golden brown on both sides and cooked through. Remove from the heat.

Put the vinegar, garlic, bay leaf, and peppercorns in a saucepan, bring to a boil, and boil for 5 minutes. Put the fried eel in a bowl and pour the marinade over it; the eel should be immersed. Let sit in a cool place for at least 15 days before serving.

Crostini di finta selvaggina · Toast with mock game
Makes 8 to 10 servings

1 small carrot
2 sage leaves
leaves from 1 small bunch parsley
needles from 1 sprig rosemary
1 garlic clove
3½ ounces (100 g) chicken giblets
3 tablespoons extra-virgin olive oil
small piece dried chile
salt
2 tablespoons white-wine vinegar
3½ ounces (100 g) oil-packed tuna, preferably Italian
½ pesticide-free lemon
1 heaping tablespoon capers preserved in vinegar
1 heaping tablespoon small gherkins
8 to 10 slices bread, toasted, or crackers

Chop together the carrot, parsley and sage leaves, and rosemary needles. Crush the garlic clove. Trim the giblets, eliminating the green bile ducts from the livers. Rinse them for a good, long time and pat dry.

Heat the oil in a skillet and sauté the garlic and chile over medium heat. When the garlic begins to color, add the giblets and the carrot mixture, sprinkle with salt, and continue cooking for about 20 minutes, adding a tablespoon of hot water if the pan begins to dry. When the giblets are cooked, add the vinegar and let it evaporate over medium heat.

Put the contents of the skillet in a food processor. Drain the tuna and add to the processor. Squeeze the juice from the lemon half and set aside. Cut the lemon rind (colored part only) away from the pith and pulp, cut it into small pieces, and add it to the processor along with the capers and gherkins. Process until the mixture is creamy and smooth. Add the lemon juice and process just until combined. Serve spread on toasted bread or crackers.

Crostini di provatura e alici · *Anchovy and cheese toast*
Makes 4 servings

14 ounces (400 g) *provatura* (see page 275) or mozzarella
8 slices *casereccio* bread (see page 273)
5½ tablespoons (80 g) butter
4 tablespoons milk
4 salt-packed anchovies, prepared as described on page 273

Slice the cheese and blot with paper towels. Trim the bread slices to the same size as the cheese slices. Thread them alternately onto wooden skewers and place in a baking pan. Melt 4 teaspoons (20 g) of the butter over low heat.

Bake the skewers in an oven preheated to 475°F (240°C) until the cheese begins to melt. Brush every so often with the melted butter. Meanwhile, bring the milk to a boil in a small pan. At the same time, put the anchovies in another small pan with the remaining butter and let them dissolve over low heat, mashing with a fork. Then add the boiling milk to the anchovies and remove from the heat.

Remove the skewers from the oven and transfer to a warmed platter. Pour the anchovy sauce over them and serve hot.

Filetti di baccalà fritti · *Deep-fried salt cod fillets*
Makes 4 servings

3½ ounces (100 g) flour
salt
2 cups (500 ml) intensely fruity extra-virgin olive oil
1⅓ pounds (600 g) salt cod, soaked to remove the salt and
    ready to cook
2 egg whites
1 lemon

Make a batter by combining a scant 1 cup (200 ml) ice-cold water, the flour, and a pinch of salt in a bowl. Add 2 tablespoons of the oil and keep mixing until smooth and thick. Let rest for at least 30 minutes.

Scrape the skin off the cod and discard. Bone the fish carefully and cut it into pieces about 2¾ inches (7 cm) long and about 1 inch (2.5 cm) wide. Meanwhile, put the egg whites in a bowl and beat with a fork or whisk until stiff peaks form. Gently fold the whites into the batter.

Heat the remaining oil in a large skillet to 300°F (150°C), then lower the heat slightly. Dip the salt cod strips in the batter, allowing the excess to drip off, and then drop them, a few at a time, into the hot oil. Fry on both sides until golden brown and crisp. Scoop them out with a slotted spoon and drain on paper towels.

Cut the lemon into wedges. Serve the cod piping hot, accompanied with the lemon wedges.

Fiori di zucca fritti · Deep-fried zucchini flowers
Makes 4 servings

3½ ounces (100 g) flour
salt
2½ cups (600 ml) lightly fruity extra-virgin
   olive oil
3½ ounces (100 g) *provatura* (see page 275)
   or mozzarella
3 salt-packed anchovies, cleaned as described
   on page 273
leaves from 1 small bunch flat-leaf parsley
1⅓ pounds (600 g) very fresh zucchini flowers
2 egg whites

Make a batter by combining a scant 1 cup (200 ml) ice-cold water, the flour, and a pinch of salt in a bowl. Add 2 tablespoons of the oil and keep mixing until smooth and thick. Let rest for at least 30 minutes.

Blot the *provatura* with paper towels and cut it into strips ¼ by 1 inch (6 mm by 2.5 cm). Cut the anchovies into strips. Chop the parsley leaves. Put the cheese and anchovies in a bowl and sprinkle with the parsley. Toss to mix.

Gently open the corollas of the flowers and discard the pistils. Insert a strip of cheese and a strip of anchovy into each flower, then gently twist the top of each flower to close and put it on a plate. Put the egg whites in a bowl and beat with a fork or whisk until stiff peaks form. Gently fold the whites into the batter.

Heat the remaining oil in a large skillet. Immerse the stuffed flowers in the batter. One at a time, remove the flowers from the batter with two spoons and put them in the oil. Fry on both sides for a few minutes, until golden brown and crisp. Drain on paper towels and serve piping hot.

Ganascione alla ciociara · Ham and cheese pie
Makes 4 servings

14 ounces (400 g) raised bread dough
3 tablespoons extra-virgin olive oil, plus more for oiling
the pan
3½ ounces (100 g) semisoft cheese
1¾ ounces (50 g) boiled ham
5 ounces (150 g) ricotta
pepper

Divide the dough in half and roll out each half into a disk about ⅜ inch (1 cm) thick. Oil a baking pan large enough to hold the dough and place a disk in the pan. Reserve the second disk. Let the dough rise for 20 minutes.

Meanwhile grate or slice the semisoft cheese. Cut the ham into narrow strips. When the dough has risen, spread both cheeses and the ham evenly over the dough disk in the pan. Sprinkle with pepper, cover with the second disk, and seal the edges. Let rise for a few minutes, then make indentations all over the surface with fingertips and brush with the oil. Bake in a preheated oven at 400°F (200°C) for 15 minutes, or until golden brown. Serve hot.

La padellaccia · Pork bits with garlic and rosemary
Makes 4 servings

1 head garlic
needles from 1 sprig rosemary
small piece dried chile
2 to 3 tablespoons medium-fruity extra-virgin olive oil,
preferably from Sabina
about 2 pounds (1 kg) small pieces mixed fresh pork (fresh
bacon, liver)
scant 1 cup (200 ml) dry white table wine
salt

Flatten the garlic without peeling. Put the garlic, rosemary needles, chile, oil, and pork pieces in a skillet and brown everything over a lively flame. Add the wine and finish cooking, stirring often, over medium heat. Just before the dish is ready, season with salt. Serve piping hot.

Pancotto alla romana
Makes 4 servings

11 ounces (300 g) very ripe small sauce tomatoes
2 garlic cloves
9 ounces (250 g) day-old *casereccio* bread (see page 273)
about 4 cups (1 liter) light meat or vegetable broth
3 tablespoons intensely fruity extra-virgin olive oil
salt
pepper
leaves from 1 small bunch marjoram
1 heaping tablespoon grated *parmigiano-reggiano*

Halve the tomatoes. Discard the seeds, then cut into small pieces. Crush the garlic cloves. Soak the bread in cold water in a small bowl. Drain it carefully and crumble it, not too finely. Put it into a pan (preferably earthenware) and pour in the broth just to cover. Add the tomatoes, garlic, 1 tablespoon of the oil, and a pinch each of salt and pepper.

Cover and cook over low heat, stirring often, for about 20 minutes. When the tomatoes have completely disintegrated, remove from the heat. Chop the marjoram leaves and sprinkle over the *pancotto,* then dust with the parmigiano. Drizzle with the remaining oil and serve immediately.

La panontella · Bread with pancetta and guanciale
Makes 4 servings

7 ounces (200 g) pancetta, sliced
7 ounces (200 g) *guanciale,* sliced not too thin
pepper
1 loaf *casereccio* bread (see page 273), about 1 pound
   (500 g)
salt

Fold each pancetta and *guanciale* slice several times to form cubes, then thread them onto a skewer. Pepper generously. Slice the bread in half lengthwise.

Put the skewer under a hot broiler or on a grill over a moderate fire to cook. Every so often, blot the skewer with the cut sides of the bread, pressing down on the crumb so it absorbs the meat juices. Continue cooking and blotting until the pancetta and *guanciale* are nicely browned. Cut the bread into pieces, scatter the pieces of crisp meat on top, salt lightly, and serve piping hot.

Panzanella · Bread salad
Makes 4 servings

CLASSIC VERSION

8 slices *casereccio* bread (see page 273), about
   1 inch (2.5 cm) thick
4 tablespoons or more intensely fruity
   extra-virgin olive oil
2 tablespoons white-wine vinegar
salt
leaves from 2 small bunches basil

MODERN VERSION

2 small salad tomatoes, not too ripe
2 small white onions, or 1 garlic clove
8 slices *casereccio* bread, about 1 inch (2.5 cm) thick
4 tablespoons or more intensely fruity
   extra-virgin olive oil
2 tablespoons white-wine vinegar
salt
freshly ground pepper

To make the classic version, hold the bread slices very briefly under running water to moisten them. Place them in a single layer on a large platter. Distribute the oil, vinegar, and a pinch of salt evenly over the bread slices. Mince the basil leaves and sprinkle over the top. Let rest for about 2 hours before serving.

   To make the modern version, halve, seed, and dice the tomatoes. Thinly slice the onions, or pass the garlic clove through a garlic press. Hold the bread slices very briefly under running water to moisten them. Place them in a single layer on a large platter. Distribute the oil, vinegar, and a pinch of salt evenly over the bread slices. Finish with the tomato and onion or garlic. Add a grinding of pepper and let rest for about 2 hours before serving.

Il pinzimonio · Crudités

combination of very fresh raw vegetables such as fennel,
    celery, and artichokes
extra-virgin olive oil
salt
freshly ground pepper

Trim the vegetables, keeping only the tender hearts (see page 273 for directions on trimming the artichokes). Cut into wedges and arrange on a platter. Each diner makes his or her own dressing with the oil, salt, and plenty of pepper for dipping the vegetables.

Supplì "al telefono" · Rice croquettes

These croquettes can also be made with a good *ragù* of giblets and sweetbreads. The name *supplì* derives from the French *surprise,* and the surprise is the melted mozzarella inside. When you hold the hot *supplì* in your hand, bite it, and pull the uneaten half away, a string of melted cheese forms connecting the two halves of the *supplì* like a telephone base and receiver. With the preponderance of cordless telephones, however, the second part of the name is increasingly being left off.

Makes 4 servings

9 ounces (250 g) Arborio, Carnaroli, Vialone Nano, or other
    rice for risotto
about 3¼ cups (750 ml) light meat broth
3½ tablespoons (50 g) butter
2½ ounces (70 g) grated *parmigiano-reggiano*
nutmeg
leaves from 1 small bunch flat-leaf parsley, chopped
3½ ounces (100 g) mozzarella
1¾ ounces (50 g) prosciutto
4 eggs
3½ ounces (100 g) flour
2 tablespoons dried bread crumbs
2½ cups (600 ml) lightly fruity extra-virgin olive oil

Make a very al dente risotto with the rice, broth, butter, half the parmigiano, a grating of nutmeg, and the chopped parsley leaves. Spread it out on a slightly damp marble or other cold surface and let it cool completely. Meanwhile, dice the mozzarella and put it in a small bowl. Dice the prosciutto and put it in another small bowl.

Place the cooled risotto in a bowl, add 3 of the eggs and the remaining parmigiano, and stir until well mixed and quite firm. Make small ovoid shapes weighing about 1¾ ounces (50 g) each, and insert a little mozzarella and prosciutto into the center of each one. Break the remaining egg into a small bowl and beat with a fork just until blended. Dredge each *supplì* in the flour, then dip in the egg, and finally coat with the bread crumbs. Put them on a plate.

Heat the oil in a deep skillet to 300°F (150°C), then lower the heat slightly. Fry the *supplì,* a few at a time, until uniformly golden brown. Drain on paper towels and serve hot.

La tiella di Gaeta · Fresh-anchovy pie

The savory pie, typical of the pretty seaside town of Gaeta,
takes its name from the pan, the *tiella,* in which it is baked.
There are numerous possible fillings
for it, with seafood and without.

Makes 8 servings

FOR THE PASTRY
¾ ounce (20 g) fresh cake yeast
1 pound (450 g) flour
3 tablespoons extra-virgin olive oil
salt

FOR THE FILLING
about 1 pound (500 g) fresh anchovies
11 ounces (300 g) Gaeta-type black olives
4 San Marzano tomatoes
2 garlic cloves
1 heaping tablespoon minced flat-leaf parsley
pinch of ground red pepper
salt
4 tablespoons extra-virgin olive oil, plus more for brushing

To make the pastry, crumble the yeast into a small bowl and add 2 tablespoons lukewarm water. Mix gently, then cover the bowl and let the yeast sit for 6 to 7 minutes, or until it begins to foam. Mound the flour on a work surface and make a well in the center. Add the yeast, oil, a pinch of salt, and ⅔ cup (150 ml) lukewarm water to the well. Begin to incorporate the wet ingredients into the flour with a fork. When the mixture is too stiff to use a fork any longer, begin forming the dough with your hands. Once it comes together in a fairly uniform ball, knead it vigorously with your hands for about 15 minutes, or until you have a smooth, firm dough. Place the dough in a bowl, cover, and let rise for about 1 hour; it should double in volume.

To make the filling, remove the heads and the guts from the anchovies. Rinse very well and blot dry. Pit the olives. Chop together the anchovies, olives, tomatoes, and garlic cloves. Mix in the parsley.

Divide the dough into two portions, one slightly larger than other. Roll out the large portion into a thin disk and use to line the bottom and sides of a round baking pan about 9 inches (23 cm) in diameter. Spoon the anchovy mixture into the pastry shell, spreading it evenly. Drizzle with the oil and sprinkle with the red pepper and a little salt. Roll out the second dough portion into a thin disk and lay it over the filling. Carefully seal together the edges of the bottom and top crust. Pierce the top crust here and there with the tines of a fork, then brush with the oil.

Bake in an oven preheated to 400°F (200°F) for about 30 minutes, or until golden brown. Serve warm or at room temperature.

Provola ai ferri · Grilled provola cheese

provola cheese, sweet or smoked
extra-virgin olive oil for brushing
freshly ground pepper

Cut the provola into slices ⅜ inch (1 cm) thick. Brush both sides of each slice with the oil, and season both sides generously with pepper. Cook the slices on a grill or in a lightly oiled skillet. Turn the slices as soon as they begin to melt on the first side, and then pull from the fire when they begin to melt on the second side. Serve immediately.

Uova "trippate" · "Triped" eggs

The term *trippate* in the recipe title comes from the fact that the
finished dish vaguely resembles a plate of tripe.

Makes 4 servings

> leaves from 1 small bunch flat-leaf parsley
> 8 eggs
> 1 heaping tablespoon grated *parmigiano-reggiano*
> salt
> pepper
> scant ½ cup (100 ml) lightly fruity extra-virgin
>   olive oil
> 1⅔ cups (400 ml) ready-made tomato sauce

Chop the parsley leaves. Break the eggs into a large bowl, add the parsley, parmigiano, and a pinch each of salt and pepper, and beat lightly with a fork.

Heat the oil in a skillet over medium heat. Pour about one-fourth of the beaten egg into the oil, forming a thin sheet, and fry just until set. Remove from the pan. Repeat with the remaining beaten egg in three batches, to make 4 thin, medium-size *frittatine* total. Let cool, then cut into very narrow strips.

Put the tomato sauce in a pan and add the strips of *frittatina*. Heat over low heat for a few minutes. Serve hot.

CONDIMENTI · SAUCES AND CONDIMENTS

Battuto

This is just pork fat chopped and crushed (*battuto*) with other flavorings. It can
be stored in the refrigerator in a glass jar for several weeks and used, a heaping
tablespoon or more at a time, as the basis of numerous sauces and stews.

> 3½ ounces (100 g) *lardo*
> 1 white onion
> leaves from 1 small bunch flat-leaf parsley
> 1 celery rib

Finely chop together the *lardo,* onion, parsley leaves, and celery. When using
the mixture, sauté it slowly, stirring it often and not allowing it to brown.

Salsa verde · Green sauce
Makes about 3¹⁄₄ cups (780 ml)

1 pesticide-free lemon

1 ounce (30 g) salt-packed capers, rinsed thoroughly
  to remove the salt

5 ounces (150 g) flat-leaf parsley

3½ ounces (100 g) basil

2 or 3 chives

4 oil-packed anchovy fillets

1 small white onion

⅓ garlic clove

1½ ounces (40 g) crustless bread

1 hard-boiled egg yolk

pepper

1¼ cups (300 ml) lightly fruity extra-virgin
  olive oil

scant ½ cup (100 ml) white-wine vinegar

salt

Grate the rind (colored part only) from the lemon and put in a small bowl. Chop the capers and add to the lemon rind. Chop separately the parsley and basil leaves and the chives. Drain the anchovies and chop. Chop together the onion, garlic, and bread. Mash the egg yolk with a fork.

Combine all the prepared ingredients in a bowl, season with pepper, and add the oil and vinegar. Mix carefully for a long time. Taste and add salt if needed. Let the sauce rest for at least a couple of hours before using.

Sugo d'umido (Garofolato di manzo) · *Clove-flavored*
meat sauce and pot roast

This sauce can be used with many types of pasta. The meat is sliced and
served separately as a main dish.

Makes enough sauce for 1 pound (450 g) pasta, with
4 to 6 servings pot roast

1¾ ounces (50 g) prosciutto rind
1¾ ounces (50 g) prosciutto fat
salt
pepper
1½ pounds (700 g) boneless beef pot roast
3 cloves
1 small bunch flat-leaf parsley
2 bay leaves
1 small white onion
1 small celery rib
1 carrot
1 garlic clove
2 tablespoons (30 g) butter
scant 1 cup (200 ml) dry red table wine
1 tablespoon tomato paste

Drop the rind into about 4 cups (1 liter) boiling water, cover, boil for 10 minutes, then drain. Scrape the rind carefully to remove any hairs and then cut
into small dice. Cut the prosciutto fat into strips. Mix a little salt and pepper
in a bowl and toss the strips of prosciutto fat in the mixture. Make small slits
all over the beef and stick half of the strips into the slits. Stick the cloves into
the beef. Tie the meat tightly with kitchen twine so it will keep its shape.

Tie the parsley and bay leaves together with twine. Chop together finely the
onion, celery rib, and carrot. Crush the garlic clove. Put the butter in a pan just
large enough to hold the meat and add the remaining prosciutto fat, the diced
rind, the onion mixture, the herb bundle, and the garlic. Cook over medium
heat for about 5 minutes. When the onion is almost translucent, add the meat.
Sear over medium heat on both sides for a few minutes, or until a nice brown
crust forms. Add the wine and let it evaporate, then dilute the tomato paste in a
ladleful of boiling water and add to the pan along with enough boiling water
just to cover the meat. Cover and cook over very low heat for a couple of hours.

Remove the meat from the sauce and set aside for the second course. Put the
sauce through a food mill before using.

Sugo finto · Meat-flavored tomato sauce

Literally "bogus sauce," *sugo finto,* a typical condiment for *paste asciutte,* was long used by poor people who could not afford costly meat. The ingredients simulated the taste of a true meat sauce. Today it is considered an essential element of the *cucina romana.*

Makes enough sauce for 1 pound (450 g) pasta

1 white onion
1 celery rib
leaves from 1 small bunch flat-leaf parsley
1¾ ounces (50 g) *lardo* or prosciutto fat
scant 1 cup (200 ml) vegetable or meat broth
1 tablespoon tomato paste
salt
pepper

Chop together finely the onion, celery, and parsley leaves. Chop the *lardo.*

Put the *lardo* in a pan and heat over low heat until it melts. Add the onion mixture and continue to cook over medium heat for about 5 minutes, stirring constantly. Meanwhile, heat the broth in a pot, and dissolve the tomato paste in the hot broth. When the onion is almost translucent, pour the broth into the pan and cook the sauce over low heat for about 20 minutes, or until it has reduced considerably. Season with salt and pepper and remove from the heat.

DOLCI · SWEETS

Bignè di San Giuseppe · Father's Day buns

Roman families still buy these traditional buns at pastry shops on Saint Joseph's day, March 19, the Italian Father's Day.

Makes about 40 pieces

3¼ ounces (90 g) flour
scant ½ cup (100 ml) water
1½ ounces (40 g) butter
pinch of salt
1½ teaspoons confectioners' sugar

½ pesticide-free lemon

2 whole eggs plus 1 egg yolk

about 2 cups (400 ml) lightly fruity extra-virgin
olive oil

10½ ounces (300 g) lard

3½ ounces (100 g) vanilla-flavored sugar (see page 275)

Sift the flour. Put the water in a saucepan and add the butter and salt. Bring to a boil over low heat and remove from the heat. Add the flour and the confectioners' sugar all at once and stir with a wooden spoon. Return the pan to low heat and continue stirring until the mixture begins to sizzle on the sides of the pan. Transfer to a bowl and let cool until tepid. Meanwhile, grate the rind (colored part only) from the lemon half.

When the mixture is tepid, add the whole eggs, one at a time, beating after each addition until perfectly incorporated, and then beat in the extra yolk. Finally, beat in the grated rind until evenly distributed, cover, and let rest for about 30 minutes.

Heat the oil and lard together in a deep skillet to 300°F (150°C), then lower the heat slightly. With the help of two teaspoons, shape hazelnut-size balls of the mixture and drop them into the hot oil. As soon as they puff up and are golden brown, transfer them to paper towels to drain.

Arrange the *bignè* in a pyramid on a large platter. Dust with the vanilla sugar just before serving.

"Bocconotti" di ricotta alla romana · Ricotta-filled pastries
The same amount of short-pastry dough
can be used in place of the *pasta frolla romana*.
Makes 10 to 12 servings

FOR THE PASTA FROLLA ROMANA

10½ ounces (300 g) flour

5¼ ounces (150 g) granulated sugar

1 pesticide-free lemon

5¼ ounces (150 g) cold lard or equal parts cold lard and
butter

3 egg yolks

1¾ ounces (50 g) mixed candied fruits
1 pound (450 g) ricotta, preferably *ricotta romana*
  (see page 275)
3 ounces (80 g) confectioners' sugar
3 egg yolks
ground cinnamon

TO ASSEMBLE
1 egg white
4 teaspoons (20 g) butter

To make the pastry, sift together the flour and granulated sugar onto a board. Grate the rind (colored part only) from the lemon. Cut the lard into small pieces. Add the lard and grated rind to the flour mixture and work them in with fingertips until the mixture is the consistency of coarse crumbs. Shape the mixture into a mound and make a well in the center. Add the egg yolks to the well and begin to incorporate them into the flour with a fork. When the mixture is too stiff to use a fork any longer, begin using your hands. Work the ingredients together quickly just until a smooth, silky dough forms. You will have 1 pound (450 g) dough. Cover and let rest in the refrigerator for about 1 hour.

Make the filling while the dough rises. Chop the candied fruits and put in a bowl. Add the ricotta, confectioners' sugar, egg yolks, and a pinch of cinnamon and mix well.

Once the dough has rested, assemble the pastries. Lightly beat the egg white and set aside. Butter the bottom of a 10-inch (25-cm) round baking pan (or a 9-inch/23-cm square pan). Divide the dough into two portions, one slightly larger than other. Roll out the large portion into a thin disk and use to line the bottom and sides of the prepared baking pan. Spoon the filling into the pastry shell, spreading it evenly. Roll out the second dough portion into a thin disk and lay it over the filling. Carefully seal together the edges of the bottom and top crust. Brush the top crust with the beaten egg white.

Bake in an oven preheated to 375°F (190°C) for about 40 minutes, or until golden brown. Remove from the oven and let cool for a while. Then, using a very sharp knife, cut the pastry, still in the pan, into 10 to 12 uniform pieces. Let cool completely before removing them from the pan.

Budino di castagne · Chestnut pudding
Makes 8 servings

3 ounces (80 g) blanched almonds, toasted

2 cups (500 ml) milk

pinch of salt

1 envelope *vanillina* (see page 275), or 4 or 5 drops vanilla
extract

1 pound (450 g) vacuum-packed peeled chestnuts (or roast
and peel fresh chestnuts)

1¾ ounces (50 g) sugar

½ ounce (15 g) sheet gelatin

2 tablespoons brandy

1 cup (240 ml) heavy cream

3 ounces (80 g) candied fruits, macerated in brandy

Put the almonds in a food processor and pulse until reduced to a powder. Set
aside. Pour the milk into a saucepan, add the salt and *vanillina* (if using vanilla
extract, reserve to add later), and bring to a boil. Add the chestnuts and simmer
over medium heat for about 20 minutes, or until tender. Put the chestnuts and
their milk in a food processor and process until smooth. Return this purée to
the saucepan, add the sugar, mix well, and evaporate any remaining liquid over
low heat. Let the mixture cool, then stir in the ground almonds and the vanilla
extract, if using.

Soften the gelatin in cold water for 3 to 5 minutes, squeeze out the excess
water, and put in a pan with the brandy. Melt over very low heat, stirring constantly. Add to the chestnut mixture and mix well. Whip the cream until stiff
peaks form.

Moisten a 2-quart (2-liter) pudding mold. Layer about one-eighth of the chestnut mixture in the bottom of the mold. Top with one-eighth of the whipped
cream, and then with one-eighth of the candied fruits. Repeat to make eight
layers total of each ingredient, finishing with a layer of candied fruits. If you
prefer to make fewer layers, that is fine; just divide the ingredients accordingly.
Put the mold in the refrigerator for a few hours.

Just before serving, dip the mold briefly in boiling water and immediately
turn the pudding out onto a platter.

Budino di ricotta · Ricotta pudding
Makes 8 servings

1 heaping tablespoon confectioners' sugar
ground cinnamon
¾ ounce (20 g) mixed candied orange and citron rinds
½ pesticide-free lemon
5 eggs
1 pound (450 g) ricotta, preferably *ricotta romana*
    (see page 275)
4½ ounces (130 g) flour
3 ounces (80 g) granulated sugar
2 tablespoons brandy
4 teaspoons (20 g) butter

Mix together the confectioners' sugar and a pinch of cinnamon in a bowl and reserve. Finely chop the candied rinds. Grate the rind from the lemon half. Separate 3 of the eggs. Beat the egg whites with a whisk or fork until stiff peaks form.

In a medium bowl, combine the ricotta, 3½ ounces (100 g) of the flour, the 2 whole eggs, the 3 yolks, the granulated sugar, the candied rinds, the grated lemon rind, a pinch of cinnamon, and the brandy. Mix well. Gently fold the egg whites into the ricotta mixture just until combined.

Grease a 2-quart (2-liter) pudding mold with the butter and dust with the remaining flour. Pour the ricotta mixture into the prepared mold; it should fill two-thirds of its capacity. Bake in an oven preheated to 325°F (165°C) for about 30 minutes, or until the pudding looks compact. Let cool. Turn the pudding out onto a platter and sprinkle the surface with the reserved cinnamon sugar.

Crostata di visciole alla romana · Sour-cherry tart
Makes 8 servings

1 pound (450 g) *pasta frolla romana* (recipe on page 255) or
    other sweetened short pastry
4 teaspoons (20 g) butter
9 ounces (250 g) sour-cherry jam *(confettura di visciole)*

1 egg white
1 tablespoon confectioners' sugar

Divide the dough into two portions, one twice as large as the other. Roll out the larger portion into a disk about ⅛ inch (3 mm) thick. Grease a 10-inch (25-cm) tart pan with a removable bottom with the butter, then line the pan with the dough disk, trimming away the overhang and setting the scraps aside. Spread the jam over the pastry and level it with the back of a wet tablespoon. Roll out the remaining dough into a thin disk the diameter of the tart pan and cut into several narrow strips. Arrange the strips in a lattice pattern on top of the jam. Gather together the dough scraps and roll them into a rope with your hands to fit the perimeter of the tart pan. Lay the rope around the rim of the *crostata*, sealing the edge of the bottom crust with the ends of the lattice strips to create a finished edge. Beat the egg white lightly in a small bowl and brush it over the lattice top.

Bake in an oven preheated to 350°F (180°C) for about 35 minutes, or until the pastry is golden brown. Let the *crostata* cool completely, then remove from the pan and dust with the confectioners' sugar before serving.

Crostata di mandorle e ricotta · *Almond and ricotta tart*
Makes 8 servings

7 ounces (200 g) blanched almonds
½ pesticide-free orange
4 eggs
9 ounces (250 g) granulated sugar
1 pound (450 g) ricotta, preferably *ricotta romana*
  (see page 275)
1 cup (250 ml) heavy cream
1 pound (450 g) *pasta frolla romana* (recipe, page 255) or
  other sweetened short pastry
4 teaspoons (20 g) butter
1 tablespoon confectioners' sugar

Put the almonds in a food processor and pulse until finely ground. Grate 1 teaspoon rind (colored part only) from the orange. Separate 1 of the eggs and set the egg white aside. Put the egg yolk, the remaining 3 eggs, and the granulated sugar in a bowl and whip with an electric mixer at medium speed for about 20 minutes. Add the ricotta, cream, ground almonds, and grated rind and mix until combined.

Roll out two-thirds of the dough into a disk about ⅛ inch (3 mm) thick. Grease a 10-inch (25-cm) tart pan with a removable bottom with the butter, then line the bottom and sides of the pan with the dough disk. Spread the ricotta mixture over the pastry and level with the back of a wet tablespoon. Roll out the remaining dough into a thin disk and cut into several narrow strips. Arrange the strips in a lattice (or other) pattern on top of the filling. Lightly beat the reserved egg white and brush it over the lattice top.

Bake in an oven preheated to 350°F (180°C) for about 45 minutes, or until the filling is set. If the pastry seems to be browning too quickly, cover with aluminum foil. Let the *crostata* cool completely, then remove from the pan and dust with the confectioners' sugar before serving.

Crostata di ricotta · *Ricotta tart*
Makes 8 servings

1¾ ounces (50 g) raisins
½ pesticide-free orange
½ pesticide-free lemon
1 ounce (30 g) mixed candied orange and citron rinds
1⅓ pounds (600 g) ricotta, preferably *ricotta romana*
  (see page 275)
10½ ounces (300 g) sugar
ground cinnamon
1½ ounces (40 g) pine nuts
3 egg yolks plus 1 whole egg
1 pound (450 g) *pasta frolla romana* (see page 255) or other
  sweetened short pastry
4 teaspoons (20 g) butter
1 egg white

Immerse the raisins in a small bowl of water to plump. Grate 1 teaspoon rind (colored part only) each from the orange and lemon. Finely chop the candied rinds. Put the ricotta in a large bowl. Drain the raisins and add to the ricotta along with the sugar, a pinch of cinnamon, the pine nuts, and the fresh and candied rinds. Mix well. Add the egg yolks, one at a time, beating after each addition until incorporated. Then add the whole egg and mix well.

Roll out two-thirds of the dough into a disk about ⅛ inch (3 mm) thick. Grease a 10-inch (25-cm) tart pan with a removable bottom with the butter, then line the pan with the dough disk. Spread the ricotta mixture over the pastry and level with the back of a wet tablespoon. Roll out the remaining dough into a thin disk and cut into several narrow strips. Arrange the strips in a lattice pattern on top of the filling. Lightly beat the reserved egg white and brush it over the lattice top.

Bake in an oven preheated to 375°F (190°C) for about 45 minutes, or until set. If the pastry appears to be browning too quickly, cover with aluminum foil. Let the *crostata* cool completely, then remove from the pan.

———————

Frappe

These very light pastries are the typical sweet of the Roman Carnival.

Makes 6 servings

1³⁄₄ ounces (50 g) butter
1³⁄₄ ounces (50 g) flour
¹⁄₃ ounce (10 g) confectioners' sugar
2 eggs
pinch of salt
1 pound (450 g) lard, or 2¹⁄₂ cups (600 ml) lightly fruity
  extra-virgin olive oil
³⁄₄ ounce (20 g) vanilla-flavored sugar (see page 275)

Put the butter in a bowl and cream it with a wooden spoon or a whisk. Sift the flour into the bowl and add the confectioners' sugar, eggs, and salt. Work quickly to form a smooth, silky dough. Wrap the dough in a dish towel and let it rest in a cool place for about 1 hour.

Divide the dough into two or three portions and roll out each portion into a sheet less than ¹⁄₁₆ inch (1 mm) thick. Cut the dough into any shapes you like, such as triangles, rectangles, or ribbons. Melt the lard in a deep skillet over high heat. Drop in the dough pieces, one at a time, and fry for just a few seconds until crisp and golden. Drain on paper towels and arrange on a platter. Let cool, then dust with the vanilla sugar.

Frittelle di mela · Apple fritters
Makes 8 servings

FOR THE BATTER
14 ounces (400 g) flour
1 tablespoon Sambuca or other anise-flavored liqueur
1 teaspoon salt
1²⁄₃ cups (400 ml) ice-cold water
2 egg whites

FOR THE APPLES
4 rennet or Granny Smith apples
2 cups (500 ml) Sambuca or other anise-flavored liqueur
2 tablespoons confectioners' sugar

FOR FRYING
2½ cups (600 ml) lightly fruity extra-virgin olive oil,
   or 1 pound (450 g) lard

To make the batter, sift the flour into a bowl. Add the Sambuca and salt, and then add the ice water, a few tablespoons at a time, while stirring constantly. When the batter is thick and smooth, cover it with a kitchen towel and let it rest in a cool place for about 2 hours.

To prepare the apples, peel them, then halve, core, and slice rather thickly. Moisten the slices with the Sambuca, dust with the confectioners' sugar, and set aside for about 2 hours.

Beat the 2 egg whites with a fork or whisk until stiff peaks form. Fold the egg whites into the batter, incorporating thoroughly. Heat the oil in a deep skillet over high heat. Dip the apple slices in the batter, allowing the excess to drip off, and drop them into the hot oil, a few at a time. Fry until golden brown, then drain on paper towels. Serve piping hot.

Frittelle di pasta lievitata · Fried dough
Makes 8 servings

2½ ounces (45 g) fresh cake yeast
7 ounces (200 g) confectioners' sugar
few tablespoons warm water for activating yeast, plus
   6 tablespoons (90 ml)

1¾ pounds (800 g) flour
generous pinch of salt
1⅔ cups (400 ml) lightly fruity extra-virgin olive oil

Crumble the yeast in a small bowl and add a pinch of the confectioners' sugar and a few tablespoons warm water. Mix gently, then cover the bowl and let the yeast sit for 6 to 7 minutes, or until it begins to foam. Sift the flour into a bowl and add the salt. Add the yeast mixture and begin to work it into the flour, gradually moistening with the 6 tablespoons (90 ml) warm water. Knead the mixture for about 20 minutes. When it begins to come away from your hands and seems elastic and silky, cover it with a kitchen towel and let it rise for about 1 hour, or until it doubles in volume.

When the dough is ready, heat the oil in a skillet over high heat. Using two teaspoons, drop walnut-size balls of dough into the hot oil, a few at a time. As soon as they are golden brown, drain them on paper towels. Dust with the remaining confectioners' sugar and serve piping hot.

Frittelle di riso all'antica · *Rice fritters*
Makes 4 servings

3½ ounces (100 g) flour
1 ounce (30 g) fresh cake yeast
pinch of salt
2 cups (500 ml) milk
1¾ ounces raisins
½ pesticide-free lemon
1 tablespoon granulated sugar
3½ ounces (100 g) Arborio or other rice for risotto
1 ounce (30 g) pine nuts
1 whole egg plus 2 egg yolks
about 2 cups (500 ml) lightly fruity extra-virgin olive oil
14 ounces (400 g) lard
3½ ounces (100 g) confectioners' sugar

Put 1½ ounces (40 g) of the flour in a small bowl, crumble in the yeast, and add the salt. Heat ½ cup (125 ml) of the milk until it is tepid, add it to the bowl, and stir well to make a batter. Cover the bowl with a dish towel and let the batter rest for about 30 minutes, or until the yeast begins to foam.

Meanwhile, immerse the raisins in a small bowl of water to plump. Grate the rind (colored part only) from the lemon half. Put the remaining milk and the sugar in a saucepan and bring to a boil. Add the rice and boil it until it is al dente. Drain the rice and let it cool somewhat in a bowl. Drain the raisins and add to the rice along with the remaining flour, the pine nuts, and the grated rind, then stir to mix. Add the whole egg and egg yolks, one at a time, mixing well after each addition until incorporated. Finally, add the batter and work the ingredients together thoroughly, adding a few tablespoons warm water only if the mixture seems too stiff.

Heat the oil and lard in a deep skillet to 300°F (150°C), then lower the heat slightly. Using two teaspoons, drop walnut-size balls of the dough into the hot oil, a few at a time. As soon as they are golden brown, drain them on paper towels. Dust with the confectioners' sugar and serve piping hot.

"Gelato" di ricotta · Ricotta "gelato"
Makes 8 servings

5 eggs
3½ ounces (100 g) sugar
5 tablespoons rum or brandy
1 pound (450 g) ricotta, preferably *ricotta romana*
   (see page 275)

Separate the eggs. Beat the whites with a fork or whisk until stiff peaks form. Put the egg yolks in a bowl and add the sugar. Whip with an electric mixer at medium speed for about 20 minutes. Stir in the rum, a tablespoon at a time, then add the ricotta, forcing it through a large-mesh sieve. Mix gently until the mixture is smooth. Finally, fold in the beaten egg whites just until combined.

Line a 1-quart (1-liter) mold with parchment paper and pour in the ricotta mixture. Put in the refrigerator to chill for about 4 hours. Turn out onto a platter to serve.

Gnocchi dolci alla romana · Sweet gnocchi
Makes 4 servings

5¼ ounces (150 g) butter
2¾ ounces (75 g) flour
1 ounce (30 g) cornstarch
1 tablespoon sugar

6 egg yolks
scant 1 cup (200 ml) milk
2 tablespoons brandy
nutmeg
2 tablespoons grated *parmigiano-reggiano*

Put 3½ tablespoons (50 g) of the butter in a small bowl and let soften for about 30 minutes. Sift the flour.

Put the softened butter and the flour in a food processor and add the cornstarch, sugar, egg yolks, milk, brandy, and a grating of nutmeg. Process until a silky cream forms. Transfer to a saucepan and bring to a gentle boil over low heat. Cook for about 10 minutes, always over low heat and stirring constantly with a whisk to prevent lumps.

Moisten a marble or other cold surface and pour the mixture onto it. Level it to a thickness of about ⅜ inch (1 cm) with the back of a wet tablespoon. Let cool completely. Cut the cooled mixture into rhombuses about 1¼ inches (3 cm) on a side.

Grease a baking pan with 4 teaspoons (20 g) of the butter. Make a layer of the rhombuses, arranging them very close together, on the bottom of the pan. Dust with a little parmigiano and dot with a few flakes of the remaining butter. Continue forming layers, always dusting with the parmigiano and dotting with the butter, until all the rhombuses are used up; reserve a little parmigiano and butter. At the end, you should have a sort of flattened dome. Dust the top with the remaining parmigiano and dot with the remaining butter.

Bake in an oven preheated to 400°F (200°C) for about 10 minutes, or until a nice, brown crust forms. Let cool for a few minutes before serving.

Maccheroni con le noci · Sweet pasta with walnuts
Makes 4 servings

5¼ ounces (150 g) skinned walnuts
5¼ ounces (150 g) sugar
1 tablespoon ground dry cookies
1¾ ounces (50 g) unsweetened cocoa powder
ground cinnamon
nutmeg
4 tablespoons alchermes (bright-red Italian liqueur used in
    pastry making)

few tablespoons milk, if needed

14 ounces (400 g) lasagne

Put the nuts, sugar, ground cookies, cocoa, a pinch of cinnamon, a grating of nutmeg, and the alchermes in a food processor and process until a thick cream forms. If it is too thick, add the milk.

Drop the pasta into about 4 quarts (4 liters) boiling salted water. Drain when al dente. Make a layer of the lasagne in a warmed serving bowl and top with a layer of the chocolate cream as though you were adding sauce to a bowl of noodles, first pasta, then sauce, then more pasta, more sauce. Repeat the layers until all the ingredients are used up, ending with a layer of the cream. Serve immediately, scooping the servings directly from the bowl.

Maritozzi quaresimali · Lenten buns
Makes 10 to 12 buns

¾ ounce (20 g) raisins

½ pesticide-free orange

1 pound (450 g) raised bread dough

3 tablespoons lightly fruity extra-virgin olive oil

3 tablespoons confectioners' sugar

¾ ounce (20 g) pine nuts

4 teaspoons (20 g) butter

Immerse the raisins in a small bowl of water to plump, then drain. Grate 1 teaspoon rind (colored part only) from the orange half. Put the bread dough on a wooden board and knead in the oil, confectioners' sugar, pine nuts, raisins, and grated rind. Work the ingredients together quickly with your hands until the dough is quite homogeneous and compact.

Grease a baking pan with the butter. Pinch off small pieces of the dough about the size of an egg and form oval buns. Put the buns in the prepared pan, spacing them about 2 inches (5 cm) apart. Let the buns rest in a warm spot for about 1 hour, or until they have doubled in volume.

Bake in an oven preheated to 400°F (200°C) for about 20 minutes. Let cool before serving.

Pangiallo

Makes 8 to 10 servings

3 ounces (80 g) sugar

scant 1 cup (200 ml) warm water

scant 1 ounce (25 g) fresh cake yeast

9½ ounces (270 g) flour

scant ½ ounce (12 g) mixed ground spices (cinnamon,
    coriander, pepper, nutmeg, cardamom)

4 pounds (1.8 kg) Zibibbo or golden raisins

3 ounces (80 g) candied orange and citron rinds

6 tablespoons (90 ml) lightly fruity extra-virgin olive oil

8 ounces (225 g) pine nuts

8 ounces (225 g) blanched almonds

Put 2½ ounces (70 g) of the sugar in a bowl, add the warm water, and stir to dissolve the sugar. Put 2 tablespoons of this sugar syrup in a bowl, crumble in the yeast, and add 1 tablespoon of the flour and a pinch of the spices. Mix well, then cover with a dish towel and let sit for 6 or 7 minutes, or until the yeast begins to foam.

Immerse the raisins in a large bowl of water to plump. Finely chop the candied rinds and reserve. Sift 9 ounces (250 g) of the flour onto a wooden board, shape it into a mound, and make a well in the center. Add the yeast mixture, the remaining spices, the remaining sugar syrup, and 5 tablespoons of the oil to the well. Begin to incorporate the yeast mixture into the flour with a fork. When the mixture is too stiff to use a fork any longer, begin forming the dough with your hands. Work carefully to make a somewhat soft dough, moistening, if needed, with a few tablespoons warm water. Drain the raisins and add to the dough along with the pine nuts, almonds, and candied rinds and knead until all the ingredients are evenly distributed and the dough is soft and smooth. Form the dough into a round loaf, cover it with a dish towel, and let it rise in a warm place for about 12 hours.

Make a quick batter with the remaining flour (about 1½ tablespoons), a spoonful of water, and the remaining oil and sugar. Brush the batter over the entire surface of the loaf, including the bottom, then put the loaf in a baking pan. Bake in an oven preheated to 400°F (200°C) for about 1 hour, or until a toothpick inserted in the center comes out clean. Let cool completely before serving.

Pizza di polenta con la ricotta · Ricotta corn cake
Makes 8 to 10 servings

1 ounce (30 g) raisins
2½ cups (600 ml) water
pinch of salt
9 ounces (250 g) finely ground corn flour (polenta)
9 ounces (250 g) ricotta, preferably *ricotta romana*
  (see page 275)
1 cup (120 g) confectioners' sugar
ground cinnamon
4 teaspoons (20 g) butter
1½ ounces (40 g) pine nuts
3½ tablespoons (50 g) lard

Immerse the raisins in a small bowl of water to plump. Bring the water to a boil and add the salt. Remove from the heat and stir in the corn flour. Keep stirring until all the water has been absorbed. Let cool somewhat, then drain the raisins and add to the bowl along with the ricotta, confectioners' sugar, and a pinch of cinnamon and mix well.

Grease a 10-inch (25-cm) round cake pan with the butter. Pour in the batter and decorate the top with the pine nuts and flakes of lard. Bake in an oven pre-heated to 350°F (180°C) for about 1 hour, or until a toothpick inserted in the center comes out clean. Let cool for a few minutes before turning it out of the pan. Then let cool completely before serving.

Pizza di visciole alla romana · Sour-cherry and custard tart
Makes 8 servings

4 egg yolks
1 envelope *vanillina* (see page 275), or 4 or 5 drops vanilla
  extract
1½ ounces (45 g) cornstarch
½ pesticide-free lemon
1 cup (240 ml) milk
5 ounces (140 g) sugar
1 pound (450 g) *pasta frolla romana* (see page 255) or other
  sweetened short pastry

4 teaspoons (20 g) butter
7 ounces (200 g) sour-cherry jam (*confettura di visciole*)
1 tablespoon confectioners' sugar

Put 3 egg yolks in a bowl and beat with the *vanillina* (if using vanilla extract, reserve to add later) and cornstarch to make a smooth cream. Grate 1 teaspoon rind (colored part only) from the lemon half.

Combine the milk, sugar, and grated rind in a large saucepan and bring to a boil. Remove from the heat and pour the egg mixture into the milk in a steady stream, stirring vigorously with a whisk to prevent lumps. Return the pan to the stove top over very low heat and cook, stirring constantly, for about 10 minutes, or until the consistency of a thick custard. Remove from the heat and stir in the vanilla extract, if using. Let cool completely.

Divide the dough into two portions, one slightly larger than the other. Roll out each portion into a disk about ⅛ inch (3 mm) thick. Grease an 8-inch (20-cm) tart pan with a removable bottom with the butter, then line the bottom and sides of the pan with the larger dough disk. Pour the custard into the pastry-lined pan, and spread the jam evenly over the custard, leveling it with the back of a wet tablespoon. Lay the smaller disk over the filling and seal together the edges of the top and bottom crust. Lightly beat the remaining egg yolk and brush it over the top crust.

Bake in an oven preheated to 350°F (180°C) for 45 minutes, or until golden brown. Let cool completely, then remove from the pan and dust with the confectioners' sugar before serving.

––––––––––

Pizza ricresciuta di Pasqua · *Easter pie*
Make 8 to 10 servings

1 pesticide-free lemon
1 pound (450 g) flour
4 eggs
5¼ ounces (150 g) ricotta, preferably *ricotta romana*
  (see page 275)
pinch of ground cinnamon
pinch of salt
14 ounces (400 g) raised bread dough
4 tablespoons lightly fruity extra-virgin olive oil

Grate 1 tablespoon rind (colored part only) from the lemon. Sift the flour onto a wooden board, shape it into a mound, and make a well in the center. Break the eggs into a small bowl and beat lightly. Pour them into the well and add the ricotta, forcing it through a large-mesh sieve, along with the salt, cinnamon, and grated rind. Add the bread dough and knead everything together vigorously, whacking the dough on the wooden board for about 20 minutes. It should be elastic and come away easily from the board.

Divide the dough in half. Grease two 7-inch (18-cm) round baking pans with the oil. Shape each dough portion into a round and put a round into each prepared pan. Cover each pan with a dish towel and let the dough rise in a warm spot for 8 to 10 hours, or until doubled in volume.

Bake in an oven preheated to 375°F (190°C) for about 40 minutes, or until golden brown. Let cool completely before serving.

Ricotta condita · Sweet ricotta flavored with rum and coffee
Serve with cookies.
Makes 8 servings

1 pound (450 g) ricotta, preferably *ricotta romana*
  (see page 275)
2 tablespoons rum
1½ ounces (40 g) finely ground coffee
2 ounces (60 g) sugar

Force the ricotta through a large-mesh sieve and let it fall into a bowl. Soften it with a wooden spoon. Add the rum, coffee, and sugar. Mix again to blend well, then serve.

Ricotta fritta · Fried ricotta
Makes 8 servings

1 pound (450 g) ricotta, preferably *ricotta romana*
  (see page 275)
3 eggs
2 ounces (60 g) confectioners' sugar
ground cinnamon
1¼ cups (300 ml) lightly fruity extra-virgin olive oil
7 ounces (200 g) flour

Make sure you have drained the ricotta thoroughly as directed, as it must be very compact. Cut the ricotta first into rather thick slices and then into rhombuses about 2 inches (5 cm) on a side. Break the eggs into a bowl and beat lightly with a fork. In another bowl, stir together the confectioners' sugar and a pinch of cinnamon.

Heat the oil in a skillet over medium heat. Meanwhile, dredge the ricotta rhombuses in the flour, shaking off the excess, and then dip in the beaten egg. Drop the coated pieces into the hot oil, a few at a time, and fry until golden brown. Drain on paper towels and arrange on a platter. Dust with the cinnamon sugar and serve piping hot.

Timballo di ricotta · Baked ricotta pudding
From the Roman Jewish tradition.
Makes 6 servings

½ pesticide-free lemon
5 eggs
8 ounces (225 g) confectioners' sugar
1½ pounds (700 g) ricotta, preferably *ricotta romana*
  (see page 275)
ground cinnamon
2 tablespoons brandy

Grate the rind (colored part only) from the lemon half. Separate the eggs. Reserve the whites in a bowl. Put the egg yolks in a second bowl and add the confectioners' sugar. Beat with an electric mixer until a soft cream forms. Add the ricotta, grated rind, a pinch of cinnamon, and the brandy and mix well. Beat the eggs whites with a fork or whisk until stiff peaks form. Gently fold the whites into the ricotta mixture, incorporating thoroughly.

Pour the ricotta mixture into a 9-inch (23-cm) flan mold or similar pan. Bake in an oven preheated to 350°F (180°C) for about 20 minutes. Lower the oven temperature to 300°F (150°C) and bake for 10 minutes longer, or until a toothpick inserted into the center comes out clean. Let cool completely before serving.

Torta di pinoli · *Pine-nut pie*
Makes 8 servings

6 ounces (170 g) butter
11¼ ounces (320 g) flour
12 ounces (340 g) sugar
1 teaspoon baking powder
5 tablespoons milk
pinch of salt
10 ounces (280 g) blanched almonds
½ pesticide-free lemon
4 egg whites
10½ ounces (300 g) pine nuts

Put 5¼ ounces (150 g) of the butter in a saucepan and melt over very low heat. Remove from the heat and let cool until tepid. Sift together 10½ ounces (300 g) of the flour, 7 ounces (200 g) of the sugar, and the baking powder onto a wooden board. Shape the mixture into a mound and make a well in the center. Add the milk, salt, and the tepid butter to the well and begin to incorporate the wet ingredients into the flour with a fork. When the mixture is too stiff to use a fork any longer, begin forming the dough with your hands and work the ingredients together until you have a smooth, evenly blended dough.

Roll out the dough into a disk about 13 inches (33 cm) in diameter and ¼ inch (6 mm) thick. Grease a 9-inch (23-cm) springform pan with the remaining butter and dust with the remaining flour. Line the bottom and sides of the prepared pan with the dough disk, creating a finished edge. Bake in an oven preheated to 350°F (180°C) for 15 to 20 minutes, or until golden. Remove from the oven and let cool. Lower the oven temperature to 325°F (165°C).

Meanwhile, put the remaining sugar and the almonds in a food processor and process until the consistency of a fine flour. Grate 1 teaspoon rind (colored part only) from the lemon half. Put the egg whites in a bowl and beat with a fork or whisk until stiff peaks form. Add the almond-sugar mixture, pine nuts, and grated rind to the egg whites and mix just until evenly combined.

Pour the mixture into the baked crust and level with the back of a wet tablespoon. Return the pan to the oven for about 10 minutes, or until the filling is golden. Let cool completely, then unmold. Serve at room temperature.

GLOSSARY OF TERMS
AND INGREDIENTS

Anchovies *(alici* or *acciughe)*. These useful and nutritious little fish are used in three forms, fresh, salt packed, and oil packed. To prepare salt-packed anchovies for cooking, rinse off all the salt and divide the fish (which will be headless) into two fillets, discarding the skeleton. Oil-packed anchovies should be drained of their oil and blotted on paper towels.

Artichokes *(carciofi)*. Paradoxically, the large, delicately flavored globe artichoke, typical of the *campagna romana,* is not the best for the recipes here, except when it is used raw. The smaller, more ovoid, often purple-tinged varieties from elsewhere in Italy are preferable. To trim artichokes: Remove the tough outer leaves of the artichoke and cut off the thorny tips from the remaining leaves. Working 1 to 2 inches (2.5 to 5 cm) above the base, turn the artichoke against the blade of a small, curved knife, removing everything tough and inedible. The stem is edible. If using, cut off the tough bottom, then peel away the stringy outer layers, exposing the tender core. Work quickly when trimming artichokes, and rub them with a cut lemon or drop them into water acidulated with lemon juice to prevent darkening.

Broccolo romanesco. This member of the genus *Brassica* comes in a head and behaves more or less like a cauliflower, which can substitute for it when needed, but the taste is rather closer to broccoli. It is distinguished by its pointed fractal florets and light but vivid green. Once unknown outside the Rome area, it is now increasingly available around the world, often misnamed simply *romanesco*.

Butter. Always use unsalted butter for the recipes.

Casereccio bread *(pane casereccio)*. The basic bread of Rome and the Castelli Romani, it is made with natural yeast in large round or long loaves (called *pagnotta* and *filone,* respectively), sometimes baked in a wood-burning oven. Its pleasantly chewy, rough texture is ideal for *bruschetta*.

Castrato. Lamb castrated at about four months and butchered between five and fifteen months. In recipes calling for it, any lamb can be used. In Rome and Lazio, *abbacchio* is milk-fed lamb that has never consumed grass.

Crostini. Cubes of bread fried, usually in oil, or toasted in the oven.

Eggs. All eggs called for in recipes are USDA large.

Flour. In recipes specifying simply flour, all-purpose flour should be used.

Frittata. Like an omelet, but cooked on both sides, not folded. To turn the frittata, slide it out of the pan onto a plate or the inside of a lid, invert the pan on top, and flip both over so the uncooked side falls into the pan.

Guanciale. Cured (but not smoked) pork jowl essential in many traditional Roman and Latian dishes. It is usually quite fatty, with a delicate, almost sweet flavor. A very good pancetta can be substituted in most cases.

Lard and *lardo.* The English term *lard,* which refers to rendered pork fat, is *strutto* in Italian. *Lardo,* which is a type of cured pork fat, appears in Italian in recipes.

Lemons. Although many Italian lemons achieve impressive sizes, normal-size lemons are called for in the recipes. Ideally, only organically grown lemons should be used, but they are indispensable when the rind is called for. Pesticides and preservatives render the rind inedible.

Mint. Romans acknowledge two main uses for mint, and each takes a different plant. *Menta romana (Mentha spicata),* or Roman mint, is similar to spearmint. *Mentuccia (M. pulegium)* is the characteristic flavoring of *carciofi alla romana* (recipe on page 209).

Nervetti. Strips of cartilage from the knee or shank of the calf, boiled and dressed variously, *nervetti* were at one time an important food source for the poor. In fact, butchers gave them away. Today, they are a niche item on traditional menus.

Olive oil. The recipes always call for extra-virgin olive oil, even for deep-frying, and usually specify whether the oil should be lightly fruity, medium fruity, or intensely fruity, the categories into which the oil from the hundreds of olive varieties in Italy, or their blends, are traditionally divided.

Ovoli. The *Amanita caesarea* mushroom is one of the most highly prized mushrooms in Italy. Today an expensive gourmet item, it is almost always served raw, but back in the day when they could be gathered easily and in quantity, *ovoli* turned up in some surprisingly homely dishes.

Pajata or *pagliata.* This is the Roman name for the first section of the intestine of the milk-fed calf, used with its chyme. Today it is difficult to find, and lamb intestine is used instead of calf. Its flavor, however, is much stronger.

Pancetta. Cured (not smoked) pork belly, pancetta comes in both slab (*tesa*) and rolled (*arrotolata*) forms. Slab is somewhat preferable, but if the recipe calls for chopping the pancetta into tiny pieces, it makes no difference which type you use. Bacon, which is smoked, is not usually an acceptable substitute for pancetta.

Pesce azzurro (literally, "blue fish"). Generic term for fish that live far from the coast and are steel blue. The most common "blue" fish are herring, anchovies, sardines, mackerel, tuna, and swordfish.

Pork rind. The Italians have two terms, *cotenna* and *cotiche,* for pork rind. Fresh rind is usually meant, but occasionally the rind of the prosciutto is called for. They need to be washed and scraped (to remove errant hairs) before use.

Prosciutto. The Italian word can mean any kind of ham, but unless indicated, *prosciutto crudo,* or so-called Parma ham, which is salted, air-dried ham, is what is meant.

Provatura. This very old Latian and Campanian *pasta filata* cheese (that is, it forms strings when melted) is made from the milk of water buffalo and is a close relative of mozzarella, which can substituted for it in recipes.

Ricotta romana. The typical ricotta of Rome is made with sheep's milk and is renowned for its good, sweet flavor and creamy, buttery texture. It needs to be left to drain in a nonmetallic colander for several hours or up to overnight before use. Cow's milk ricotta is not typical of Lazio. Use the best, creamiest ricotta you can find, but know that it will never be as good as the Roman kind.

Telline. Also known in Italian as *arselle,* or wedge shells in English *(Donax trunculus),* *telline* are small clamlike bivalves with a roughly triangular shell. In their place, use the smallest clams you can find.

Vanilla-flavored sugar *(zucchero vanigliato).* Put confectioners' sugar and one or two vanilla beans in a hermetically sealed jar and leave untouched for about a month before using. It keeps for a long time.

Vanillina. In Italy, vanilla for baking comes in powdered form in little envelopes. You can use four or five drops of vanilla extract in place of an envelope of *vanillina.*

NOTES

1. On the food of ancient Rome, see, among many others, J. André, *L'alimentation et la cuisine à Rome* (Paris: Klincksieck, 1961); and A. Dosi and F. Schnell, *A tavola con i romani antichi* (Rome: Edizioni Quasar, 1984).

2. In the foundation myth of Rome, the Aventine Hill, which slopes steeply down to the Tiber, was connected with the figures of Romulus and Remus. According to the story, Remus chose the top of this hill for observing and reading the auspices of the flight of birds. In reality, the Aventine was probably the site of the first village, from which it was easy to watch the river and defend against the marshes that surrounded it. Today the hill is an exclusive residential area with numerous Romanesque and other churches, and it still has a marvelous view over the city.

3. On the Italian diet in the Middle Ages, see M. Montanari, *L'alimentazione contadina nell'alto Medioevo* (Naples: Liguori Editore, 1979).

4. Corresponding to today's provinces of Viterbo and Rieti, respectively.

5. The terms Campagna and Marittima were used during the regime of the papal states to indicate the administrative divisions of southern Lazio and a part of what is today the Campania region.

6. A magnificent old *caffè* on Via del Corso near the Italian Parliament. Its famous private room was frequented by painters, politicians, and writers. The building is still there, but the premises of the *caffè* have been taken over by an Italian chain restaurant.

7. The icon of the gentleman farmer called back to arms, L. Quintus Cincinnatus (519–430 B.C.) was a Roman statesman and aristocrat who famously retired from public life to tend his own farm. But when Rome needed him, he reluctantly returned, did his duty, and then went back to the plow (Livy 3:26–29).

8. Malarial fevers were already known in the second century B.C. and were believed to have been brought to Italy by the Carthaginians. The Romans had carried out large-scale hydraulic projects in an attempt to contain the stagnant ponds that formed owing to the rising and lowering of the coast in relation to the level of the sea. Malaria, by now widespread, was well known by such Roman writers as Columella, Seneca, and Livy. From the physician Galen, who died in A.D. 201, we learn that even in the city it was not uncommon to encounter daily people with jaundice and dropsy caused by the fevers.

Starting in the High Middle Ages, mild forms of malaria are documented in the countryside and in Rome. Some said they were brought by the winds from the Sahara, others that they proliferated in marsh waters. Still others attached importance to the use of cotton clothing instead of wool. Some attributed the disease to rapid oscillations of the temperature, some to the woods, some to the absence of crops and habitations. Many centuries had to pass, until almost the beginning of the twentieth century, for medicine to realize that malaria develops in the presence of decomposing organic substances and is transmitted by the anopheles mosquito. The bacillus lives in the air only at a temperature of at least 68°F (20°C) and at a specific humidity level. That is why the fevers disappeared in winter or in very dry summers. But with the first rainfall, the bacillus, transported by air currents, spread through the countryside.

9. Cicero, *De re agraria contra Rullum* (Chear GL 1:95). We are in the 60s B.C. The agrarian law proposed by Julius Caesar established the distribution among the Roman citizens of a part of the *ager publicus*.

10. After numerous sieges, Totila finally entered Rome in 549.

11. The story of the Lombard king Agilulf is told by Paulus Diaconus in his *Historia Langobardorum* (3:35).

12. He lived in Rome during the 1800s and was one of the most cultivated figures of his day, author of numerous works, among them the celebrated *Liber pontificalis*.

13. In the ninth century, Pope Leo IV built a 1.9-mile (3-kilometer) extension to the existing city wall to enclose the Vatican Hill.

14. These ancient towns still survive in the middle Tiber valley, along the Via Cassia and Via Flaminia.

15. Pirates who infested the Italian coasts for centuries.

16. Many of these fortified walls, adapted and reinforced over the centuries, are still visible in some towns of the *campagna romana*.

17. The gardens alongside the walls of Rome survived until the late 1800s.

18. The confraternities, which existed in Lazio from time immemorial, were religious organizations but also political. The "universities," which were political, had the function of organizing the workers, of assisting them in case of illness in their own hospitals, of giving shelter to pilgrims of fellow confraternities of the same trade, of providing for their members' unmarried daughters, and more.

19. The oldest confraternity included not only the animal raisers but also all those whose work had to do with the butchering and distribution of meat, tanning of hides, and other related activities.

20. Almost all these towers are located along the Tyrrhenian coast, both north and south of Rome, on promontories from which it was possible to watch the sea.

21. The barons who owned vast estates outside Rome often requisitioned the goods on their way to the city. They especially favored wheat, which they bought up to sell at a high price during famines.

22. The giulio was the coin circulated by Pope Julius II (1503–13), for whom it is named.

23. A Roman agrarian measurement, the *rubbio* corresponds to about 1.25 acres (0.5 hectare), or 5,980 square yards (5,000 square meters).

24. An estate that still survives in Monte Mario, a quarter on the north side of Rome next to the Via Cassia.

25. J. Le Gall, *Il Tevere, fiume di Roma nell'antichità* (Rome: Quasar, 2005). See also *Il territorio della media valle del Tevere. La pianificazione territoriale comprensoriale* (Rome: Università La Sapienza, Dipartimento di Architettura, 1966).

26. The new conquerors of Rome, Piedmont's House of Savoy, lacking in sensitivity to history, traditions, and territory, destroyed the magnificent archaeological parks to build new quarters to make the recently named capital more like Paris.

27. J. Carcopino, "Les fastes de la cuisine romaine," in *La Cuisine considerée comme une des Beaux-arts* (Paris: Tambourinaire, 1951), 43–71.

28. Sergius Orata (140–90 B.C.) was a wealthy Roman entrepreneur and engineer who loved fishing and had a particular fondness for the fish named *orata,* the gilt-head bream. Columella (*De re rustica,* 8:16) attributes his cognomen to his passion for this fish.

29. *Letters to Atticus,* 1:19.

30. Juvenal, *Satires,* 4:37–136.

31. The two city ports on the banks of the Tiber, now obscured by the nineteenth-century embankments.

32. As Rome expanded, the waters of the Tiber became an important transport route. Different types of vessels plied it, among the most important of which were the *caudicariae,* ships for carrying foodstuffs. Large cargo ships, or *onerariae,* arrived loaded with wheat. *Scaphae* and *lenunculi* were small craft used only in port for transferring goods from the large ships that could not dock.

33. The humanist Andrea Bacci (1524–1600), in his *Del Tevere della natura et bontà dell'Acque & delle Inondationi* (Rome, 1558), also marvels at how full of fish the Tiber and its tributaries are.

34. In 2002, the market was moved outside the city to modern headquarters in Guidonia, on the Via Tiburtina, but the old structure remains near the beginning of the Via Ostiense in Rome.

35. This was the church where Jews were obliged to listen to sermons every Sunday.

36. Trade of the maritime republics, especially Genoa and Pisa, which during the Middle Ages pushed their goods as far as northern Europe, must have spread the use of Norwegian stockfish even in its own country.

37. A very old legend has it that the witches hold their Sabbath around a walnut tree in the countryside outside Benevento, in Campania.

38. From the word *fagotto,* or "bundle," the wrapping, usually a colored cloth, used to wrap and carry the lunch.

39. *De Aquis urbis Romae.* Sextus Julius Frontinus, who held the office of *curator aquarum* (water commissioner) under Nerva and Trajan, and was therefore responsible for the city's water supply, gives a detailed account of the nine aqueducts in function in his day.

40. The ancient Forum Boarium or Bovarium, where animals were bought and sold, was located at the foot of the Capitoline Hill.

41. Remains of it can be seen beneath the American Academy in Rome.

42. An enormous bibliography exists on the Roman aqueducts. This account is based principally on the classic T. Ashby, *The Aqueducts of Ancient Rome* (Oxford: Clarendon, 1935). On the aqueducts and fountains of Rome in general, see H. V. Morton, *Fountains of Rome* (London: Macmillan, 1966).

43. J. André, 52 ff.

44. *Farro* was a great resource for making bread in Lazio during World War II, since *farro* flour was not rationed.

45. In the Roman hinterland, *mola* is still the word for both flour mill and the milling of olives for oil.

46. The great Byzantine general Flavius Belisarius (500–65) was sent to Italy by the emperor Justinian to defend Rome from the Goths.

47. One Roman *libbra* was equivalent to a little more than a pound (about 500 grams).

48. The bolognino was a coin struck in Bologna between the twelfth and seventeenth centuries; it circulated in other parts of Italy as well.

49. *Capitoli e leggi da osservarsi inviolabilmente per ordine espresso della Santità di Nostro Signore da le milizie a piedi e a cavallo dello Stato Ecclesiastico* (Rome, 1658), s.e. art. 4, p. 8.

50. For an exhaustive treatment of traditional homemade pastas, see O. Zanini De Vita, *Encyclopedia of Pasta,* translated by M. B. Fant (Berkeley: University of California Press, 2009).

51. G. Moroni (1802–83), great scholar of things Roman, private secretary of Pope Gregory XVI, compiled, at the pontifical court and curia, with the help of a large staff, an enormous and useful collection of items that he published in the 103 volumes of the *Dizionario di erudizione storico ecclesiastica.*

52. Between the end of the nineteenth century and the 1930s, the Pontina, or the Pontine marshland, was finally successfully drained with the aid of labor from the Veneto and Emilia. The workers who helped complete this massive work were rewarded with plots of the reclaimed land.

53. As late as the 1950s in the *agro romano,* a favorite remedy for every sort of illness was the famous *olio fiorito.* Oil was taken from the lamps that burned in front of sacred images and placed in a glass jar. Large quantities of fragrant herbs were added to the oil, where they macerated in a warm place for fifty days. The herbs included chamomile, mallow, mint, wild lettuce, thyme, arugula, elderberries, hemp flowers, myrtle, rue, nettles, and *erba grassa* (*Veronica beccabunga,* or European speedwell).

54. *I Regesti dei Bandi, Editti e Notificazioni,* emanated almost until the arrival of the Kingdom of Italy, constitute a very rich documentation on the production and consumption of the products of Rome's gardens.

55. Pellegrino Artusi wrote *La scienza in cucina e l'arte di mangiar bene* (The science of cooking and the art of eating well), published between the end of the nineteenth and beginning of the twentieth century in several highly successful editions. It remains a perennial best-seller in Italy and nearly every Italian household has a copy.

56. 1: 2, 19.

57. Istituzione del Governo pontificio, which had control of the entire food sector.

58. C. Marigliani and O. Zanini De Vita, *Castelli Romani, il paesaggio agrario, il territorio e la sua gente* (Rome, 2010).

59. A campaign promoted by the Mussolini government to boost wheat production and achieve self-sufficiency, which was one of the pillars of the policy of autarky. Every free space in the city was sown with wheat, and farming in the countryside was intensified.

60. The Opera Nazionale Combattenti (ONC) was founded at the end of World War I to assist returning veterans and their families.

61. The major highways radiating from Rome like the spokes of a wheel, called thus because they correspond in name and, roughly, route to the great roads of ancient Rome.

62. General Pietro Badoglio was called by the king to lead the government after the fall of Mussolini.

63. Pliny the Elder, *Natural History,* 10:139–140.

64. The quattrino was a copper coin in circulation throughout Italy from the Middle Ages to the nineteenth century. In Rome, it was worth 0.53 of a bajocco (see n. 107).

65. Called *vino di Ripa,* an obvious reference to imported wine unloaded at the Ripa Grande, the river port near what is today Piazza dell'Emporio, at the end of Via Marmorata, in the Testaccio quarter.

66. Summaries of public and private acts relating to the life of the medieval Abbey of Farfa, in the Sabine hills.

67. Guarcino and Aspra are small towns, one in the province of Frosinone, the other in the province of Rieti.

68. The bridges called Mammolo, Nomentano, and Salario are found along the Via Tiburtina, Via Nomentana, and Via Salaria where they leave Rome and used to cross the Aniene River.

69. During the French occupation of Rome, in 1798, the government, from Paris, charged the agronomist De Tournon with drafting a report on the condition of the *campagna romana.* The result of his careful work was *Études statistiques sur Rome et la partie occidentale des états romains: contenant une description topographique et des recherches sur la population, l'agriculture, les manufactures, le commerce, le gouvernement, les établissements publiques et une notice sur les travaux exécutés par l'administration française* (Paris, 1831).

70. A civil and religious organization that looked out for the interests of its members, much as a labor union does today.

71. The Annona and the Grascia were public institutions, governed by the central administration, which directed all operations regarding the production, commerce, and distribution of wheat and meat, respectively.

72. Its fragrance was believed to repel insects.

73. Low-flying birds, such as partridge, quail, woodcock, and the like.

74. The pilgrims' road toward the three most important destinations of medieval Christianity, Rome, Santiago de Compostela, and Jerusalem. The route to Rome was also called the Via Romea, and pilgrims to Rome were called *romei.*

75. The beautiful valley along the Via Cassia 12.4 miles (20 kilometers) from Rome, today intensely cultivated and inhabited was, in the nineteenth century, still a vast marshy depression that was drained by the Chigi princes, owners of the lands.

76. Attributed by legend to the king Servius Tullius, whence the name, the Servian walls, which actually date to the fourth century B.C., were the first and only walls to surround Rome until those built by the emperor Aurelian in the third century A.D. Short stretches of the Servian walls are preserved in a handful of spots around the city, notably beneath the Stazione Termini and at the foot of the Aventine Hill. —M.B.F.

77. *History of Rome,* 7:39 and 9:29.

78. The nomenclature of Capua is a bit confusing: ancient Capua is today's Santa Maria Capua Vetere; the town known today as simply Capua was founded in 856 on the site of the ancient Casilinum.

79. These were constructions where horses were changed and where the mail was deposited for the hinterland. They survived until the nineteenth century.

80. *Philippics,* 12:9.

81. Henry V, last of the Holy Roman emperors, came down to Rome to be crowned by Pope Paschal II and, in February 1111, signed an accord with him on his rights of investiture called the *giuramento di Sutri*, "oath of Sutri," not in a cathedral or palace but in an osteria.

82. Landowners hired the *caporale,* a sort of foreman, to organize and supervise the farmwork. Today the term can also mean a recruiter of farmworkers, legal and illegal.

83. The marshy lands and the consequent malaria caused much sickness and death among the peasants who worked the estates of the *agro romano.*

84. The minister of the Camera Apostolica in charge of distribution of charity.

85. The *arrosto morto* (literally, "dead roast") is a pot roast cooked in a covered pan with the gradual addition of wine and broth.

86. M. de Montaigne, *Journal de voyage en Italie par la Suisse et l'Allemagne en 1580–1581* (Rome: Le Jay, 1775).

87. In this connection, see the interesting contribution of F. Irsigler, "La fonction des foires dans l'intégration des économiques européennes au moyen âge," in S. Cavaciocchi, ed., *Fiere e mercati nella integrazione delle economie europee: secc. XIII–XVIII* (Bagno a Ripoli: Le Monnier, 2001), 49–69.

88. It was Frederick II, rightly known as Stupor Mundi, who in 1233 greatly encouraged the fairs held in the cities of his realm. This was the origin of the important fairs of Sulmona, Lucera, Capua, Bari, Taranto, Cosenza, and Reggio. But of their success and duration we know nothing certain.

89. Archivio Vaticano, armadio IV, t. 56, p. 59.

90. To attest the continuity over time of this fair, we have the written *avviso* (notice) of Cardinal Flavio Chigi and his brothers that informs that "the day 28 May 1662 will take place at Galloro di Ariccia the usual fair free of taxes and duties, except those due to the Camera" (Archivio Vaticano, armadio IV, t. 56, p. 53).

91. A Breve of Clement VIII dated July 2, 1593 receives the petition of the Jews to be allowed to do business at the fairs; and another *motu proprio* of the same pope authorizes the Jews to participate in all the fairs held in the papal states. In Comune di Roma, *Regesti di bandi, editti, notificazioni e provvedimenti diversi relativi alla Città di Roma ed allo Stato Pontificio,* pp. 116 and 150.

92. These venerable organizations, although burdened by an 1890 decree of abolition from the parliament of the Kingdom of Italy, still survive in many localities around the region. Of the many, we mention the Confraternity of Palestrina, which survived until the outbreak of World War II. It organized the procession for the feast of Saint Martin: The club of the *cornuti* (cuckolds) followed those more strictly devotional participants with their own insignia, and the men burdened by this unwanted designation had to wear their jackets inside out, thus becoming the brunt of jokes and japes. Everything concluded with wonderful fireworks, as at other civil and religious events.

93. A cloth twisted into a ring shape and placed between the head and the water jar for trips from the fountains.

94. Local associations whose aim is to promote the territory.

95. An edict of August 16, 1630 suspends the Farfa fair because of the plague and dictates severe health measures for the fair of the following year. In Comune di Roma, *Regesti di bandi, editti, notificazioni e provvedimenti diversi relativi alla Città di Roma e allo Stato Pontificio,* pp. 114 and 123.

96. Dining room cupboard, with open shelves, where the silver and crystal were displayed.

97. The poets Carlo Goldoni, Pietro Metastasio, and Vincenzo Monti were all the rage in the 1700s; Ludovico Ariosto's romantic epic, *Orlando furioso,* written in the early sixteenth century, was also still popular.

98. Luigi Cherubini, Giovanni Paisiello, and Nicolò Piccinni are the illustrious musicians whose works filled theaters from the middle of the 1700s.

99. *Il tempo del papa-re, diario del principe don Agostino Chigi dall'anno 1830 al 1855* (Milan: Il Borghese, 1966), 161.

100. "Priest-stranglers," a very old but imprecise name for a number of hand-formed pasta shapes; see Zanini De Vita, *Encyclopedia of Pasta,* 264.

101. *Rione* was and is the term used for the divisions of the center of Rome, some of which correspond to the fourteen ancient *regiones* into which the emperor Augustus divided the city.

102. For example, the use of the artichoke stem, which is chopped together with garlic, parsley, and *mentuccia (Mentha pulegium)* for the filling of the famous *carciofi alla romana;* and also the use of animal parts of little value, such as the neck of the goose, turkey, or chicken, which can be stuffed.

103. The term *conclave* indicates the place where the cardinals meet to elect the new pontiff. It was locked with a key, in Latin, *cum clave.* See especially D. Silvagni, *La Corte e la società romana nei secoli XVIII e XIX* (Naples: Arturo Berisio Editore, 1880).

104. In this connection see the beautiful plates 20 and 21 in *Opera di M. Bartolomeo Scappi cuoco secreto di Papa Pio V divisa in sei libri* (Venice: Tramezzino, 1570; repr., Forni, 1981).

105. Today, this fish-filled lake in the province of Viterbo still supplies the tables of the area's restaurants with excellent fish, principally eel, pike, pike perch, chub, trout, and carp.

106. Among his most significant works was the completion of the dome and piazza of Saint Peter's, as well as the completion of the Sistine Chapel. Among his initiatives aimed at eradicating poverty and injustice, he started the work of draining the Pontine marshes, but this was to be accomplished only in the 1930s, with the advent of modern technology.

107. Coins circulating in the papal states. At the beginning of the Kingdom of Italy, the bajocco was worth five centesimi, or hundredths of a lira. See *Tavole di riduzione delle antiche e nuove misure pesi e monete per lo stabilimento del nuovo sistema metrico negli Stati romani* (Rome: Mariano De Romanis, 1811), 201.

108. In the 1800s, Cassandrino was considered the typical mask of Rome. He is represented with powdered wig, three-cornered hat, swallow-tailed coat, light-colored britches, and shoes with buckles. He speaks with a nasal voice and represents the credulous bourgeois father whose daughters have no trouble wrapping him around their little finger. He often is the voice of the people who complain about the power of the pope-king.

109. *Reichardia picroides,* literally, "chase hare."

110. For example, Aldo Fabrizi, *La pastasciutta, ricette e considerazioni in versi* (Milan: Mondadori, 1970).

111. Ceccarius, pseudonym of Giuseppe Ceccarelli (1889–1972), great journalist and a scholar of the folklore and traditions of Rome, left to the state his important library and rich archive of documents on the history of the territory of Lazio.

112. J. André, 213 ff.

113. A. Dosi and F. Schnell, 195 ff. Also E. Salza Prina Ricotti, *Ricette della cucina romana a Pompei e come eseguirle* (Rome: L'Erma di Bretschneider, 1968).

114. It will be sufficient to have a look at the *servizi di credenza* in the monumental work of Bartolomeo Scappi, cook of Pope Pius V: *Opera di M. Bartolomeo Scappi, cuoco secreto di papa Pio 5. diuisa in sei libri, nel primo si contiene il ragionamento che fa l'autore con Gio. suo discepolo. . . . Con il discorso funerale che fu fatto nelle esequie di papa Paulo 3. Con le figure che fanno bisogno nella cucina, & alli reuerendiss. nel Conclaue* (Venice: Michele Tramezzino, 1570).

115. The branding of the animals was an important event. The owners of the flocks or the herds of water buffalo and horses invited relatives and friends to observe the operation, which took place on the meadow. It was the occasion for jaunts to the countryside and outdoor meals.

116. Apicius (1:14) suggests keeping olives whole and to press them only when needed to preserve the fragrance and flavor of the fruit.

117. The powerful imperial Abbey of Farfa, about 23 miles (about 37.5 kilometers) from Rieti, with its extensive holdings in Lazio and elsewhere; olive culture, from the Middle Ages on, was one of its important activities. The abbots possessed a fleet of trading ships that they anchored at a port on the Tiber, which at the time was navigable as far as Perugia. In the Middle Ages, the most important fair in central Italy was held at Farfa. The Benedictine abbey of Subiaco (about 43 miles/70 kilometers east of Rome), one of the fourteen founded by Saint Benedict, is located in the upper valley of the Aniene River and is still a religious pilgrimage destination.

118. Mountain chains in the central Apennines.

119. "Tucking in at the foot," that is, a process of pushing manure beneath the roots of the tree.

120. C. Corsi, "Attività produttive e commerciali nell'Etruria marittima," in Società tarquiniese di arte e storia, *Bollettino dell'anno 1994*. The large numbers of food containers found in excavations tell us that wheat, oil, and wine were the main commodities traded.

121. These are ancient towns along the coast north of Rome, some of which are still industrious small cities. The ruins of others are preserved and remain the object of archaeological excavations and studies.

122. The so-called Pyrgi Tablets, now in the National Etruscan Museum housed in the Villa Giulia in Rome, are three gold sheets found in Pyrgi (today Santa Severa) inscribed in Etruscan and Phoenician. They are considered the earliest Italic written sources and are of enormous interest for the history of language.

123. Varro, *De re rustica*, 1:2

124. C. Marigliani and O. Zanini De Vita, *Da Civitavecchia ad Anzio e Nettuno. Il paesaggio agrario del litorale romano* (Rome: Provincia di Roma, 2009), 11 ff.

125. Caeretan wine was famous (Martial, *Epigrams*, 3:124) and better than that produced at Veii, and not only in antiquity. According to Sante Lancerio, the famous enologist of the 1500s, who, in his *I vini d'Italia giudicati da papa Paolo III, e dal suo bottigliere Sante Lancerio,* mentions is a wine produced in the Cerveteri area, which he describes as light and, unfortunately, not easily transportable.

126. Diodorus Siculus (90–27 B.C.), great historian of Magna Graecia, is the author of the encyclopedic *Bibliotheca historica*.

127. For example, that of the married couple in the Villa Giulia museum in Rome.

128. An excellent collection can be seen in the Villa Giulia museum in Rome.

129. *Aeneid,* 7:116. The Harpy Celaeno had prophesied (3:257) that Aeneas and his men would eventually be so hungry they would eat their tables.

130. See especially M. Montanari, *Alimentazione e cultura nel Medioevo* (Rome-Bari: Laterza, 1988).

131. During the Middle Ages, *vino cotto,* or "cooked wine," that is, partially condensed, was widely added to wine as a preservative.

132. C. De Cupis, *La caccia nella Campagna Romana secondo la storia e i documenti* (Rome: A. Nardecchia, 1922).

133. The so-called Babylonian Captivity, when the popes were held in Avignon, lasted from 1309 to 1377.

134. Geographic term used to indicate all the territory of the papal states and the Kingdom of Naples, which extended along the coast.

135. Also known as *cicerbita,* a wild plant of the genus *Sonchus.*

136. R. Di Mario, *Viaggio nel Medioevo Sabino tra storia, costumi e tradizioni* (Teramo, [no pub.], 1989), 17 ff.

137. Picked by hand, one by one. Today a special tool that resembles a large pair of scissors is used. It is run along the branches and makes the olives drop off into waiting baskets below. This prevents blemishing that might give rise to fermentation of the fruit.

138. R. Di Mario, 53.

139. For the various pasta shapes, see Zanini De Vita, *Encyclopedia of Pasta.*

140. See Hans Barth, *Osteria, guida spirituale delle osterie italiane da Verona a Capri* (Florence: Le Monnier, 1921).

141. Andrea Bacci, *De naturali vinorum historia accessit De Factitiis, ac cervisiis, de quibus Rheni, Galliae, Hispaniae et de totius Europae vini set de omni vinorum usu compendiaria tractatio* (Rome: Officina Nicholai Mutis, 1596).

142. Cooked over a fire made with vine branches.

143. Today all Italians associate the name of Anagni with this legendary affront to the papal face. In 1300, political controversies that arose from the Jubilee of that year put Pope Boniface VIII (Caetani) head to head with the king of France. Irritated by the Vatican's requests for funds, the king called a council and demanded that the pope attend. He sent an emissary to Rome, who, with the assistance of the noble Sciarra Colonna, went to Anagni, ancient feud site of the Caetani family, to fetch the pope and take him to France. At Boniface's resistance, the story goes, he delivered the famous slap.

144. Originally the territory of the city of Capua, in the Kingdom of Naples, it expanded later to include all the lands that had the papal states on their northern border. The name *felix* (happy) was bestowed in antiquity for its particular fertility.

145. Athenaeus 7 a-b; 104 f.

146. The *fuochi* that were counted throughout Italy; the peasant families refer to the hearth, always present in poor homes.

147. The *tomolo* was an old area measurement of farmland in almost all of Italy, but the exact meaning differed from place to place. In Lazio a *tomolo* was equivalent to about an acre (four thousand square meters).

148. Marigliani and Zanini De Vita, *Da Civitavecchia ad Anzio e Nettuno,* 11 ff.

149. On the situation of the landscape all along the coast, from Civitavecchia to Anzio and Nettuno, see C. Calisse, *Storia di Civitavecchia* (Florence: Barbera, 1898).

150. F. Gregorovius, *Passeggiate per l'Italia* (Rome: Avanzini e Torraci, 1968), 2:150.

151. A system whereby fish are forced to gather in a particular spot.

GENERAL INDEX

Page numbers in italic refer to illustrations.

abbacchio. See lamb

Abruzzo, xii, 4, 31, 67, 87

acorns, 19

acquapazza (crazy water), 88

acquecotte (soups), 74

Africa, 19, 29, 66, 89

Agilulf (Lombard king), 6, 278n11

agriculture, ix–xi, 5–10, 26–28; Castelli zone vineyards, 79–80; in coastal region, 91; in Etruscan lands, 69, 70–71; irrigation in, 23; olive culture in, 66–67; papal aid for, 8, 9; and pasturage, 9, 31–32, 73, 91; plow, x, 69, 71; in Pontine area, 89–90; pre-World War II, ix; in Sabina, 75–80; state central policy, 28; use of fallow fields, 69, 89, 91

agro romano, 5–6, 9, 28; De Tournon's study of, 31; honey in, 62; olive culture in, 66–67; osterias in, 36; pasturage in, 31–32, 73; sweets in, 63; wine trade in, 72. *See also* agriculture; *campagna romana*

Alban Hills, 16, 17, 43, 85

Albano, 67, 80

Alfredo (pasta dish), 61

almonds, 51, 63

Amalfi, 4

Amatrice, 4, 75, 77; *pasta all'amatriciana,* 22, 111–12

Anagni, 86, 285n143

anchovies, 273

Aniene River, x, 16, 85, 281n68

animals, 29–33; in Lazio region, ix–x; taxes on, 30; for traction, 11, 69. *See also* livestock, raising; meat; *specific animals*

Annona dei grani, 32, 281n71

Apicius, xi, 25, 284n116

apples, 9

aquaculture, 10–11, 73. *See also* fish and fishing; Tiber River

aqueducts, 6, 8, 16–18. *See also* water supply and management

Arab cooking, influence of, ix, 63

Ariccia, 33, 79; fair at, 41, 282n90

Ariosto, 32, 47, 283n97

artichokes, ix, 9, 16, 24, 25, 82, 273, 283n102

Artusi, Pellegrino, 26, 280n55

arugula, 24, 59, 70; recipe, 223

arzilla (ray, skate), ix, 15

asparagus, wild, 24

aubergine. *See* eggplants

Augustus (emperor), 10, 17, 283n53

Aventine Hill (Rome), 4, 277n2, 281n76

Baccano valley, 33, 281n75

Bacci, Andrea, 79, 80

badger, 77

bakers, 19, 20. *See also* bread; sweets

banquets, 3, 45, 70; papal, 44, 53, 55, 56. *See also* Carnival

barbel, 12

barley, 7, 19, 70, 76, 89

basil, 5

battuto, 21

beans, 6, 76; green, ix. *See also* fava beans

beccaficos (fig peckers), 29

beef, 29, 30, 73, 74, 84

Belisarius, Flavius, 19–20, 280n46

Belli, Giuseppe Gioacchino, 58–60

Bibliotecario, Anastasio, 6, 278n12

borage, xi, 24

Borghese family, 75

Borgia, Lucrezia, 54

Borgia, Rodrigo. *See* popes: Alexander VI

bread, 3, 18–21, 59, 63, 74, 88; ancient types, 18–19; *casereccio, 273; crostini, 273; pizza ricresciuta,* 64

broccoli, 74

broccoli rabe, ix

broccolo romanesco, 15, 273

bruschetta, 21, 72

bucalossi, 24

butteri (cowboy), 73, 84

cabbage, xi, 3, 6, 9, 24, 50, 70, 76

caccialepre, 24

Caetani, Enrico, 30

Caffè Aragno, 5, 277n6

Camera Apostolica, 14, 30, 31, 41, 73, 282n84. *See also* papacy and popes

Campagna, 4, 277n5

Campagna e Marittima. *See* Ciociaria

campagna romana, 5–10, *17,* 26, 61–62, 63, 64, 65, 82, 278n16, 278n20, 281n69; De Tournon's study of, 31–32; invasions of, 6, 11; towers and farmhouses in, 8, 278n20. *See also* agriculture; Rome

Campania, 11, 88

Caracalla (emperor), 16, 86

caraway, 70

cardoons, 25, 74

cariota, 24

Carnival, 14, 43–49; sweets for, 61, 63

carp, 12

carrots, 70

casali (large farmhouses), 8

Casilinum, 33, 281n78

Castelgandolfo, 7, 80

Castelli Romani, 18, 23, 26, 28, 35, 79–82; fairs in, 41; wine from, 38, 39, 46, 79–82

castrato. See lamb

cattle, 29, 70, 77, 84. *See also* beef

caviar, 12, 56

Ceccarelli, Giuseppe (Ceccarius), 61, 283n111

celery, 9, 24

Cerveteri, 68, 284n125

chanterelles, 24, 26

chard, 24

cheeses, *13,* 19, 21, 25, 85, 88; for barter, 42; making, 31; in Pontine area, 90; *provatura,*

275; in sweets, 63, 64. *See also specific cheeses*

cherries, 9, 78, 91

chestnuts, ix, 9, 76, 77

chickens, 3, 29, 77, 90, 283n102

chickpeas, 3, 76, 83

chicory, xi, 33, 67, 76

Chigi, Agostino, 48, 55; family, 281n75, 282n90

churches (Rome): Basilica of St. John Lateran, 7; Santa Maria dell'Orto, 24; Sant' Angelo in Pescheria, 14; Santa Susanna, 23; St. Peter's Basilica, 48, 65, 283n106

Cicero, xi, 6, 11, 86, 278n9

Cincinnatus, L. Quintus, 5, 277n7

Ciociaria, ix, 5, 82–86, 92

ciriole (eels), 12; recipe, 192–93. *See also* eels

clams, 11, 92, 98

Claudius (emperor), 17

cococciata, 76

cocozze. See zucchini

cod, salt, 15

coffee, 17, 64

Columella, xi, 277n8, 279n28

Commodus (emperor), 10, 86

confraternities, 8, 278n18; *Ars bobacteriorum urbis,* 8, 278n19; Confraternity of Bakers, 20; Confraternity of the Oil Men, 8; Confraternity of the Vegetable Men, 7–8; at fairs, 42, 282n92

consular roads. *See* roads

coriander, 70

Coricio, Messer, 23

corn (maize), ix, 3, 9, 89; polenta, 22

credenzieri, 52, 57

crespigno (herb), 24, 74

Crusades, impact of, 4

cucumbers, 25, 70, 76

Curius Dentatus, 25

cuttlefish, 88, 89, 92

Dante, Alighieri, 53

date shells, 11

De Tournon (French prefect), 31, 66–67, 74, 281n69

Diodorus Siculus, 69

Domitian (emperor), 11

domuscultae (villages), 7

DOP (Protected Denomination of Origin), 72, 75

dormice *(glires),* 29

doves, 14, 29, 77
drainage projects, 6, 28, 75, 88, 91. *See also*
    water supply and management
ducks, 29, 77

East, trade with, 4
eels, xiv, 11, 12, 53, 73, 283n105
eggplants, 25–26
eggs, 3, 35, 42; egg pasta, 5, 78
Egypt, contact with, 19, 56, 62
elder flowers and berries, 62, 280n53
emmer, 3, 76. See also *farro*
endive, 24, 76
Etruscan lands, 6, 68–74; Viterbo and Tuscia,
    70–74, 277n4

Fabrizi, Aldo, 60, 283n110
fairs, 40–43, 281n88
fallow system. *See* agriculture
famigliole (mushrooms), 26
far, 3. *See also* emmer; *farro*
Farfa, Abbey of, 66, 75, 76, 77, 281n66,
    284n117; fair at, 41, 282n95
Farnese, Cardinal, 80
farro, 63, 70, 279n44. *See also* emmer
fasting. *See* Lent
fava beans, 3, 9, 25, 70, 76, 90
feasts and feast days, 9, 70; families'
    celebrations, 61; meat on, 77; sweets on,
    61, 62, 65
fennel, wild, 25, 70, 72, 74
fern roots, 76
festivals, 43, 44, 67; at Ceprano, 82–83;
    Jewish, 50–51. *See also* Carnival; feasts and
    feast days
figs, 53, 91; syrup, 63
Fiora River, 90
fish and fishing, 10–16, 76; in coastal Lazio,
    91–93; importance in diet, 14, 15, 279n36;
    pesce azzurro, 274; in Pontine area, 88–89;
    in Viterbo/Tuscia area, 72–73
fishmongers, 12–14
fly agaric mushrooms, 24
focaccia, 3, 18, 63, 70. *See also* bread
Fondi, 33, 85, 89
food policy: central agricultural policy, 28;
    papal liberalization of market, 27; statutes
    on wine, 72; taxes on food/meat, 30; of
    towns, 70
Formia, 33, 38, 89
Forum Boarium (Rome), 16, 30, 279n40

fountains, 16, 23, 24, 43, 279n42
francolins, 29
Frascati, 35, 82; wine, xi. *See also* Castelli
    Romani
fraschetta, 39. *See also* osterias
Frontinus, Sextus Julius, 16, 279n39
Frosinone, xii, 87
fruit and fruit trees, 4, 9, 28, 57, 71, 78;
    candied fruits, 19; in Pontina, 90; in
    sweets, 63, 64
funghi. *See* mushrooms
fuochi (fires), 89

Gaeta, 38; onions from, 56; *tiella di Gaeta*, 89
game, xiv, 29, 72, 77, 80, 86, 87–88
gardens, 8, 23–28, 70–71
garlic, 21, 90
geese, 29, 77
Genoa, 4
Genzano, 28, 82
Ghetto (Rome), 13, 14, 47, 49–51. *See also*
    Jews; Jewish cooking of Rome
Giovio, Paolo, 12, 23
gnocchi, 51, 85
goats, 77, 78
Goethe, Johann von, 5, 6
Good Friday, 15
Gothic War, 17, 19
Gothic War (Procopius), 19
grains, ix, 19, 75, 76; mills, 19–20; regulation
    of, 26–27; in Sabina, 76 77; for sweets,
    63. *See also specific grains*
Grand Tour, 26, 74
Grand Tour in Italy (Goethe), 5
grapes, ix, 4, 8, 24, 71; *pizzutello*, ix. *See also*
    wine
Grappasonne, Abele, 35
Grascia, 32, 281n71
gray mullet, 11
Greece, influence of, 4, 10
greens, xii, 24, 25, 59, 280n53. *See also*
    vegetables; *specific greens*
Gregorovius, 39, 85, 91
Grottaferrata, Abbey of, 40, 41, 80, *81*
guanciale, 22, 77, 274
guazzetto, 12
guilds, 24; animal raisers and shepherds, 30,
    32; fishing, 12–14; innkeepers, 38; millers
    and bakers, 20; pasta makers, 21; vegetable
    gardeners, 23–24
guinea fowl, 29

hares, 29, 70
hazelnuts, 74, 76, 90
heart, xi
herbs, 19, 21, 71, 74, 90; *olio fiorito*, 280n53.
　See also specific herbs
holidays. *See* feasts and feast days;
　festivals
honey, 3, 4, 19, 62–63, 90. *See also*
　sweets
Horace, xi, 75, 86, 87
horseradish, 74
Hostaria dell'Orso (Rome), 36
hunters. *See* game

innkeepers, 36, 38. *See also* osterias
inns. *See* osterias
iron, 69, 75, 91
irrigation, 6, 23; wells for, 8. *See also*
　agriculture; water supply and
　management

Janiculum Hill, 17, 279n41
Jewish cooking of Rome, xi, 49–51, 283n102;
　recipes, 130, 133, 141–42, 144–45, 175–76,
　179–80, 181–82, 183–84, 199, 203–4, 209,
　217–18, 227–28, 271
Jewish quarter. *See* Ghetto (Rome)
Jews, xiii, 41, 47, 279n35, 282n91.
　See also Ghetto (Rome); Jewish cooking
　of Rome
Justinian (emperor), 17
Juvenal, xi, 11

Kingdom of Italy, 4, 23, 48, 282n92, 283n107
Kingdom of Naples, 38, 56, 85, 87, 88,
　285n144

laganum, 3
Lake Baccano, 68
Lake Bolsena, 53, 71, 73, 283n105
Lake Bracciano, 18
Lake Garda, 47, 55, 56
Lake Lucrinus, 11
Lake Martignano, 17, 18
lamb, ix–x, 5, 30–31, 32, 74, 77, 83, 85, 88, 90;
　castrato, 273
land management, under papacy, 6
lard, 4, 88, 274
latifundium (farming estate), 9, 26, 91
Latina, xii, 22, 87
Latium, xiii

Lazio region, ix–xi, xii–xiii, 4, 277n5;
　agriculture in, 26–28; ancient cuisine of,
　3–4; coastal area, 90–93; fairs and
　markets in, 26, 40–43; Lombard invasion,
　6; olive culture in, 67–68. See also
　campagna romana; specific provinces
leeks, 25, 70
legumes, 4, 7, 24, 76, 83, 84, 89. *See also*
　specific legumes
lemon balm *(melissa),* 35, 76
lemons, 23, 48, 274
Lent, 14, 15, 44, 64, 80
lentils, 3, 77
Leonine wall (Rome), 7, 278n13
leporaria. See hares
lettuce, 24, 76, 280n53; lamb's, 24; romaine,
　ix, 9, 70
liver, xi, 77, 90
livestock, raising, ix–x, 8, 9, 29, 278n19; in
　Ciociaria, 83–84. *See also* meat; *specific
　animals*
Livy, 33
lobster, 88
Lombards, 6
Lucullus, L. Licinius, 11; banquets of, 3

mackerel, 11
maize. *See* corn (maize)
malaria, 6, 8, 9, 36, 73, 87, 277–78n8
Marcus Aurelius (emperor), 10, 86
Maremma Laziale, xi, 73
Mare Nostrum (Mediterranean), 90
Marforio ("talking statue"), 57
Margherita di Savoia, Queen, 35, 49
marignani. See eggplants
Marino, 35, 43, 82
Marittima, 4, 73, 85, 277n5, 285n134. *See also*
　Lazio region
marjoram, 90
markets, 26, 40–43; fish, 10, 13–14, 279n34
marrane (streams), 20, 23. *See also* water
　supply and management
Martana. *See* Lake Bolsena
Marta River, 73, 90
Martial, xi, 19, 24, 25, 89, 284n125
marzipan, 64. *See also* sweets
meat, 3, 29–33, 70, 84; kosher, 50; meatless
　days, 14, 15; in Pontina, 88, 90; trade in
　and taxes on, 30; in Viterbo and Sabina,
　74, 77. *See also specific types*
melons, 25, 70

Michelangelo, 8
millet, 19, 63, 76; foxtail, 70, 90
mills, 19–20, 76
mint, 274
misticanza (salad), 24
mollusks, 11
monasteries, land holdings of, 8, 9
monk's beard, 24
Montaigne, 34, 37
Montefiascone, 71, 73
Monti Lepini, 67, 87, 88, 89
moorhens *(folaghe),* 88
moray eel *(murena),* 10. *See also* eels
Moroni, Gaetano, 22, 280n51
Murena, Licinius, 11
mushrooms, xii, 24, 26, 61. *See also specific types*
mussels, 11
mustard, 70

Napoléon (Bonaparte), 47, 59
nassa (basket), 72–73. *See also* fish and fishing
Nemi, ix, 43. *See also* Castelli Romani
nervetti, 274

oats, 89
octopus, 92
offal, xiv, 84; *padellotto,* xi; sweetbreads, 5
oiosa, 24
olives and olive oil, ix, xii, 3, 4, 5, 41, 62, 65–68, 69, 274; *olio fiorito,* 280n53; in Sabina, 75, 76, 285n137; in Viterbo, 72
onions, 6, 21, 24, 56, 70, 76, 90
oranges, 4
Orata, Sergius, 11, 279n28
oregano, 90
Orvieto, 71
osterias, 34–40, 82
Ostia, 10, 11, 14, 75, 91
ovoli (mushrooms), 26
oxen, 3, 73, 77, 84
oxtail, 24
oysters, 11, 19, 88

padellotto, xi
paiolo (pot), 76, 79
pajata, 274
panarda (ceremony), 83
pancetta, 77, 274

pancotto, 21
pangiallo, 64
panpepato, 5
panzanella, 21
papacy and popes: aid for agriculture, 8, 9; conclave (papal election), 52, 283n103; creation of Ghetto, 49; eating habits of, 52–57; land management of, 6; papal states, 87, 285n134, 285n144; temporal power of, 7, 11, 14, 18, 20, 27, 30, 31, 47, 48. *See also* popes
parmigiano-reggiano, 25, 85
parsley, 70, 90
parsnips, 74
Pascarella, Cesare, 86
Pasquino ("talking statue"), 57
pasta, 4–5, 21–22, 61, 78
pasta shapes: *bucatini,* 22; *capelli d'angelo,* 22; *cecamariti,* 5, 78; *ciufulitti,* 5; *cordelle,* 5; *curuli,* 5; *fieno,* 5; *frascarelli,* 4, 78; *fregnacce,* 4, 78; *frigulozzi,* 5, 78; *fusilli,* 5; *lacchene,* 5; *manfricoli,* 5; *paglia,* 5; *pencarelli,* 5; *pizzicotti,* 5; *sagne,* 78; *sfusellati,* 5; *stracci,* 4; *strozzapreti,* 5, 48; *tagliolini,* 22
pasticceria (pastry shop), 64–65
pasturage, 8, 9, 31. *See also* sheep, raising
peaches, 9, 78
peacocks, 29, 45
pears, 9, 78
peas, 16, 24
pecorino, x, xi, 9, 21, 85
peddlers, food, 39
Peretti, Felice. *See* popes: Sixtus V
pheasants, 14, 29
piè di gallo, 24
pigeons, 14, 29
pigs, 7, 14, 30, 70, 77; "parade dish," 45; wild, 72. *See also* pork
pike, 11, 73
pilgrims, 36, 38, 74, 281n74
Pincio (hill), 24
pine nuts, 63
Pisa, 4
placenta (sweet), 63
plague, 8–9, 282n95
plow. *See* agriculture
plums, 78
polenta, 22. *See also* corn (maize)
Pontine area: food of, 88–90; marshes, 22, 57, 73, 87–88, 280n52

wheat, 18, 19, 28, 63, 70, 76, 280n59. *See also* bread; pasta

wine: in Castelli zone, 79, 80–81, 82; Etruscan, 69, 284n125; Frascati, xi; Malvasia, 54; for osterias, 38; tax on, 30, 281n65; from Viterbo area, 71–72

witches, 15, 279n37

women: in agricultural labor, 26, 67; Etruscan, 69–70, 284n127; at fairs and festivals, 42, 43, 82

wood grouse, 29

wood sorrel, 24

zampogna (bagpipe), 32, 85

zucchini, 25, 76

RECIPE INDEX

beef *(continued)*
    kidney, stewed, 176
    leftover boiled, with onions, 166
    leftover boiled, with potatoes, 167
    oxtail, stewed, 156–57
    rolls, 164–65
    tongue, sweet-and-sour, 167–68
    See also veal
bell peppers
    chicken with, 171–72
    salt cod with, 188
    stuffed, 230–31
    with guanciale, 230
    with onions and tomatoes, 229–30
bietole al pomodoro, 205–6
bignè di San Giuseppe, 254–55
boar, sweet-and-sour, wild, 155–56
boccette in brodo, 130–31
"bocconotti" di ricotta alla romana,
    255–56
borage fritters, 224–25
borragine, frittelle di, 224–25
boscaiola, spaghetti alla, 117
brasato di manzo ai funghi, 152–53
bread
    salad, 247
    toast with mock game, 242
    with pancetta and guanciale, 246–47
    See also *bruschetta*
broccoletti "strascinati," 207
broccoli
    al prosciutto, 207–8
    stufati, 208
broccoli
    with prosciutto, 211–12
broccoli rabe, sautéed, 207
broccolo romanesco
    in red wine, 208
    ray broth with pasta and, 143
brodetto pasquale, 129
brodo, boccette in, 130–31
"broken" soup, 141–42
broth
    curly endive in, 133
    "grated" pasta in, 142
    meatballs in, 130–31
    rice in, with turnips, 144–45
bruschetta
    classica, 240–41
    con il pomodoro, 241
bucaniera, spaghetti alla, 115

budino
    di castagne, 257
    di ricotta, 258

cacio e pepe, spaghetti alla, 116–17
calamari ripieni alla romana, 190–91
calf's liver, fried, 162
cannellini beans
    and chard, soup of, 135
    with tuna, 217
capitone marinato, 241–42
cappelle di porcini arrosto, 208–9
carbonara, spaghetti alla, 112
carciofi
    alla giudia, 209
    alla romana, 209–10
    con i piselli, 210–11
    con il guanciale, 211
    coratella di abbacchio, con i, 159
    frittata di, 222
    fritti alla romana, 211–12
    in fricassea alla romana, 212–13
    tortino di sarde e, 199
carrettiera, spaghetti alla, 113
castrato
    con le patate, spezzatino di, 183
    con i fagioli cannellini, spalla di, 180–81
cauliflower
    batter-fried, 213
    with anchovies, 213–14
cavolfiore
    fritto in pastella, 213
    in tegame con le alici, 213–14
ceci
    al rosmarino, 214
    e "pennerelli," minestra di, 133
    laganelle con i, 134–35
    pasta e, 144
cefalo in gratella, 191
celery, stewed, 235
chard
    cannellini beans and, soup of, 135
    with tomatoes, 205–6
checca, spaghetti alla, 114
cheese
    baked pasta with meat and, 105
    pie, ham and, 245
    provola, grilled, 250
    toast, anchovy and, 243
    See also pecorino; ricotta
chestnut pudding, 257

CALIFORNIA STUDIES IN FOOD AND CULTURE

Darra Goldstein, Editor